preserves

preserves

the complete book of jams, jellies,
pickles, relishes and chutneys,
with over 150 stunning recipes

Catherine Atkinson
& Maggie Mayhew

HERMES
HOUSE

This edition is published by Hermes House, an imprint of Anness Publishing Ltd,
Blaby Road, Wigston, Leicestershire LE18 4SE
Email: info@anness.com

Web: www.hermeshouse.com; www.annesspublishing.com

If you like the images in this book and would like to investigate using them for
publishing, promotions or advertising, please visit our website
www.practicalpictures.com for more information.

Publisher: Joanna Lorenz
Managing Editor: Linda Fraser
Senior Editor: Susannah Blake
Editorial Reader: Jane Bamforth
Photographer: Craig Robertson
Home Economist: Sarah O'Brien
Assistant Home Economist: Emma Robertson
Stylist: Helen Trent
Production Controller: Don Campaniello

ETHICAL TRADING POLICY
Because of our ongoing ecological investment programme, you, as our customer,
can have the pleasure and reassurance of knowing that a tree is being cultivated
on your behalf to naturally replace the materials used to make the book you are
holding. For further information about this scheme, go to
www.annesspublishing.com/trees

NOTES

Bracketed terms are intended for American readers.

For all recipes, quantities are given in both metric and imperial measures
and, where appropriate, measures are also given in standard cups and spoons.
Follow one set, but not a mixture, because they are not interchangeable.

Standard spoon and cup measures are level.
1 tsp = 5ml, 1 tbsp = 15ml, 1 cup = 250ml/8fl oz

Australian standard tablespoons are 20ml. Australian readers should use 3 tsp in
place of 1 tbsp for measuring small quantities of gelatine, flour, salt, etc.

Medium (US large) eggs are used unless otherwise stated.

contents

THE HISTORY OF PRESERVING

Preserving seasonal fruits and vegetables as jams, jellies, chutneys and relishes is one of the oldest of culinary arts. Once essential for basic survival, preserving is nowadays more often employed to store seasonal vegetables or fruits. It can be done in two ways: by heat sterilization, which destroys enzymes and bacteria, or by creating an environment where contaminants are unable to thrive – by drying, salting, or adding sugar, vinegar or alcohol.

AN AGE-OLD TECHNIQUE

Preserving was one of the earliest skills acquired by man, essential for survival during the cold, dark winter months when fresh food was scarce. Sun and wind were the first natural agents to be used: fruits and vegetables laid out in the hot sun or hung in the wind to dry were found to last longer than fresh produce and were lighter and easier to carry. In colder, damp climates, smoke and fire were used to hasten the drying process.

These discoveries meant that travelling to new territories became easier and new settlements were built where it was feasible for people to both grow and store food. It wasn't long before early man found that salt was a powerful dehydrator, far more consistent and reliable than the natural elements of sun and wind. Salt soon became a highly prized commodity – so much so that wars were fought over it. In fact, sometimes the salt was more valuable than the food it preserved, hence the saying that something is not worth its salt. Using salt to preserve foods made long-distance travel more possible because produce that had previously been perishable could be taken on board ships for journeys that lasted months and sometimes even years.

The preservative properties of vinegar and alcohol were discovered around the same time as those of salt, and people also realized that food could be flavoured at the same time that it was being preserved. Vinegar, which creates an acid environment that contaminants cannot live in, was used throughout the world. Malt vinegars were common in countries where beer was brewed, wine vinegar where vines were grown and rice vinegar became popular in the Far East.

Surprisingly the use of sugar as a preservative wasn't discovered until many centuries later. Cane sugar, brought to Europe by Arab merchants in the 12th century, remained a scarce luxury in the Western world for 400 years. It wasn't until the 16th century, when it was introduced to Europe from the West Indies, that sugar became a sought-after ingredient. Soon the demand for it became so great that it encouraged the rise of colonialism and the slave trade. In the 18th century, beetroot (beet), which had always been enjoyed as a vegetable, began to be cultivated specifically for its sugar content. Eventually sugar became plentiful and cheap, and the liking for sweet preserves started to grow.

It was during the 19th century that preserving really came into its own and was considered to be a skilled craft. Many of the recipes we use today are based on those that first appeared in cookbooks

Left: Rich, fruity chutneys were first made in India and became popular in Britain in the 19th century.

Above: Bottling fruits in flavoured syrups was one of the earliest ways that sugar was used for preserving.

during that era. Housewives took pride in filling capacious larders (pantries) with bottles and jars of preserves made from summer and autumn fruits while they were plentiful. These were then enjoyed during the lean winter months to supplement their diet, which would otherwise have consisted mainly of salted meats and root vegetables.

In the 20th century, preserving became less fashionable. Many homes had less storage space and, as the range and use of commercially prepared foods and preserves increased, huge stocks of home-made preserves were no longer needed or desirable. Imported produce meant that many fruits and vegetables were available all year round – soft fruits could be bought in the winter months and citrus fruits never disappeared from grocers' shelves. By the middle of the century, refrigerators could be found in most homes, followed by freezers in the 1960s and 70s, and during those decades freezing became the preferred way of preserving fruit and vegetables and the old-fashioned techniques became less popular.

PRESERVE-MAKING TODAY

Nowadays though, the art of preserving is coming back into its own, not because food needs to be processed to make it keep for long periods but for reasons of quality and variety. Improved travel and communication have increased knowledge of preserves from around the world and more unusual varieties of fruit, vegetables and flavouring ingredients are now readily available. Many people prefer to make their own preserves instead of buying mass-produced products with artificial flavourings and colourings. The satisfaction that comes from being able to create a unique product is also being rediscovered.

This book contains a comprehensive and detailed reference section showing how to make sweet and savoury preserves. All the main techniques are shown, including jam-, jelly- and marmalade-making; bottling fruits; pickling; chutney- and relish-making; candying; and drying. There is also a fabulous full-colour guide to the ingredients used for preserving – from seasonal fruits and vegetables to flavourings and preservatives.

The stunning recipe collection includes a whole host of traditional and contemporary ideas that will prove to be an inspiration and pleasure to both the novice jam-maker and the experienced preserver.

Below: Nowadays jams and conserves are made with a huge range of exotic ingredients.

SOFT FRUITS AND BERRIES

These delicate fruits are the epitome of summer and early autumn and can be made into wonderful jams and jellies. Despite their distinctive flavours and appearance, many are interchangeable in recipes. They can also be preserved in alcohol, but are less successful when bottled in syrup and are almost never included in pickles and chutneys. Soft berries are most often used in jams and conserves, while currants and cranberries are particularly good made into jellies.

STRAWBERRIES

These fruits are one of the most popular berries for jam-making and have a wonderfully fragrant flavour. Choose medium-size berries with an intense fragrance as these will give the preserve a good fruity flavour. Look for just-ripe, firm, fresh berries and use them for jam-making as soon as possible after picking, as this is when the

Below: Strawberries are one of the most popular fruits for jam-making.

Right: Raspberries can be made into intensely flavoured jams, jellies and conserves.

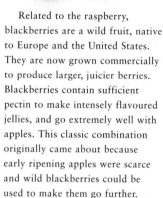

pectin content is highest. Rinse them only if absolutely necessary; if you do wash them, don't cut or hull them beforehand, or water will penetrate the fruit.

Tiny wild strawberries (*fraise de bois*), also known as alpine strawberries, have a pungent aroma and flavour and can be used whole in conserves.

THE RASPBERRY AND BLACKBERRY FAMILY

Technically, each berry is composed of multiple fruits as every tiny segment contains a hard seed. Jams made from these fruits have a high seed content, so they are often strained and made into seedless jams or jellies. The true raspberry is a bright crimson colour; yellow and white raspberries are also available and these have a deliciously delicate flavour, but make less attractive preserves.

Related to the raspberry, blackberries are a wild fruit, native to Europe and the United States. They are now grown commercially to produce larger, juicier berries. Blackberries contain sufficient pectin to make intensely flavoured jellies, and go extremely well with apples. This classic combination originally came about because early ripening apples were scarce and wild blackberries could be used to make them go further.

Dewberries are closely related to the blackberry and are similar in appearance. Cloudberries, which grow in North America and Canada, are a bright orange-red colour; the Scandinavian (or Arctic) cloudberry, which also grows in Scotland, is a pinky yellow colour with an almost caramel flavour. Loganberries (a cross between the raspberry and the Pacific blackberry) look like elongated, very dark raspberries but have a juicier, fuller flavour. Tayberries are a similar hybrid and are large, conical and deep purple. Boysenberries are long, dark red berries with a sharp flavour. All these berries can be successfully preserved in the same way as raspberries and blackberries.

CURRANTS

Black-, red- and whitecurrants have a sharp, intense flavour and are picked in bunches on stems. Blackcurrants and redcurrants are most common; whitecurrants are an albino strain of redcurrants and have a less acidic flavour. High in both pectin and acid, currants need little cooking. Blackcurrants are usually made into jam, and red- and whitecurrants into jelly.

The simplest way to remove currants from the stalk is to run the prongs of a fork gently down the stalk over a bowl.

BLUEBERRIES AND BILBERRIES

Blueberries and bilberries are small, dark fruits that grow wild in Britain, Europe and the United States. Bilberries, the European species, are dark bluish black with a soft bloom. The slightly flattened sphere-shaped berries measure no more than 1cm/½in across. The larger cultivated blueberry and the wild huckleberry have a similar appearance but a sweeter flavour.

Below: Blueberries have a mild, fragrant flavour and can be made into richly coloured jams.

CRANBERRIES

Small, hard, shiny, deep red cranberries are a member of the blueberry and bilberry family. They are much too sour to eat raw but, once cooked with sugar, can be transformed into sparkling bright red jellies and rich, jam-like sauces, which are traditionally served with turkey.

GOOSEBERRIES

Popular in northern Europe, gooseberries are rarely eaten in other parts of the world. Most bushes produce hard oval berries, dark green in colour with paler stripes, and a smooth or, more usually, fuzzy skin. There is also a softer, pale purple variety.

The fruit is usually too sour to eat raw, but can be made into jellies, jams, chutneys and relishes. Gooseberries are rich in pectin, especially when slightly unripe, so they produce jams and jellies with a good set. Unless the mixture is being strained or sieved, they should be "topped and tailed" (trimmed) before preserving.

PHYSALIS

Also known as Cape gooseberries, although they are unrelated to gooseberries. The golden berries are enclosed in an inedible papery husk. They make good, if rather expensive, jams and bottled fruits.

Above: Tiny redcurrants have a distinctive, tart flavour and are particularly good made into sparkling jellies.

HEDGEROW FRUITS

Elderberries are the fruit of elderberry trees, which grow all over Europe and West Asia and the United States. The berries are small and very dark bluish black and hang in umbrella-like clusters. They can be stripped from the sprigs with a fork and are excellent preserved with crab apples or cooking apples.

Haws are the small dark berries of the hawthorn or May tree. They are slightly astringent and very good cooked with apples to make a dark red jelly.

Hips or roseships are the orangey red seedpods of the rose and can be made into a bittersweet jelly.

Sloes, a type of plum, are the fruit of the blackthorn bush, which is found in Europe and West Asia. The fruits are black with a blue bloom, and measure only about 1cm/½in across. They can be combined with apples and made into a fragrant jelly.

ORCHARD FRUITS

Apples and pears, which are available all year round, are the most common members of this family of fruits. They can be made into jams, jellies and chutneys, bottled in syrup or dried into chewy rings. Other, more unusual, orchard fruits include quinces, japonicas and medlars.

APPLES

There are thousands of varieties of apples, although choice in the shops is usually limited to just a few. Among the most popular eating apples are Gala, Russet, Granny Smith, Braeburn, Golden Delicious and Cox's Orange

Above: Pears are equally good bottled in sweet syrups or spiced vinegars and make a tasty addition to sweet-and-sour chutneys.

Below: Apples are used in almost every type of preserve – from sweet jellies to spicy relishes.

Pippin. These all have their own individual flavours that are captured when the apples are bottled in spiced or flavoured syrup. Well-flavoured eating apples may also be used in chutneys and relishes when retaining the texture of the fruit is desirable. Cooking apples are more frequently used in preserves and give a good pulpy texture to chutneys.

Apples are high in pectin and, on their own, produce rather bland, colourless jams. They are therefore often combined with fruits with a good flavour and low pectin content to produce a jam or jelly with a better set. Using apples as a base is also a good way to make expensive fruit go further. Mild-flavoured apple jelly makes a good base for herb jellies. The jelly usually takes on a pinkish colour, so traditionally a few drops of green food colouring are added.

Most of the pectin in apples is found in the skin and seeds so apple peelings and cores are often used to make a pectin stock. This is then stirred into other fruit jams and jellies to improve their set, without affecting their flavour.

CRAB APPLES

These small apples can be gathered from the wild, from cultivated garden trees or, very occasionally, bought from independent food stores. They have a sharp, rich flavour and are very good used on their own or combined with other hedgerow fruit.

CORING APPLES AND PEARS

To core apples, place a corer over the stalk end and push it right through the fruit. Gently twist the corer and carefully pull out the core.
To core pears, start at the base of the fruit and push the corer only halfway through.

To remove the core from halved fruit, scoop out the cores using a melon baller or a teaspoon to make a neat round hole.

PEARS

Unlike apples, pears are low in pectin, so are less frequently used in jams and jellies. Their sweet, mild flavour and tender texture makes them popular for chutney-making and they are superb preserved in syrup or alcohol, or pickled in raspberry vinegar, either whole, halved or quartered. Pears are divided into eating and cooking varieties, although some eating pears are also suitable for cooking. The British Conference and the American Bosc are particularly good for preserving.

QUINCES

Golden yellow quinces can be the shape and size of a small squat pear or a small apple, or as large as big pears, depending on the variety. The flesh is hard, granular and sour when eaten raw, but cooking makes it smooth and tender, with a delicate tinged soft pink colour and a sherbet-like aromatic flavour. Quinces are rich in pectin and they can be made into jellies, fruit cheeses and butters; these may be a rich golden or a deep pink colour depending on the variety of quince used.

JAPONICAS

These small, round, green fruits are also known as Japanese quinces. They can be preserved in the same ways as quinces, but have a slightly sharper, lemony flavour.

Above: Medlars are not widely available but, if you can find them, they can be made into really delicious preserves.

MEDLARS

Medlars are small brown fruit with a squashed round shape and an open end revealing the seeds. The flesh is very hard and mouth-puckeringly acidic when first picked. To soften and sweeten the fruit, it must be "bletted" or allowed to ferment slightly. The flesh is dry and sticky and tastes a little like the flesh of dried dates. A mixture of unripe and "bletted" medlars can be made into aromatic preserves such as jams, jellies and cheeses.

Above: Quinces have a distinctive, aromatic flavour and can be made into delicious jellies, which are good spread on bread or toast.

STONE FRUITS

These are all fruits of the *prunus* genus, recognized by their single central woody stone (pit), soft flesh and thin skin. They are well-suited to jam-making and can also be used whole or halved in bottled preserves. These fruits come in a wide variety of colours, textures and flavours, from tender pale orange apricots and yellow-skinned tart plums, to glossy sweet red cherries, and they can be made into numerous types of preserves. Plums are available all year round, and although cherries, apricots, peaches and nectarines are sometimes available at other times of the year, they are at their peak in summer and early autumn.

PLUMS

These fruits range in colour from pale gold through red and crimson to deep purple. When buying, choose firm, unwrinkled fruit, which still have a slight bloom. They will keep for several days at room temperature, but will

Below: Plums are most plentiful in the summer, so it is well worth making a batch of jam to enjoy during the rest of the year.

Above: Sweet black cherries can be made into the most delicious, richly flavoured preserves.

continue to ripen. Once they are almost ripe, they can be stored in the refrigerator for a few more days. Use them when just-ripe to make richly flavoured jams.

Mirabelle plums are a French speciality, grown particularly around Alsace. They are small, round, red-flushed yellow plums with a powerful sweet scent. They are usually preserved whole in a liqueur-enriched syrup. Greengages are small, green, fragrant plums, primarily dessert fruits, but excellent bottled or made into luxurious jams.

Purple-black damsons are available only in the early autumn months. Small and sour-tasting, they make superb jams and damson cheese. Bullaces are small, round plums that grow wild throughout Europe and can be used in the same way as damsons.

CHERRIES

These fruits are divided into two main groups: sweet cherries, which may be black (actually deep red) or white (usually yellow), and sour cherries, of which the best known are Morellos. When buying, the cherry's stem is a good indicator of freshness – it should be green and flexible not brown and brittle. Avoid any fruit that is overly soft or split. Cherries are low in pectin, so must either be combined with apples or other pectin-rich fruit, or commercial or home-made pectin stock needs to be added when making jam or other set preserves. Both sweet and sour cherries are excellent pickled or bottled.

Below: Ripe, juicy peaches are delicious preserved in sweet syrups, spirits and liqueurs.

STONING FRUITS

Large stone fruits such as peaches, nectarines, plums and apricots can all be stoned (pitted) in the same way. Cherries can also be stoned in this way, but because they are so small, it is much easier to use a special cherry stoner.

1 Using a sharp knife, carefully cut around the middle of the fruit through the crease that runs from the stem to the tip, right through to the stone.

2 Twist the halves in opposite directions to separate; the stone will remain in one of the halves.

3 To remove the stone, carefully lever it out of the fruit with a knife.

Stoning cherries To remove the stones from cherries, use a cherry stoner. Pull the stalk from the cherry, then place the fruit in the cup of the stoner and squeeze the handles of the tool together. The short prong will push through the fruit and force out the stone.

SKINNING STONE FRUITS

1 Raw peaches, nectarines and thick-skinned plums are difficult to peel with a knife. To loosen the skins, put the fruits in a heatproof bowl and pour over enough boiling water to cover.

2 Leave to stand for 1 minute, then drain and cool the fruit under cold running water. The skin should now come off easily, using the point of a small knife to peel it away.

PEACHES AND NECTARINES

A good peach or nectarine will be richly coloured and heavy, with a strong aroma. Peaches have downy skins and the most common types have yellow or pink flesh. The white-fleshed and pale-skinned variety is the sweetest of all.

Nectarines are similar to peaches but they have smooth and shiny skins and a slightly sharper taste – like a cross between a peach and a plum. They make great jams, are good pickled or bottled, and are also excellent made into fruity chutneys. Peaches and nectarines should be skinned when making jams and chutneys.

APRICOTS

With their slightly sweet-and-sour flavour, soft texture and downy skins, apricots are delicious eaten fresh and raw. Cooking with sugar intensifies their flavour. Slightly under-ripe apricots can be poached in a sugar syrup with a dash of lime juice and bottled. Just-ripe fruit can be cooked with sugar to make jams.

Right: Smooth-skinned nectarines can be preserved in the same way as peaches.

Apricots and almonds are a very popular combination and split almonds can be added to special conserves for extra flavour and texture. When choosing apricots, pick those with the strongest colour for the sweetest flavour.

CITRUS FRUITS

With their aromatic acidity, citrus fruits are the main ingredient of nearly all marmalades and fruit curds. They are also often added to other preserves because they have a high pectin and acid content, and they are frequently used in jams and jellies to help achieve a good set. Their pungency and sharpness adds not only flavour but also offsets sweetness. Members of the citrus family include lemons, limes, oranges, grapefruits and tangerines as well as the more exotic Ugli fruit, citrons and kumquats, and hybrids such as the clementine and limequat. All are covered in a thick peel, which consists mainly of white pith and a colourful outer layer of zest or rind.

Below: Sweet, juicy oranges are most commonly preserved as tangy breakfast marmalades.

ORANGES

There are three types of sweet oranges: the common orange is a medium-size fruit with a fine-grained skin, and popular varieties are Valencia, Jaffa and Shamouti, which is available only in the winter. These are the juiciest oranges and are ideal for sweet marmalades and orange curds. They often contain a lot of pips (seeds), which are essential for marmalade-making because they are high in pectin.

Navel oranges are seedless, so are better preserved whole, in segments or in slices. Red-flushed blood oranges have ruby-coloured flesh and a rich, almost berry-like flavour. These make excellent marmalade when combined with sharper lemons, but are less successful for curd-making because their deeply coloured juice looks rather unappetizing when mixed with yellow butter and eggs.

Bitter Seville oranges have a high pectin and acid content, as well as an excellent, punchy flavour and make the finest marmalades. (The bulk of the Spanish crop is exported to Britain for this purpose.) The season is a fairly short one and they are only available for a few weeks during the winter. However, bitter oranges can be successfully frozen whole or chopped. Alternatively, the oranges can be chopped and cooked without sugar until very soft before cooling and freezing. When ready to use, they can be thawed and then boiled with sugar to setting point.

Above: Sharp, zesty lemons are widely used in both sweet and savoury preserves.

LEMONS

In the preserving kitchen, lemons are indispensable. They add acid and pectin to jams and jellies made from low-pectin fruit such as strawberries and peaches, which are difficult to set. Adding lemon juice to jellies also gives them a sparkling appearance. A dash of lemon juice added to preserves made from soft fruit such as strawberries and exotic fruits such as papayas, helps bring out their flavour. A few spoonfuls of lemon juice added to cold water makes an acidulated dip that will prevent cut fruit such as pears and apples from discolouring.

Small, thin-skinned lemons are juicier, so are perfect for making curds; bigger, more knobbly ones have a higher proportion of peel and pith to flesh, so are better for marmalades and candying.

Above: Limes have a distinctive, sharp flavour and are equally delicious made into sweet marmalades and salty pickles.

LIMES

These small green fruits flourish in near-tropical conditions. They have a distinctive, tangy flavour and are one of the most sour citrus fruits. A squeeze of lime juice can be added to jams and jellies instead of lemon juice to enhance the flavour of the fruit and to improve the set. It goes particularly well with tropical fruits, such as mangoes and papayas.

Right: Tiny orange kumquats look delightful preserved in syrup.

GRAPEFRUITS

One of the largest citrus fruits, with a diameter of up to 15cm/6in. The flesh of grapefruits varies in colour from pale yellow to the dark reddish pink of sweeter ruby grapefruit. The yellow skinned and fleshed varieties have a sharp and refreshing flavour that makes good marmalade. Sweetie grapefruits are a less sharp variety with a vibrant bright green skin.

CITRONS

This large, lemon-shaped fruit grows to 20cm/8in in length. It has a fairly thick lumpy greenish yellow peel that is often candied and is used in commercial candied peel. The very sour-tasting pulp is sometimes made into sweet preserves, but it has no other culinary use.

POMELOS

Also known as the shaddock, this large citrus fruit resembles a pear-shaped grapefruit. The flesh can be used to make jams and the rind can be candied with sugar or used to make marmalade.

Left: Pink grapefruits have a milder flavour than yellow ones and can be made into very pretty preserves.

TANGERINES AND MANDARIN ORANGES

These are the generic names for small, flat citrus fruits with loose skins and a sweet or tart-sweet flavour. Satsumas, clementines and mineolas also fall into this group. Satsumas are slightly tart and very juicy; clementines (a cross between the tangerine and the bitter orange) are similar but have a thinner, more tight-fitting skin. Both fruits are almost seedless so are the best choice for preserving whole in sugar syrup. Mineolas are larger. They are hybrids of the grapefruit and tangerine, have a sharp, tangy flavour and resemble oranges in size and colour.

KUMQUATS AND LIMEQUATS

The tiny, orange, oval kumquat with its distinctive sweet-sour flavour can be eaten whole and unpeeled; the rind has a sweeter flavour than the flesh. Kumquats are delicious pickled, preserved in syrup or candied.

Limequats are a cross between a lime and a kumquat. The small, bright green fruits have a fragrant flavour and can be preserved in the same way as kumquats, although they have a slightly more sour flavour. The two fruits look very pretty bottled together in the same jar and make a lovely gift.

HYBRID FRUITS

There are a huge number of citrus hybrids that are bred for flavour, colour or to be seedless.

ugli fruit

Available in winter, this hybrid of the grapefruit, tangerine and orange has a loose, rough, greeny yellow skin and a slightly squashed appearance. It is very juicy and sweet and can be used instead of grapefruit in marmalades. The peel is very good candied.

temple oranges

These loose-skinned fruits are a cross between a tangerine and an orange. Slightly oval in shape, they have rough, thick, deep orange skin, which makes them popular for marmalade-making in the United States. The flesh is sweet, yet tart and contains a fair number of seeds. Temple oranges are in season from December to March.

buying and storing

Look for firm, plump citrus fruits that feel heavy for their size as this indicates that the fruit will be juicy. Avoid dry, wrinkled specimens, soft squashy fruit or any with brown spots. Green patches on lemons and yellow patches on limes are a sign of immaturity.

Citrus fruits can be kept at room temperature for several days, but for longer storage, keep them in the refrigerator, putting unwaxed fruit in a plastic bag. Always wash and scrub citrus fruits before using them in preserves.

GRATING CITRUS RIND

To make long, thin shreds, scrape a canelle knife or zester along the surface of the fruit, applying firm pressure.

To make finer shreds, gently rub the fruit over the fine side of a grater to remove the rind without taking off any bitter white pith. Use a dry pastry brush to brush off any rind that sticks to the grater.

CUTTING RIND INTO FINE STRIPS OR JULIENNE

1 Using a vegetable peeler or a sharp knife, remove strips of rind as thinly as possible, without taking off any of the bitter white pith.

2 Stack several strips of rind on top of each other and, using a sharp knife, cut them into fine strips or julienne.

FLAVOURING SUGAR

To add a hint of citrus flavour to a preserve, rub the fruit's skin with 1 or 2 sugar cubes, turning the cubes as each side becomes saturated with the oil. Weigh the cubes with the sugar.

PEELING CITRUS FRUIT

1 To peel large citrus fruit such as grapefruit, cut a slice from the top and bottom of the fruit, through the flesh, then cut away the rind, pith and skin, working from top to base, following the curve of the fruit.

2 To peel smaller fruits such as oranges, cut off the rind, pith and skin in a long spiral.

SEGMENTING CITRUS FRUIT

1 Holding the peeled fruit in one hand and the knife in the other, slice the knife down one side of a segment, cutting it away from the membrane. Cut down the other side and pull out the segment.

2 Repeat with the remaining segments, turning back the flaps of membrane like a book. When all the segments are removed, squeeze the remaining fruit to extract the juice.

TROPICAL FRUITS

With imports from many parts of the world, tropical fruits are now available all year round, but tend to be at their best during the winter months. They are often vibrantly coloured with fabulous flavours and make fragrant jams and luxurious chutneys.

PINEAPPLES

This distinctive fruit has extremely juicy, sweet and refreshing golden flesh. It can be made into lovely jams and crisp-textured relishes, which are ideal for serving with chicken, pork and ham. Pineapple rings are also good candied.

Once picked, pineapples do not ripen so always buy ripe fruits. (If you do buy an unripe fruit, leaving it for a few days may help reduce the acidity.) Ripe fruits should give off a sweet aroma and be orange all over with no brown parts. They can be stored in a cool place for up to a week.

PREPARING A PINEAPPLE
1 Using a sharp knife, slice off the base and plume of the pineapple. Rest the cut base on a board. Cut away the peel thinly, working from the top downwards, then cut out the "eyes" following their spiral around the fruit.

2 To make pineapple rings, cut the peeled fruit into thick slices, then remove the central core from each slice using a 2cm/¾in round cookie cutter.

GUAVAS

These fruits have a sweet, almost spicy aroma and flavour, with granular flesh that becomes creamy when ripe. The small oval fruits, no larger than 7.5cm/3in long, have a number of small seeds in the centre. Buy fruits with smooth skins and no wrinkling or brown patches around the stalk. Guavas will keep for a few days in the refrigerator but always wrap them in clear film (plastic wrap) because their aroma will permeate other foods. Peel them thinly, then halve and remove the seeds. They can be made into fragrant jams, cheeses and sparkling jellies, with a honey-like

Right: Pineapples have a sweet, sharp, tangy flavour and are good in jellies, jams and tangy relishes.

aroma, and pink or gold colour, depending on the variety used. It is essential to add lemon or lime juice to preserves that are made with guavas to achieve a good set and to heighten the flavour.

PAPAYAS

Also known as pawpaw, these pear-shaped fruits have a green skin that turns a speckled yellow when the fruit is ripe. The creamy textured flesh is a vibrant orange-pink colour with a wonderful sweet flavour and lovely perfumed aroma. To prepare papayas, cut them in half lengthways and scoop out the numerous black seeds. Use ripe fruits to make jams and butters, and firm, slightly under-ripe fruits to make chutneys.

MANGOES

The skins of these luscious fruits range in colour from green, through yellow and orange to red. Ripe fruits have deep-orange flesh, which will yield slightly when the uncut fruit is gently squeezed. Just-ripe and green under-ripe mangoes can be made into excellent, highly flavoured chutneys and pickles, but over-ripe fruit should be avoided as mangoes tend to become more fibrous when very ripe and soft. When mangoes are scarce or expensive, substitute up to half the total weight of mangoes with cooking apples.

BANANAS

These long, yellow fruits make delicious, though not particularly attractive, jams. Their sweet flavour and soft, pulpy texture combine well with dried fruits such as dates and figs, which need a relatively short cooking time. They are also good in fruity chutneys,

PREPARING A MANGO
The simplest way to prepare a mango is to remove the skin with a vegetable peeler and slice the flesh off the stone (pit). To cut mango flesh into cubes, use the following method.

1 Hold the mango with one hand and cut vertically down one side of the stone. Repeat on the other side.

2 Cut into the flesh, but not all the way through the peel, lengthways and widthways.

3 Holding the mango slices with the flesh side upwards, press each slice inside out, opening the cuts in the flesh. Cut the mango cubes from the peel. Cut any remaining flesh from the stone, remove the peel and cube.

particularly spicy Indian-style preserves. It is best to use just-ripe bananas for preserves; choose ones with smooth, yellow skins that have only a few brown speckles.

Dried bananas are sun-dried in their skins, then peeled to reveal dark, sticky fruit inside. They have a concentrated flavour and can add sweetness to chutneys. Do not confuse them with banana chips, which are hard, dried slices of banana, unsuitable for preserving.

Below: Fragrant mangoes are fabulous made into sweet and tangy chutney.

Plantains, another member of the banana family, are "cooking" bananas. Green-skinned with flecks of brown, turning black when fully ripe, they may retain much of their shape after cooking and are good in vegetable chutneys.

Above: Although not traditionally throught of as a preserving fruit, bananas can be made into surprisingly good chutneys.

Left: Kiwi fruit can be made into pale green jams and chutneys.

KIWI FRUIT

Although completely unrelated to the gooseberry, these fuzzy, brown, egg-shaped fruits were once known as Chinese gooseberries. The flesh is bright green with a sunray pattern of black seeds. Just-ripe fruit (when it yields to gentle pressure) should be used for jam-making. Kiwi fruit has a slightly sharp flavour so it is usually better to use sugar with pectin than to add lemon juice to get a good set.

PASSION FRUIT

These oval fruits have leathery reddish purple skins that become dimpled when the fruit is ripe. Inside are small, hard edible seeds, surrounded by fragrant, intensely flavoured orange pulp. The pulp and seeds may be scooped out of halved passion fruit shells and made into jam. Alternatively, the pulp can be rubbed through a fine sieve with a spoonful of boiling water to extract the juice, leaving the seeds behind. The juice can then be used with other fruit to make intensely flavoured, aromatic jams, jellies and curds.

Grenadillas are a larger, but less fragrant, member of this fruit family.

PERSIMMONS AND SHARON FRUIT

Rather like squarish, squashed tomatoes in shape, persimmons have a deep orange, smooth and shiny skin, and are about 6cm/2½in in diameter. Before they are ripe, the flesh has an astringent taste and pithy texture. The fruits tend to ripen suddenly, transforming into a soft, sweet fruit with no trace of bitterness. This quality encouraged the growers to develop the Sharon fruit, a golden-orange persimmon that is almost entirely seedless and sweet even when firm. The skins are tough, so the fruit should be peeled before making into jam, but this is not necessary when making jellies.

TAMARILLOS

This egg-shaped fruit of the tomato family (sometimes known as a "tree tomato"), may be yellow, red, or dark red; the yellow variety has the finest flavour. Tamarillos can be used in the same way as tomatoes to make pickles and chutneys, but the skin has a very bitter taste so the fruit should be peeled; blanch the fruits first to loosen their skins. Tamarillos can also be made into sweet jellies.

POMEGRANATES

The shape and size of an orange, pomegranates have tough, leathery skin and a large calyx, and range in colour from deep yellow to crimson. Inside are dozens of white seeds surrounded by transluscent pinkish-red flesh, encased in a cream-coloured membrane. The seeds, pith and membranes are bitter so it is the juice that is extracted to make jams and jellies. The simplest way to do this is to cut the fruit in half and use a lemon squeezer to squeeze out the juice, taking care not to crush the seeds. Grenadine, a sweet syrup used in cocktails and mixed drinks, is made from pomegranate juice, and a dash of this can be used to flavour preserves.

Below: The bright pink flesh of pomegranates can be made into beautiful glistening jellies.

MELONS, GRAPES, DATES AND FIGS

These fruits don't fit into any particular category. They were among the first to be cultivated and all come in a vast array of shapes, sizes and colours.

MELONS

There are two kinds of melon: the dessert melon and the watermelon. Dessert melons may have green or yellow skins, sometimes streaky or netted (with fibrous markings), and fragrant, dense flesh, ranging from pale green to deep orange. Most are ripe if they yield under your thumb when pressed on the stem end. They should also give off a sweet aroma. Once ripe, they should be kept in a cool place and used within a few days. When cut they will keep for a day or two in the refrigerator. The flavour of melon in preserves is not intense. They work well if combined with strong flavourings such as ginger, or other fruits such as pineapple, passion fruit, peach and mango. They are also good scooped into balls with a melon baller or cut into cubes and pickled. Watermelons have a high water content, at around 90 per cent, so the flesh is rarely used in preserves. The skin though, can be diced and pickled.

GRAPES

Of the many grape varieties that are available, the smaller seedless grapes are preferable for preserves as they need less preparation and have thin skins with little tannin. Usually, grapes are referred to as either black or white, although the colours vary a great deal from pale green to pinkish red and dark purplish black. Grape flavours range from honey-sweet to sharp and almost lemon-scented. When buying, choose fruits that are firm with smooth skin and no sign of turning brown near the stem end. Store them in the refrigerator and bring to room temperature before using. Grapes make good jams, conserves and jellies that are sometimes flavoured with alcohol such as wine. They can also be pickled or included in chutneys and relishes.

Above: Juicy black grapes are good for making into delicate, fragrant, sparkling jellies.

Left: The orange flesh of cantaloupe melons is excellent scooped into balls and preserved in a sweet syrup.

RHUBARB
Technically, rhubarb is the stem of a vegetable. Outdoor-grown rhubarb is available in late spring and has crimson and green stems; forced rhubarb, cultivated indoors without light, has thin, tender, pale stems. The former can be made into chutney, the latter into a delicately flavoured jam. Rhubarb has a very sharp, intense flavour and goes particularly well with orange and ginger.

Above: Naturally sweet dates make the perfect addition to tangy sweet-and-sour chutneys.

DATES

Plump and glossy, fresh dates are soft and packed with concentrated sugar. The thin papery skins should be slipped off and the long stone (pit) removed before the flesh is added to chutneys. When the date is squeezed at the stem end, the flesh should pop out of the skin, then you can use a sharp knife to cut the fruit in half and carefully prise out the stone.

The sweet flavour of dates combines very well with vinegar to make a wonderful sweet-and-sour preserve that goes particularly well with cheese. Semi-dried and dried dates are also widely available and can be added to chutneys.

FIGS

These fragile fruits have thin skins that may be purple or greenish gold; inside is a glorious soft, scented flesh filled with tiny round seeds. Fresh figs need careful handling as they damage easily. When figs are ripe and yield to a light pressure, they can be poached whole in syrup for bottling; they do not need to be peeled, simply snip off the tough stem. Avoid sour-smelling figs; this indicates

DRIED FRUITS

All kinds of fruits are available dried and they can successfully be made into jams and pickles, or included in chutneys and relishes. Jams made with dried fruits have a concentrated fruity flavour and often require less sugar than fresh fruit jams. Modern tenderized dried fruit, often labelled "ready-to-eat", requires a short soaking time, or sometimes none at all, before being made into jam. Any soaking liquid may be used as part of the recipe. If the fruit needs to be chopped into small pieces, do this after soaking, or it will absorb too much water.

Many dried fruits, including mangoes, apricots, prunes, figs and pears, make good pickles. Less sugar is needed than with fresh fruit and pre-soaking is unnecessary; the fruit is put straight into sterilized bottles and hot vinegar poured over.

Dried fruits are also good added to chutneys, particularly when vegetables with a high water content such as marrows (large zucchini) and squashes are used. The dried fruits help to soak up the liquid. Chopped or whole small dried fruits may be added part way through cooking. They add flavour and also speed up the time it takes the chutney to thicken. The shorter cooking time helps to retain the fresh flavour of the other ingredients.

Raisins, sultanas (golden raisins) and currants are often referred to as vine fruits and are popularly added to chutneys to give a sweet-and-sour result. They are made from grapes that have been dried in the sun. Raisins are made from seeded and seedless grapes, sultanas are produced from seedless white grapes, and currants from small black grapes.

they are over-ripe. When figs are plentiful, they can be made into luxurious conserves and chutneys. Warm spices such as cinnamon and vanilla go very well with figs. Dried figs, with their concentrated flavour, make a thick, dark

and delicious jam. A little grated orange rind added to the mixture heightens the flavour.

Below: Figs have a subtle, sweet flavour and are particularly good bottled whole in syrup.

VEGETABLE FRUITS

Sweet (bell) peppers, tomatoes and aubergines (eggplant) are fruits, but they are treated like vegetables.

THE PEPPER FAMILY

From mild peppers to hot chillies, this family of vegetable fruits can be preserved in pickles, chutneys or relishes, or used to add flavour and texture to preserves made with a variety of other vegetables.

sweet peppers

These are the mildest members of the capsicum family. Young peppers have a sharp flavour and are bright green. As they mature, they become sweeter and turn yellow, then orange and finally red. Preserved green peppers tend to lose their colour with long-term

Above: Sweet peppers can be used in all savoury preserves. Roasting them first brings out their flavour.

storage, which is unimportant in dark chutneys, but best avoided in clear pickles.

chillies

These small peppers with a spicy kick are the world's most popular spice. Green chillies are immature, while red ones are ripe. As a very general rule, chillies sweeten as they ripen so dark green chillies tend to be hotter than paler green ones and red ones. Heat is influenced by a combination of variety and the climate. Anaheim and Dutch chillies are mild, jalapeño and Scotch bonnets are much hotter, and tiny Thai or bird's eye chillies are very hot. Dried chillies are used in most pickling spices.

Left: Crisp green peppers are good in dark-coloured relishes.

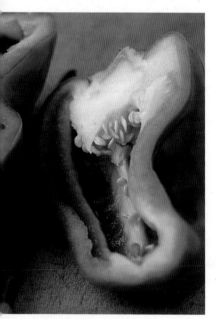

PREPARING FRESH CHILLIES

When handling fresh chillies, either wear gloves or wash your hands in soapy water directly afterwards. Chillies contain capsaicin, which can cause severe irritation to skin, especially on the face.

1 Using a sharp knife, halve the chilli, then cut off and discard the stalk and the very top part of the chilli.

2 Carefully scrape out and discard the seeds and core, then cut out and discard the white membrane, keeping the knife close to the flesh.

3 To chop finely, cut the chilli flesh lengthways into very thin strips, then cut the strips across to make tiny pieces.

TOMATOES

From unripe green tomatoes to ripe red ones, tomatoes are used in all types of pickles and preserves. Ripe tomatoes may be yellow or red, depending on variety and their sweetness or acidity varies according to types as well as how ripe they were when picked. The common round tomato is juicy and fairly acidic. Italian plum tomatoes have an elongated shape with denser flesh and a sweeter flavour. Tiny cherry tomatoes are very sweet, while beefsteak tomatoes are very large and can weigh up to 450g/1lb. Unripe green tomatoes are usually picked at the end of the season when there is not

Above: Tomatoes have tough skins so are often better peeled before adding to pickles and preserves.

enough summer sunshine to ripen them. They are often made into green tomato chutney, but may also be included in tart relishes such as piccalilli. Green tomatoes are slightly bland so are best combined with apples or other fruit and plenty of flavourings.

Ripe tomatoes may be made into sweet jams and marmalades as well as savoury jellies, chutneys, relishes, sauces and pickles. If the tomatoes are not going to be strained after cooking, their tough skins should be removed before cooking; the easiest way to do this is to blanch them first. Ripe tomatoes can also be dried in the oven, then bottled in oil.

Choose firm, unblemished tomatoes, preferably with the calyx intact. Once ripe, they should be preserved as soon as possible, although they can be stored in the salad drawer of the refrigerator for a few days.

PREPARING TOMATOES

1 To peel tomatoes, make a shallow cross at the base of each one. Place in a bowl and pour over boiling water. Leave for 30 seconds, or until the skin curls away at the cut.

2 Drain the tomatoes, dip in cold water and peel.

3 To remove the seeds, cut the tomatoes into quarters and cut out the seeds with a knife.

AUBERGINES/EGGPLANT

The most common aubergines are large, dark purple and oval but there are also smaller round purple ones and a little oval, ivory-white variety that inspired the American name eggplant. Aubergines may be pickled raw, either sliced or whole, but they are more usually chopped and cooked in pickles. Aubergines are often salted when making chutneys and pickles to extract some of the moisture, which would otherwise dilute the mixture. When buying, look for small to medium-size aubergines with smooth and shiny skins; they will have sweet, tender flesh. Larger specimens with wrinkled skins are too mature and may be tough and slightly bitter. Aubergines can be stored in the refrigerator for up to two weeks before preserving.

Below: Baby aubergines are great pickled whole in brine or vinegar with whole spices.

THE ONION FAMILY

ONIONS

These include strongly flavoured brown-skinned onions, used for everyday cooking, and the larger mild, sweet and juicy Spanish onions, which are also known as yellow onions. White onions with papery skins and red onions are mild and sweet, the latter adding a good colour to preserves. All types of onion can be made into onion chutneys and relishes, sliced and pickled in rings, or dried.

Pickling onions have brown papery skins and are also called button or pearl onions. They are main-crop onions, picked when very small. The milder-tasting and smaller silverskin onions, which are harvested when they have a diameter of no more than 2.5cm/1in, can also be pickled. Soaking them in a wet brine for 24–36 hours draws out some of the moisture and gives them a crunchier texture when pickled. It is important to use a stainless steel knife when preparing onions to prevent the cut surfaces of the onion from darkening.

Above: Red onions have a sweet, mild flavour and can add a lovely colour to preserves.

Above: Shallots have a strong flavour and are very good pickled in malt or cider vinegar.

SHALLOTS

These are a different variety of onion, grown in clusters rather than as single bulbs. They have an elongated shape and papery russet skin. Shallots have a fuller, sweeter flavour than onions and are delicious pickled.

SPRING ONIONS

Also known as green onions or scallions, these are young bulb onions, pulled while the tops are still green and before the bulb has had a chance to swell. Long cooking does not suit spring onions, so they are rarely used in chutneys. They may, however, be added to relishes with short cooking times.

PEELING PICKLING ONIONS

1 Place the onions in a bowl and pour over boiling water to cover. Leave for 1–2 minutes.

2 Drain the onions and rinse under cold water to cool. Using a sharp knife, trim the tops and root end, then slip the skins from the onions.

Below: Spring onions can be pickled whole, or chopped and added to relishes and chutneys.

LEEKS

Long, thin leeks are the mildest members of the onion family. They are included in chutneys to add texture and flavour, or pickled on their own. To clean leeks, slit them lengthways and rinse under cold water to remove any trapped grit.

GARLIC

This is the most pungent member of the onion family. One or two cloves can be used to add a subtle flavour to chutney and relishes. Vinegar can be flavoured with garlic, then used to make preserves; peel the cloves and add 5–6 to each 600ml/1 pint/2½ cups vinegar. Leave for 2 weeks to infuse. Use within 4 months.

Above: Garlic can be pickled whole, or used as a flavouring in all kinds of savoury preserves.

MUSHROOMS

There are dozens of edible mushrooms. The common cultivated mushroom is sold at various stages in its growth. Button (white) mushrooms are the youngest and these are the best for pickling and preserving as they are firm and their round, compact shape means that they are less likely to be damaged by packing into jars. When the cap has partially opened, mushrooms are sold as cup mushrooms and, when opened out completely, as flat or Portabello mushrooms. The larger they grow, the more flavour they have and the darker their juices. Mushroom varieties such as pale,

fan-shaped oyster and dark brown, cup-shaped shiitake are less suitable for preserves because they lose their delicate texture and become rubbery. Buy really fresh firm-textured mushrooms and preserve promptly after buying. Wipe them clean with a damp cloth and wash only if very dirty; do not leave mushrooms to soak. Keep them whole or halve or quarter them, depending on size. Mushrooms are often flavoured with herbs such as dill, and warm spices such as mace. They can also be dried successfully – shiitake mushrooms and wild fungi dry particularly well.

Above: Large flat mushrooms have a good, strong flavour and a rich, dark colour so are perfect for making into mushroom ketchup.

ROOTS AND TUBERS

Vegetables that grow underground include roots such as carrots and turnips, and tubers such as potatoes and Jerusalem artichokes. Roots and tubers tend to become starchier with age, so they are usually preserved while young, sweet and tender.

When preparing beetroot, be careful not to damage the skin, or the colour will leach out. Trim the stalks to 2.5cm/1in above the root. When pickling whole, choose even-size beetroot that require the same cooking time; small beetroot are preferable as they are sweeter and more tender than larger ones.

CARROTS

These sweet-tasting orange roots can be chopped or grated and used in chutneys, relishes and wonderful sweet jams. Carrot jam probably originated during the Second World War, when fruit was scarce, but it is every bit as good as fruit jams and can be made more luxurious with the addition of almonds and citrus flavouring.

PARSNIPS, SWEDES/ RUTABAGAS AND TURNIPS

Closely related to the carrot, but with a sweeter taste and a nutty flavour, creamy-coloured parsnips should be scrubbed before preserving and peeled if tough. Use young vegetables because large roots can be very woody.

The globe-shaped swede has creamy orange flesh and a delicate, sweet flavour.

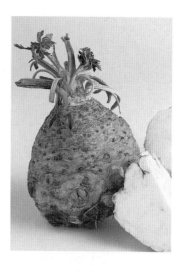

Above: Big, knobbly celeriac have a distinctive yet delicate flavour.

Turnips are smaller than swede, and they have a smoother skin and white flesh with a peppery flavour. Tender young spring turnips are ideal for pickling and preserving.

Above: Baby carrots are delicious pickled whole in spiced vinegar.

BEETROOT/BEET

Dark ruby-red beetroot has a rich, earthy, sweet flavour and is one of the most commonly preserved root vegetables. Pickled beetroot is eaten throughout Europe, and sweet-and-sour Harvard beets are popular in the United States. There are two varieties of beetroot: globe and a long, slender variety. The former is usually preserved whole and the latter sliced into rounds.

Right: Tender, crunchy baby turnips are excellent pickled.

CELERIAC

Related to celery, this knobbly root has a similar flavour. In shape and size it looks a bit like a rough-skinned swede (rutabaga), but the flesh is ivory coloured. It should be thickly peeled before using and immediately immersed in acidulated water to prevent it from turning brown. Choose small celeriac, as older ones can be stringy and may have large hollows in the flesh. Celeriac can be cubed and added to chutneys instead of celery or coarsely shredded and pickled with other root vegetables such as carrots. Dill and orange go especially well with celeriac.

RADISHES

These have a refreshing, but very peppery flavour. The familiar small round or slightly elongated red or white varieties are sold all year round. The white Japanese radish, known as mooli or daikon, is considerably larger and longer; it looks like a large, very smooth parsnip. Mooli has a mild flavour and can be cut into paper-thin slices and pickled.

HORSERADISH

This extremely pungent root is never eaten as a vegetable. The knobbly root is peeled and then grated before being made into a condiment, usually with oil and vinegar. The astringency of its flavour makes horseradish the perfect accompaniment for rich or fatty foods. The vapours that are given off while grating horseradish are extremely irritating and quite unpleasant but the end result makes the process worthwhile.

KOHLRABI

The edible part of kohlrabi is the stalk or tuber that swells above the ground. They are similar to turnips in size, appearance and taste. It is best to use small kohlrabi, no more than 5cm/2in across, for preserving because they toughen with age and their flesh becomes course and fibrous. To prepare kohlrabi, trim off the base and leaves, and peel thinly. Put the cut vegetable into acidulated water immediately to prevent it browning. Use sliced or chopped in chutneys.

Below: Tiny, peppery radishes are delicious pickled and served with cold meats or cheeses.

JERUSALEM ARTICHOKES

These small, knobbly tubers have a delicious nutty, sweet flavour when cooked. Peeling off the brown skin is time-consuming but essential – use a swivel-bladed peeler or a small sharp paring knife. These tasty vegetables can be used in chutneys and are delicious in spicy Indian relishes.

PREVENTING DISCOLORATION

Many vegetables, including parsnips, radishes, celeriac and Jerusalem artichokes, discolour very quickly when their cut flesh is exposed to air. To avoid discoloration, always prepare these vegetables with a stainless steel rather than a carbon-steel knife, and prevent the flesh browning either by submerging them or blanching them in acidulated water.

Acidulated water In a large bowl, combine 30ml/2 tbsp vinegar or lemon juice for every 600ml/1 pint/2½ cups cold water. Add the vegetables and keep them immersed by weighing them down with a plate. Use as soon as possible.

Blanching Make a paste with 15ml/1 tbsp plain (all-purpose) flour and 45ml/3 tbsp cold water, then stir in 30ml/ 2 tbsp lemon juice. Whisk the paste into a pan of salted boiling water, then add the vegetables and blanch them briefly before preserving.

SQUASHES

There are two main categories of this vegetable: summer squash and winter squash, but most are now available all year round. They vary in size and shape from small, dark green courgettes (zucchini) to large, round, orange pumpkins.

Above: Butternut squash has sweet orange flesh that is great added to chutneys and pickles.

WINTER SQUASHES

These squashes have tough inedible skins, fibrous flesh and large seeds, and include butternut squash, acorn squash, and pumpkins. Their dense, sweet flesh cooks to a thick pulp and can be made into tasty jams but they can also be used to add sweetness and a rich orange colour to chutneys.

SUMMER SQUASHES

When young and immature, these squashes have thin, edible skins and seeds. They are used to make chutneys, but may also be made into relishes and salsas because they become tender after a fairly short cooking time.

marrows

Known as large zucchini in the United States, marrows have a pleasant, but bland, flavour and high water content, so they are best brined before making into chutney. Although the skin is edible, it is quite tough so marrows are usually peeled, and the seeds discarded. Marrow can be combined with stronger-tasting vegetables and warm spices such as ginger.

Right: Courgettes are best pickled when young and tender.

Above: Mild tasting cucumbers are perfect for pickles and relishes.

cucumbers

Due to their high water content, cucumbers are usually brined before preserving. As a rule, small ridged cucumbers are pickled; long salad ones are used in relishes.

courgettes/zucchini

Picked when small, courgettes have a dark green shiny skin with light streaks, and creamy coloured flesh. The seeds are very tender.

patty pan squashes

Shaped like flying saucers, patty pan squashes are green, yellow or striped. They look attractive cut into triangular wedges, then pickled.

BRASSICAS

This family of vegetables range from pale leafy Chinese leaves (Chinese cabbage) to compact Brussels sprouts. Cabbages and cauliflower, in particular, are widely used in pickles, chutneys and relishes. Softer leafy greens such as spinach, spring greens (collards) and Swiss chard, are less suited to preserving because they discolour and lose their texture.

CABBAGES

The many types of cabbage range from dark green, crinkly-leafed Savoy to smooth, tightly wrapped white cabbages. From a preserving point of view, it is the firm white and red cabbages that are most suitable. Red cabbage is similar to white cabbage in texture, but has a sweeter taste and takes slightly longer to cook. If it needs to be blanched before preserving, a little vinegar should be added to the

Below: Firm red cabbage can be made into a delicious pickle with a fabulous dark pink hue.

water to help retain the red colour. Preserved cabbage is found in many cuisines, from the German fermented sauerkraut to sour Korean *kimchee*, which is flavoured with ginger, chilli and garlic. Hot and warm spices such as caraway seeds and juniper berries, go particularly well with cabbage. Choose firm, young cabbages and discard any tough outer leaves.

CAULIFLOWER

The creamy white florets of this mild-flavoured brassica feature in many savoury preserves, notably piccalilli, in which it is lightly cooked to retain its shape and crisp texture. It soaks up spices well and so is often used in hot and spicy Indian pickles and chutneys. When buying, check that the florets are not discoloured and that the remaining leaves are fresh and green, not yellow and wilted.

Above: Firm, white cauliflower is delicious broken into florets and pickled.

BROCCOLI

Dark green broccoli isn't often used in preserves because it tends to discolour when stored for any length of time. The long cooking required for chutneys would make the broccoli disintegrate, so cut it into tiny florets and add towards the end of the cooking time in piccalilli and relishes.

MAKING SAUERKRAUT
This classic pickled cabbage from Germany has a sharp, pungent flavour that goes very well with meats and cheeses.

1 Finely shred 1.2kg/2½lb white cabbage. Toss it with 25g/1oz coarse kosher salt and 7.5ml/1½ tsp spices such as caraway seeds, crushed juniper berries and black peppercorns. Leave the cabbage to stand for about 10 minutes, mix again, then pack into a large sterilized crock or bowl, pressing down well.

2 Weight the cabbage with a large plate, cover the crock or bowl with a lid and leave it in a cool place (below 20°C/70°F) for 1 week.

3 Remove the plate and skim off any scum with a spoon. Repeat daily for about 1 month until no more scum appears. (This means that the cabbage has stopped fermenting and it is ready.)

4 Pack into sterilized jars, cover and store in the refrigerator for up to 1 month.

SHOOTS

These tender vegetables have mild but distinctive flavours and are very good used in preserves.

ASPARAGUS

White and purple asparagus are grown in Spain, Holland and France under mounds of earth and picked just as the tips begin to show, while the spears of green asparagus, popular in Britain and America, develop their colour because it grows above ground. Asparagus can be included in luxurious preserves. Use when very fresh; the stalks should be firm and the tips plump.

Below: Young tender asparagus makes a very upmarket chutney to serve with light meats or shellfish.

FENNEL

Florence fennel has squat, plump bulbs with a similar texture to celery, and green feathery fronds. It has a mild aniseed flavour that mellows and sweetens when pickled. Keep it in the refrigerator and use within a few days, while the bulb is firm and the greenery still fresh. Use white wine or sherry vinegar without pickling spices. Small fennel bulbs can be pickled whole; larger ones should be halved or quartered. Blanch the fennel in brine, then leave to cool; pack into jars and top up with cold vinegar. Chopped fennel can be added to chutneys, and the green fronds may be chopped and used in apple jelly.

CELERY

Crisp, crunchy celery may have white or green stalks, which should snap easily and not bend. Celery does not make a good pickle on its own, but is often added to mixed pickles, chutneys and relishes. Wrapped in a plastic bag, celery will keep in the refrigerator for a week or more. Sometimes the outside stalks are removed and the top of the celery trimmed, leaving the sweet celery hearts.

GLOBE ARTICHOKES

These look like enormous thistle-heads with purple-tinged green leaves. They are difficult to preserve whole, but the hearts can be pickled in a mild vinegar, such as white wine or cider (apple cider) vinegar, then drizzled with olive oil to serve.

Above: Globe artichokes are difficult to preserve whole, but their leaves can be removed and the hearts preserved in vinegar.

PREPARING GLOBE ARTICHOKES

1 Hold the artichoke firmly and, using a sharp knife, cut off the stalk close to the base.

2 Peel away the leaves from the artichoke, rubbing the exposed parts with lemon juice to stop them browning.

3 Trim the artichoke heart with a paring knife, removing any tough areas and rubbing frequently with lemon juice.

4 Using a teaspoon, scoop out and discard the hairy choke from the middle of the artichoke, then immerse the heart in a bowl of cold water with 30ml/2 tbsp lemon juice.

PODS AND SEEDS

This group of vegetables, which includes peas, beans and corn, are all good in chutneys and relishes.

PEAS

Fresh peas in their pods have a delicate sweet flavour and make a tasty addition to chutneys and relishes. They should be added about 10 minutes before the end of cooking time, so that they stay firm and keep their colour.

BROAD/FAVA BEANS

These can be used in the same way as peas, but choose young fresh ones because the skins become tough as the beans mature.

GREEN BEANS

All types of green beans can be used to add flavour, colour and texture to preserves. French beans are small, narrow green beans with round pods that are available all year round;

Above: Corn kernels can be stripped from the cobs and used to make a delicious relish.

American green beans are similar, but much larger; flat runner beans are popular in Britain and are at their best when the home-grown crop is available in summer. Top and tail beans before use; some varieties of runner beans, and particularly older ones, may need stringing.

Below: Broad beans, runner beans and French beans can all be added to chutneys and preserves.

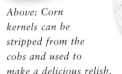

SWEETCORN

Corn cobs should be used as soon as possible after picking, before their natural sugars turn to starch. Choose cobs with plump, fresh kernels that are unwrinkled and show no signs of browning. Shuck the cobs and strip off the kernels using a sharp knife. Baby corn cobs have a more delicate flavour than mature ones; they can be sliced into rounds and used in the same ways. Store corn cobs in the refrigerator for no more than a few days.

DRIED BEANS

These can be pickled or added to chutneys and relishes. The beans need to be soaked, then boiled for 10 minutes before simmering in unsalted boiling water until tender. They can then be drained and bottled in vinegar flavoured with fresh herbs or spices. Cooked beans can also be added to chutneys and relishes – stir them in about 10 minutes before the end of the cooking time.

HERBS AND FLOWERS

Flavourings are an essential part of most preserves and using the right amount is as important as selecting the correct one. In some preserves a subtle hint is all that is needed; in others the flavouring is one of the main ingredients.

HERBS

Fresh and dried herbs are invaluable in savoury preserves, and are included occasionally in sweet ones. They can be added during the initial cooking, then removed, or finely chopped and stirred in towards the end of cooking. If dried herbs are used instead of fresh, then reduce the quantity by a third to half.

Below: Oregano has a lovely, aromatic flavour that is very good with summer squashes.

tender herbs

Herbs with fragile leaves need careful handling to avoid bruising. Once picked, they should be used within a few days. Tie the whole herb stalks in muslin (cheesecloth) and add to the simmering preserve, or stir chopped leaves into the preserve at the end of cooking.
Basil This highly aromatic herb bruises and discolours easily, so rather than adding it to a preserve, it can be steeped in vinegar until it imparts its flavour, then removed.
Chervil Use these tiny, soft and lacy leaves soon after picking. They have a flavour similar to parsley with a hint of aniseed, which goes well with mild, delicate vegetables.
Mint The many varieties of this aromatic herb include peppermint, spearmint, apple mint, lemon mint and pineapple mint. It adds a fresh flavour to preserves, but should be used sparingly.
Parsley Curly and flat leaf varieties are available. It is an essential herb in a bouquet garni.
Tarragon This herb is excellent for flavouring vinegars but is rarely used in its fresh form because it darkens and discolours on heating.

robust herbs

Often woody, with pungent leaves, these herbs are added to preserves during cooking to extract and mellow their flavour.
Bay leaf Essential in bouquet garni, these dark green glossy leaves should be dried for a few days before use. They add a slightly spicy flavour to preserves.

Above: Parsley has a mild flavour and is often used with other herbs.

Marjoram and oregano Popular in tomato preserves, these herbs are also good with marrow (large zucchini). They should be added towards the end of cooking.
Rosemary Powerfully aromatic, fresh or dried rosemary should be used in small quantities. It goes very well with citrus fruits.
Sage A strong herb that often partners garlic and tomatoes.
Thyme This robust herb works well with preserves made from roasted vegetables and beans.

aromatic and spicy herbs

Some herbs have aromatic citrus flavours, others aniseed tones; a few have a warm, spicy pungency.
Coriander/cilantro Every part of this aromatic herb can be used – from its delicate leaves and sturdier stalks to its hard brown seeds. Also known as Chinese parsley, the leaves resemble slightly

rounded flat leaf parsley. They have a warm, spicy taste and add pungency to Middle Eastern, Asian and Indian chutneys and fresh, Mexican-style relishes.

Dill This delicate herb has dark green, feathery leaves and has a subtle aniseed taste. It is an excellent flavouring for mild-tasting courgette (zucchini) and cucumber relishes and pickles.

Fennel Part of the same family as dill, with a similar, but stronger flavour, it is particularly good for flavouring vinegars.

Kaffir lime leaf This strong-tasting, aromatic leaf is used to flavour Thai and Malaysian preserves.

Lemon grass A tall hard grass, with a distinctive lemony aroma and taste, lemon grass is often used in Thai preserves and should be bruised to release the flavour.

Lovage Similar to celery leaves with a peppery flavour, lovage is good with root vegetables and in mixed vegetable chutneys.

FLOWERS

Many types of edible flowers and their leaves can be used to add fragrance and flavour to preserves, including the flowers of herbs such as rosemary, thyme, marjoram, fennel and chives.

Borage The tiny, brilliant blue or purple flowers of this plant can be candied or used to decorate jellies. Borage leaves have a fresh cucumber-like taste and can be used to flavour jellies.

Geranium leaves These give jams and jellies a subtle flavour. There are several different varieties with apple, rose or lemon aromas.

Lavender Intensely fragrant, sprigs of lavender can be used to flavour sugar, jams and jellies. The sprigs also look very pretty suspended in jelly: dip them in boiling water first, then shake off the excess before putting them in the jar and pouring over the hot jelly.

Rose Scented red, pink or yellow petals make wonderful jams and jellies. They are often combined with fruit juice, such as grape, and with added pectin, so that the preserve sets quickly without destroying the aroma of the petals. Be sure to use unsprayed roses.

Left: Tender-leafed basil has a fragrant, peppery flavour that goes particularly well with tomato-based preserves.

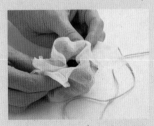

SPICES

These can be hot and spicy or warm and fragrant and are used in all kinds of preserves both for flavour and decoration. Store spices in a cool, dark place: ground ones will keep for up to six months, whole spices for a year.

HOT SPICES

These spices are used to add heat to preserves, and can be mild and subtle or exceedingly fiery.
Cayenne Made from ground dried chillies, cayenne is extremely hot and should be used sparingly.
Chillies Fresh chillies may be cooked in preserves to add heat, or added whole or chopped to clear pickles when bottling.

Below: Sweet, mild paprika is used to add both flavour and colour to chutneys and relishes.

Chilli powder This hot spice is made from ground dried chillies. Mild chilli powder and chilli seasoning are both blends of ground chilli and milder spices such as cumin, oregano and garlic.
Galangal Related to ginger, with pink-tinged flesh, galangal is often used in Malasian- and Thai-style preserves. Ginger may be used as a substitute.
Ginger Good in both sweet and savoury preserves, root ginger may be used fresh, dried or ground. Preserved stem ginger can be added to conserves and marmalades.
Mustard There are three types of mustard seed: white, brown and black; the latter is the hottest. The taste and aroma develops when the seeds are crushed or mixed with liquid. Whole mustard seeds are often included in pickles and ground mustard powder in relishes. The intensity diminishes with long simmering, so mustard powder is often added towards the end of cooking. Salt and vinegar also reduce its pungency.
Paprika This rich, red spice is sold ground and used for its colour and flavour, which ranges from mild and sweet to strong and pungent.
Peppercorns Often added whole to pickles, these tiny round berries may be green, black or white. Green ones are unripe and mildly flavoured, black ones are hot and pungent. White peppercorns have a mild aromatic flavour.
Turmeric Although yellow turmeric has a distinctive warm, spicy taste, it is often used simply for its colour as a cheap alternative to saffron in pickles and relishes.

Above: Fresh root ginger adds warmth and a lively fresh flavour to all kinds of preserves.

SEED SPICES

Some plants such as coriander and dill are cultivated for both their leaves and seeds; others, including caraway and cumin, are grown for their seeds alone.
Caraway seeds These are mildly pungent and feature in many northern European preserves, notably sauerkraut. The seeds need long soaking or cooking to soften them and release the flavour.
Cumin seeds Tiny light brown seeds with a distinctive warm flavour, cumin is used in Indian, Mexican, North African and Middle Eastern preserves. Cumin seeds are widely available both whole and ground.

GRINDING WHOLE SPICES
Spices may be bought ready-ground but most are best when freshly ground because, once ground, they quickly lose their flavour and aroma. Grind spices by hand using a mortar and pestle, or use a spice mill or coffee grinder reserved solely for this purpose.

Above: Whole cinnamon sticks are often used to flavour sweet syrups for preserving fruits.

Coriander seeds These small round seeds have a mild orange flavour and taste very different from the green leafy herb. They are usually included in pickling spice.

Dill seeds Small oval seeds with a similar flavour to caraway, these are often used with cucumber pickles and relishes.

Left: Golden saffron threads can be used to impart a subtle flavour and glorious colour.

FRAGRANT SPICES

Spices with a warm, fragrant flavour are good used in both fruity and sweet preserves.

Allspice With an aroma and flavour that is reminiscent of cloves, cinnamon and nutmeg, this is good used with orchard fruits.

Cassia and cinnamon The bark of evergreen trees, these are available ground or in sticks. The sticks are best used whole for flavouring pale or clear preserves.

Cloves These tiny dried flower buds, sold whole or ground, have a distinctive taste that goes well with apples and citrus fruit.

Juniper Used to give gin its distinctive flavour, blue-black juniper berries may be used fresh, but are more usually dried.

Nutmeg and mace Nutmeg has a warm nutty flavour. It is best bought whole and grated fresh. Mace is the orange-coloured lacy outer covering of the nutmeg; it is sold as blades.

Saffron Made from the dried stigmas of the *Crocus sativus*, saffron is the most expensive of all spices. Only a few threads are needed to produce a golden colour and impart a bitter-sweet flavour.

Star anise This star-shaped, aniseed-flavoured spice looks wonderful in pickles and bottled preserves. It can also be used sparingly in chutneys.

Tamarind This dark brown pulp from the pod of the tamarind tree adds a unique sour flavour to preserves and pickles.

Vanilla Used to flavour bottled fruits and occasionally jams and jellies, long, dark brown vanilla pods (beans) have a sweet, warm, aromatic flavour. The pods can be re-used if rinsed thoroughly, dried and stored in an airtight jar.

PICKLING SPICES

Various blends of pickling spices are available. It is worth searching for a preferred blend or making your own. Typical mixtures include allspice, bay leaf, cardamom, coriander and mustard seeds, cassia or cinnamon, dried chillies, whole cloves, dried root ginger and peppercorns. Add 5–15ml/1–3 tsp of pickling spices to each 600ml/ 1 pint/2½ cups vinegar and simmer for 5–15 minutes, then cool and strain. Alternatively, tie the spices in muslin (cheesecloth), cook in the preserve, then remove.

Below: Vanilla, star anise, ground ginger and cinnamon sticks are all widely used in preserves.

PRESERVING INGREDIENTS

A few special ingredients are essential when making preserves, because they contribute to the keeping quality of the final jam, jelly or pickle. The four main preservatives are sugar, vinegar, salt and alcohol. These all help to prolong the life of the other ingredients used in the preserve by creating an environment in which micro-organisms such as moulds and bacteria cannot grow.

SUGAR

This is the key preservative used in jams, jellies, marmalades, curds and many preserved fruits. A high proportion of sugar is needed and if the sugar content is less than 60 per cent of the total weight of the preserve (for example, in low-sugar

jams), this will affect the keeping quality of the preserve. These low-sugar jams and fruit preserves should be used within a few months or kept in the refrigerator to prevent the growth of mould.

Sugar also plays an important role in the setting of jams, jellies and marmalades. To achieve a good set, sugar should make up between 55 and 70 per cent of the total weight of the preserve. (High acid content in the fruit makes the exact amount of sugar less crucial.)

white sugars

These refined sugars produce clear, set, sweet preserves.
Preserving sugar has quite large, irregular crystals and is ideal for jams, jellies and marmalades. The large crystals allow water to percolate between them, which helps to prevent the preserve burning and reduces the need for stirring (which is important to avoid breaking up fruit too much). Use this sugar for the clearest preserves. If preserving sugar is unavailable, granulated sugar can be used instead.
Preserving sugar with pectin Also known as jam sugar, this sugar is used with low-pectin fruit. The sugar contains natural pectin and citric acid to help overcome setting problems. Preserves made with this sugar tend to have a shorter shelf-life and should be stored for no longer than six months.

Left: White and golden sugars are a key ingredient used in sweet fruit preserves, jams and jellies.

Granulated sugar is slightly coarser than caster (superfine) sugar, less expensive and gives a clear result.
Cube sugar is made from white granulated sugar that has been moistened, moulded into blocks, dried and cubed. It gives the same results as preserving sugar.

brown sugars

These sugars give a pronounced flavour and darker colour to both sweet and savoury preserves.
Demerara/raw sugar is a pale golden sugar with a mild caramel flavour. Traditionally an unrefined sugar with a low molasses content, it may also be made from refined white sugar with molasses added.
Golden granulated sugar may be refined or unrefined. It can be used instead of white sugar for a hint of flavour and colour.
Soft brown sugar is moist, with fine grains and a rich flavour. It may be light or dark in colour and is usually made from refined white sugar with molasses added.
Muscovado/molasses sugar may be light or dark and is usually made from unrefined cane sugar. It has a deeper, more pronounced taste than soft brown sugar.
Palm sugar is made from the sap of palms and has a fragrant flavour. Sold pressed into blocks, it needs to be chopped before use. Light muscovado (brown) sugar is a good alternative.
Jaggery is a raw sugar from India with a distinctive taste. It must be chopped before use. Use a mixture of light brown muscovado and demerara sugar as an alternative.

Right: Raspberry and white wine vinegar are used both to preserve ingredients and to add a sharp, tangy flavour.

VINEGARS

The word vinegar comes from the French *vin aigre*, meaning sour wine. Vinegar is made by exposing fruit or grain-based alcohol to air; a bacterial reaction then turns the alcohol into acetic acid and it is this acid that helps to prevent the growth of micro-organisms in pickles and preserves. Vinegar used for pickling must have an acetic acid content of at least 5 per cent.

Malt vinegar is made from a type of beer. It usually has an acetic acid content of 8 per cent, which allows it to be safely diluted by moisture and juices from fruit and vegetables. Malt vinegar usually contains caramel, which turns it a dark brown colour. Its strong flavour makes it ideal for pickles, chutneys and bottled sauces.

Pickling vinegar is simply malt vinegar flavoured with spices.

Distilled malt vinegar has the same strong flavour as ordinary malt vinegar but is colourless and therefore suitable for making clear pickles and light preserves.

Wine vinegar may be red or white, depending on the colour of the original wine. Most wine vinegars contain about 6 per cent acetic acid. White wine vinegar is mild and better for delicate preserves; red wine vinegar is slightly more robust and good for spiced fruits.

Raspberry vinegar, made by steeping the fruit in wine vinegar, is excellent for pickled fruits.

Balsamic vinegar has a smooth, mellow flavour. Its low acidity makes it unsuitable for use on its own, but it can be used as a flavouring for mild preserves, stirred in at the end of cooking.

Sherry vinegar is slightly sweet with a fairly strong flavour.

Cider vinegar has a slightly sharp taste and a fruity flavour. It is excellent for fruit preserves.

Rice vinegar Colourless, mild rice vinegar is made from rice wine and is often used for pickling ginger.

SALT

This is used in preserving both as a seasoning and as a dehydrator. It is often used in a process called brining to draw out moisture from vegetables such as cucumber and marrow, making them crisp and preventing the dilution of the preserve, which would reduce its keeping quality. Ordinary table and cooking salt is fine for this process, but use pure crystal salt, also known as kosher salt, or preserving or rock salt for clear pickles as ordinary table and cooking salts contain anti-caking ingredients that cause clouding.

ALCOHOL

Spirits, such as brandy and rum, and liqueurs, which are at least 40% ABV (alcohol by volume), can be used. Fortified wine, wine, beer and cider have a lower alcohol content so are not effective alone and should be either heat treated or combined with sugar.

ACIDS

These help to set jams and jellies and prevent discoloration.

Lemon juice adds pectin, prevents fruits from turning brown and enhances both flavour and colour. Use either freshly squeezed or bottled lemon juice.

Citric acid is sold as fine white crystals and can be used instead of lemon juice in preserves.

Tamarind is a spice used both for its acid flavour and its character.

Above: Many different kinds of salt – from coarse sea salt to preserving salt – can be used for pickling.

EQUIPMENT

While very few specialist items are essential for preserving, having the correct equipment for the job will make the whole process easier and helps to ensure success. You will probably have most of the basic items such as a large heavy pan, weighing scales or calibrated measuring cups, wooden spoons, a chopping board and a few sharp knives. However, a few specific items such as a jam funnel for potting preserves and a jelly bag for straining fruit juices will prove invaluable. The following is a brief outline of the more useful items, all of which are readily available from large department stores and specialist kitchen equipment stores.

PRESERVING PAN

A preserving pan or large, heavy pan is essential. It must be of a sufficient size to allow rapid boiling without bubbling over (a capacity of about 9 litres/ 16 pints/8 quarts is ideal); wide enough to allow rapid evaporation of liquid, so that setting point is reached quickly; and have a thick heavy base to protect the preserve from burning. Preserving pans are fitted with a pair of short-looped handles, or a carrying handle over the top. A non-corrosive preserving pan such as one made of stainless steel is the best choice for making all types of preserves, especially for pickles, chutneys and relishes that contain a high concentration of acid. Traditional copper preserving pans, usually very wide at the top and sloping to a narrow base, are intended only for jam- and jelly-

making and are unsuitable for preserves containing vinegar or lemon juice, or for acidic or red fruit, as both the flavour and colour will be spoilt. Enamel pans do not conduct heat fast enough for preserving and they burn easily.

SUGAR THERMOMETER

Invaluable for cooking preserves to the exact temperature needed for a perfect set. Choose a thermometer that goes up to at least 110°C/ 230°F, and has a clip or a handle that can be attached to the pan, so that it does not slip into the boiling preserve.

JELLY BAG

Used to strain fruit juices from cooked fruit pulp for jelly-making, jelly bags are made from calico, cotton flannel or nylon. The close weave allows only the fruit juice to flow through, leaving the pulp behind. Some jelly bags have their own stands; others have loops with which to suspend the bag.

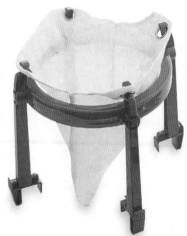

MUSLIN/CHEESECLOTH

Used for making spice and herb bags, muslin is also useful for tying together pips and peel, particularly when making marmalade. It can also be used instead of a jelly bag. To do this, layer three or four squares of muslin together and tie lengths of strong string (twine) securely to each corner. Either knot the ends together to hang from a single support, or make four loops so the bag can be suspended on the legs of an upturned stool or chair. Alternatively, line a large strainer with the muslin squares and place over a bowl to catch the juices.

JARS AND BOTTLES

When making preserves, a selection of containers is needed. Clear glass is ideal because it is non-corrosive, you can easily check for trapped air bubbles when potting preserves, and it looks very pretty when filled. As well as ordinary jam jars and bottles, there are specialist preserving jars that are designed to be heated to a high temperature. Non-corrosive seals are essential, particularly when potting acidic preserves and pickles.

Be sure to choose appropriately shaped and sized containers. Wide-necked jars are essential for recipes using whole or large pieces of fruit or vegetables, but for most preserves it is better to use several smaller jars than one or two large

Left: A jelly bag with its own stand can make an easy job of straining jellies.

ones. Preserves stored in very large jars are likely to deteriorate more quickly once the seal is broken; the preserve is not consumed as quickly and the contents are exposed to the air for longer than a preserve stored in a small jar.

PRESERVE COVERS

The cheapest way to cover jams, jellies and marmalades is to use a waxed paper disc and cellophane cover, secured by an elastic band; these covers are available to fit 450g/1lb and 900g/2lb jars. However, paper and cellophane are not vinegar-proof so are unsuitable for preserves containing vinegar. These should be potted in preserving jars with acid-resistant seals or jam jars with plastic-lined lids.

FUNNELS

These make potting preserves considerably easier. A jam funnel with a wide tube (10–13cm/4–5in diameter) that fits into the top of the jar or container can make quick, clean work of filling jars.

An ordinary funnel with a slimmer tube is useful for adding liquid to jars of pickles or fruit as well as for bottling smooth sauces and jellies. Choose funnels made of heat-proof plastic or stainless steel.

HYDROMETER

Also known as a *pese syrop*, a hydrometer measures the density of sugar syrup and is sometimes used when bottling fruit and for jam- and jelly-making. The tube is marked from 0 to 40 and measures the point to which the weighted tube sinks. The more sugar a syrup contains, the higher the hydrometer will float in it.

Above: A jam funnel can prove to be a real time-saver when potting jellies, jams and conserves.

SALOMETER

This works in the same way as a hydrometer but is used to measure the amount of salt dissolved in brine for pickling. Salometers are marked from 0 to 100.

Below: A selection of jars with either clamp-top, screw-top or two-piece screw-band lids are perfect for preserving.

BOWLS

Several non-corrosive bowls in different sizes are essential for salting, soaking and mixing.

CHOPPING BOARDS

Plastic chopping boards are considered more hygienic than wooden ones because they are easier to clean properly. However, a wooden board comes into its own during potting and is an ideal surface to stand jars on when they are cooling; placing hot jars on cold or damp surfaces can sometimes cause the jars to crack.

SIEVES AND COLANDERS

Use nylon, plastic or stainless steel sieves and colanders when straining acidic fruit or preserves. Some metals may spoil the colour and give a faint metallic taste to the finished preserve.

WOODEN SPOONS

Choose long-handled spoons to keep your hand at a safe distance from hot simmering preserves. If possible, keep separate spoons for sweet and savoury recipes. Avoid metal spoons as these conduct heat and may discolour the preserve.

SLOTTED SPOONS AND SKIMMERS

These are useful for lifting and draining solid ingredients and packing them into jars. A fine-mesh skimmer may be used for skimming jams and jellies to keep them clear.

LADLES

A large deep-bowled ladle is useful for transferring preserves to jars. Some ladles have pointed lips for easy pouring. Stainless steel ladles are best for this purpose.

Below: Fixed and swivel-blade vegetable peelers are good for peeling both fruits and vegetables.

Below: A corer is useful for preparing orchard fruits such as apples and pears.

VEGETABLE PEELERS

There are a number of different types of vegetable peeler available. Those with a swivel action follow the contours of the fruit or vegetable closely and allow peel to be pared very thinly. Some peelers have a bean slicer attachment on the handle.

CORERS

When pickling or preserving whole fruits such as pears and apples, a corer can be used to cut out and remove the cores neatly without damaging the fruit. When coring halved fruits, a melon baller or teaspoon are the best tools to use.

Left: Slotted skimmers and spoons are good for skimming jellies.

STONERS

It can be fiddly to stone (pit) small fruit such as cherries with a knife and almost impossible to keep the fruit whole. There are different types of stoners for different sized fruits. The fruit is placed in a holder, and the handles are squeezed together, which causes a prong to push through the fruit and pop out the stone.

ZESTERS

The cutting edge of a zester has five little holes, which, when pulled firmly across the fruit, remove fine strands of citrus rind, leaving the white pith behind.

CANELLE KNIVES

These have a v-shaped tooth that pares 6mm/¼in strips of peel from fruit and vegetables leaving grooves and creating a striped effect. If the fruit is then cut into slices, these will have attractively notched edges. A mushroom fluter is a similar tool for creating a pattern on mushroom caps.

Below: A cherry stoner effortlessly removes the stones from fiddly fruit.

MANDOLINS

Firm fruits and vegetables such as apples, beetroot (beet) and turnips can be sliced or shredded finely and evenly using a mandolin. Most mandolins have adjustable cutting blades and supporting struts that hold the mandolin at the desired angle. Choose one with a safety guard to hold the food being sliced because the blades are extremely sharp and it would otherwise be very easy to cut yourself.

Above: A canelle knife and zester are excellent for paring off thin strips of citrus rind.

GRATERS

Box graters usually have a choice of at least three different surfaces, from fine (for nutmeg and lemon rind) to coarse (for hard fruits and vegetables). They often have slicing blades for vegetables such as cucumbers. Most have a handle to hold them steady during use. Flat graters take up less space and are easier to clean, but usually have only one or two different-size grating surfaces.

MINCERS AND FOOD MILLS

Both hand and electric mincers can save a good deal of time and energy when processing large quantities of fruit or vegetables. Rotary food mills are especially useful when making fruit butters and smooth sauces because they reduce cooked fruit to a purée, leaving the skins and stones (pits) behind. Pressing the mixture through a fine sieve using the back of a wooden spoon or metal ladle is just as effective, although it may take a little more time and effort.

GRINDERS

The traditional mortar and pestle is perfect for coarsely grinding small quantities of spices. For larger amounts or when a fine powder is required, use a spice mill or coffee grinder kept solely for that purpose.

Left: A box grater with several different cutting surfaces is useful for preparing fruits, vegetables and spices.

preserving techniques

From jewel-like jams and jellies to sweet fruits preserved in sugar syrups and alcohol, and from spicy chutneys and relishes to tart sauces and pickles, there are so many fabulous ways to preserve fresh fruits and vegetables that it's sometimes hard to know where to begin. This easy-to-follow guide leads you through all the main preserving techniques, offering advice on how to preserve and how to avoid the potential pitfalls.

POTTING AND COVERING PRESERVES

Make sure you have enough jars and bottles, and the correct sterilizing equipment before you start to make any preserve. Preparing, covering and storing preserves correctly helps to ensure the preserve retains its colour, flavour and texture.

CHOOSING CONTAINERS

To make the most of preserves, always pot them in the right type of container. Pickles made from whole or large pieces of fruit or vegetables should be packed into medium or large jars or bottles with a wide neck. Smooth, pourable sauces or relishes can be stored in narrow-necked bottles, but thicker, spoonable preserves should be packed in jars. It is generally better to pack preserves into several smaller containers rather than one large one, especially those that need to be consumed soon after opening.

STERILIZING JARS AND BOTTLES

Before potting, it is essential to sterilize jars and bottles to destroy any micro-organisms in containers. An unsterilized jar or bottle may contain contamination that could cause the preserve to deteriorate or become inedible. Sterilizing is important for all containers, but you should take particular care when re-using jars and bottles.

Check jars and bottles for cracks or damage, then wash thoroughly in hot, soapy water, rinse well and turn upside-down to drain. Jars and bottles may be sterilized in five different ways: by heating in a low oven, immersing in boiling water, heating in a microwave, hot-washing in a dishwasher, or using sterilizing tablets.

Below: Medium, wide-necked jars with plastic-coated screw-top lids are ideal for most preserves.

oven method

Stand the containers, spaced slightly apart, on a baking sheet lined with kitchen paper. Rest any lids on top. Place in a cold oven, then heat to 110°C/225°F/Gas ¼ and bake for 30 minutes. Leave to cool slightly before filling. (If the jars or bottles are not used immediately, cover with a clean cloth and warm again before use.)

boiling water method

1 Place the containers, open-end up, in a deep pan that is wide enough to hold them in one layer.

2 Pour enough hot water into the pan to cover the containers. (Do not use boiling water because this can crack glass.) Bring the water to the boil and boil for 10 minutes.

3 Leave the containers in the pan until the water stops bubbling, then carefully remove and drain upside-down on a clean dishtowel. Turn the containers upright and leave to air-dry for a few minutes.

4 Immerse lids, seals and corks in simmering water for 20 seconds. (Only ever use corks once.)

microwave method

This method is particularly useful when sterilizing only a few jars for potting a small amount of preserve. Follow the microwave manufacturer's instructions and only use for jars that hold less than 450g/1lb and short squat bottles.

1 Half fill the clean jars or bottles with water and heat on full power until the water has boiled for at least 1 minute.

2 Using oven gloves, remove the jars or bottles from the microwave. Carefully swirl the water inside them, then pour it away. Drain upside-down on a clean dishtowel, then turn upright and leave to dry.

dishwasher method

This is the simplest way to clean and sterilize a large number of containers at the same time. Put the containers and lids in a dishwasher and run it on its hottest setting, including drying. If the jars are already washed and clean, you can run the cycle without adding detergent.

sterilizing tablet method

This method is not suitable for delicately flavoured preserves because the tablets may leave a slight taste. However, it is fine for robustly flavoured preserves such as chutneys and relishes. Following the instructions on the packet, dissolve the tablets and soak the containers in the sterilizing solution. Drain and dry before use.

FILLING JARS AND BOTTLES

Most preserves should be potted into hot containers as soon as they are ready, particularly jellies and fruit preserves with a high pectin content; a jam funnel can make quick work of this. Whole fruit jams, marmalades with peel, and jellies with added ingredients such as fresh herbs should be left to cool for 10 minutes until a thin skin forms on the surface. The preserve should then be stirred to distribute the ingredients and prevent them sinking once potted.

Some preserves such as fruits bottled in alcohol or vegetables preserved in vinegar are potted when cold rather than hot. The ingredients may be cooked, or simply washed, then packed into jars and cold alcohol or vinegar poured over them.

SEALING JARS

Different types of preserves need to be covered and sealed in different ways. Jams, conserves, jellies, marmalades and fruit cheeses can be covered with a waxed paper disc and the jar covered with cellophane held in place with an elastic band. Or, the jar can be sealed with a screw-top lid. (Waxed discs and cellophane covers should not be used together with a screw-top lid.)

Bottled fruits and pickled vegetables must be sealed in jars with new rubber seals and vacuum or clamp top lids. Chutneys and pickles should be sealed with vinegar-proof lids; the acid in the vinegar will corrode metal lids.

using waxed discs and cellophane covers

1 Using a heat-resistant ladle or jug (pitcher) and a jam funnel, carefully fill the jars with hot jam, almost to the top. Leave a small space of no more than 1cm/½in.

2 Using a clean, damp cloth, wipe the rim of the jar, making sure there are no dribbles of jam.

3 Place a waxed paper disc (waxed side down) on top of the preserve and smooth it down to form a good fit over the hot preserve.

4 Moisten a cellophane disc with a damp cloth and place on the jar, moist side up, then secure with an elastic band. Do this either when the preserve is very hot, or leave it to cool completely. (If sealed while warm, mould will grow on the surface.) As it dries, the cellophane will shrink, creating a tight seal.

using lidded jars

There are a number of different types of lidded jars available – from ordinary screw-top jars to large jars with clamped lids. Different types of jars are suitable for different types of preserves. **Screw-top lidded jars** are suitable for most sweet preserves, but uncoated metal lids should be avoided when potting acidic preserves containing vinegar because the metal lid may corrode and rust when it comes in contact with the acid.

Two-piece lidded jars are also known as lid and screw-band jars. They consist of a flat rubber- or plastic-coated lid that fits exactly over the top of the jar and a ring that screws on to the neck of the jar to hold the lid in place.

To use, fill the sterilized jar, wipe the rim and cover with the sterilized rubber-coated lid. Holding the jar steady with a cloth, position the metal ring over the lid and screw down tightly.

If the potted preserve needs to be heat-treated, release the lid by a quarter turn, or according to the manufacturer's instructions. (The glass expands during heating and may crack if the metal ring is too tight.)

Clamp-top jars can be used for any kind of preserve from jams and jellies to bottled fruits and pickles. To use, fit the sterilized rubber ring on to the lid before filling the jar to within 1cm/½in of the top, or to the manufacturer's mark on the jar. Holding the jar steady with a cloth, clamp the lid shut. An airtight vacuum will form as the preserve cools.

sealing with paraffin wax

The surface of preserves can also be sealed with paraffin wax, which is available from hardware stores.

1 Break the wax into small pieces and heat in a bowl set over a pan of hot water until just melted. (If the wax becomes too hot, it will shrink away from the sides of the jar as it cools, breaking the seal.)

2 Pour a very thin layer of wax over the hot preserve. Using a wooden cocktail stick (toothpick), prick any air bubbles, then leave the wax to set.

3 When the wax has set, pour on a second layer to make the seal about 3mm/⅛in thick. As the wax sets it will become opaque and dip slightly. To use the preserve, break and remove the wax seal. Re-cover with clear film (plastic wrap) and store in the refrigerator.

FILLING AND SEALING BOTTLES

Bottles are perfect for storing sauces and pourable relishes. They can be stoppered with a sterilized cork, then dipped in wax to seal.

1 Using a ladle and funnel, fill the hot sterilized bottles to within 2.5cm/1in of the top. Wipe the bottle rim clean with a damp cloth.

2 Soak the corks in very hot water for 3–4 minutes, then push into the tops of the bottles as far as they will go. Gently tap the cork into the bottle using a rolling pin or wooden mallet until the cork is within 5mm/¼in of the top of the bottle. Leave the bottles until cold.

3 To seal, tap down the corks as far as possible, then dip the top of each bottle in melted candle or sealing wax to coat. Leave to set, then dip a second time.

PRESENTATION, LABELLING AND STORING

Left: Preserves stored in clamp-top and two-piece lidded jars make very attractive gifts.

STORING PRESERVES

Although they look very attractive arranged on a sunny kitchen shelf, preserves should always be kept in a cool, dark, dry place because warmth and light will affect their colour and flavour, and shorten their shelf-life. Many pickles, chutneys and bottled fruits need time to mature before using.

STORAGE TIMES
Most preserves will keep for a year if packed and stored properly. Once opened, they should be eaten within 3 months. Some preserves have a shorter shelf-life:
Fruit curds, butters and cheeses can be stored in the refrigerator for 2–3 months and, once opened, should be used within 4 weeks.
Relishes with a low proportion of vinegar and sugar and a short cooking time can be stored for up to 4 months. Once opened, they should be stored in the refrigerator and used within 4 weeks.
Low-sugar jams and similar specialist preserves rely on sterilizing for their keeping qualities. They are usually processed commercially. Home-made versions are made in small quantities for short keeping in the refrigerator.

The way in which a preserve is packaged, labelled and stored is almost as important as the way it is made.

PRESENTATION

Glass jars and bottles look very pretty because they allow you to see the preserve inside. Preserving jars are practical and attractive for savoury preserves, while shaped or decorative jars with fluted and embossed designs are good for sweet preserves. Small jars, no larger than 350g/12oz capacity, look very pretty and are perfect for preserves that have a short shelf-life once opened. Glazed earthenware pots are good for storing chutneys and mustards.

No matter how much care you take, jars and bottles usually become sticky when filling. While still warm, wipe the outside of the containers with a damp cloth and a little detergent. When the preserve is cold and set, the jars may be polished with a little methylated spirit (denatured alcohol).

You can use cellophane covers or new plastic or coloured lids in place of old lids to seal jars. Pretty fabric, or coloured or brown paper can be placed over plain lids. Cut these at least 4cm/1½in bigger than the lid and secure with an elastic band, then tie with ribbon.

LABELLING PRESERVES

All preserves should be clearly labelled, especially if they are to be offered as gifts. Self-adhesive, cardboard, wooden or metal labels may be used. Always write the date, the name of the preserve and any special notes on the label. It is a good idea to add an "eat-by" if giving as a gift.

JAMS, JELLIES AND MARMALADES

These are made from fruit boiled with sugar until setting point is reached. They rely on pectin, sugar and acid for a good set. Pectin is a natural, gum-like substance, which is essential in jam-, jelly- and marmalade-making. Found in the cores, pips (seeds), pith and skins of fruits, it reacts with sugar and acid to form the gel that helps to set jams, jellies and marmalades.

testing pectin content

Pectin content can vary according to the variety of fruit, when it is picked, and growing conditions. It is best to test for pectin content at an early stage in jam-making, and add extra pectin if necessary.

1 To test for pectin content, cook the fruit until soft, then spoon 5ml/1 tsp of the juices into a glass. Add 15ml/1 tbsp methylated spirits (denatured alcohol) and shake.

2 After 1 minute a clot should form: one large jelly-like clot indicates high pectin content; two or three small clots indicate the pectin content is medium and should achieve a set; lots of small clots, or no clots at all indicate low pectin content and that extra pectin will be needed for a set.

3 If the pectin content is medium, add 15ml/1 tbsp lemon juice for every 450g/1lb fruit. If the pectin content is low, add 75–90ml/5–6 tbsp pectin stock for every 450g/1lb fruit. Alternatively, add pectin powder or liquid, or use sugar containing pectin.

making pectin stock

Home-made pectin stock is very easy to make and can be stirred into low-pectin fruit jams and jellies to improve their set. Stir in after the initial cooking of the fruit and before the sugar is added. A teaspoon of the juices can be taken from the pan at this stage and tested for pectin content.

1 Roughly chop 900g/2lb cooking apples, including the cores, peel and pips. Place in a large heavy pan and pour over cold water to cover. Bring to the boil, then reduce the heat, cover and simmer for 40 minutes, or until very soft.

2 Pour the mixture into a sterilized jelly bag suspended over a bowl. Leave to drain for at least 2 hours.

3 Pour the drained juices into the cleaned pan and boil for about 20 minutes, or until the volume is reduced by one-third.

4 Pour the pectin stock into 150ml/¼ pint/⅔ cup sterilized containers and store in the refrigerator for up to 1 week or freeze for up to 4 months.

5 To use frozen pectin stock, defrost at room temperature, or overnight in the refrigerator, then stir into the preserve.

TESTING FOR A SET
Some preserves reach setting point quickly, so check early in the cooking time.

Wrinkle test Remove the preserve from the heat and spoon a little preserve on to a chilled plate. Leave to cool for 1 minute, then push the preserve with a finger; the top should wrinkle. If it wrinkles only slightly, return the preserve to the heat and cook for 2 minutes more, then test again.

Flake test Coat a spoon in the preserve; cool for a few seconds, then hold the spoon horizontally. When shaken, the jam should run off the side in one flat flake.

Thermometer test Briefly stir the preserve, dip a jam thermometer into very hot water, then place in the preserve. Move it around, but do touch the pan base. Jams and marmalades reach setting point at 105°C/220°F; jellies and conserves a degree lower.

MAKING JAM

Usually made with whole or cut fruit, jam should have distinct flavour, bright colour and soft set.

making summer fruit jam

Use sound, slightly under-ripe fruit; over-ripe fruit contains less pectin and will not set well.

Makes about 1.6kg/3½lb

INGREDIENTS

900g/2lb mixed fruits, such as cherries, raspberries, strawberries, gooseberries, blackcurrants and redcurrants

2.5–20ml/½–4 tsp lemon juice

900g/2lb/4½ cups preserving or granulated sugar

1 Weigh each type of fruit, then prepare. Rinse and drain cherries, gooseberries, blackcurrants and redcurrants; wash raspberries and strawberries only if necessary; remove any stems and leaves and cut off any damaged parts.

2 Put the lemon juice in a large heavy pan: strawberries and cherries are low in pectin, so add 10ml/2 tsp lemon juice for each 450g/1lb fruit; add 2.5ml/½ tsp for each 450g/1lb raspberries; and add no lemon juice for high-pectin gooseberries and currants.

3 Put the prepared gooseberries, blackcurrants and redcurrants in the pan with 60ml/4 tbsp water and cook over a low heat for 5 minutes until the skins soften.

4 Add the raspberries, cherries and strawberries to the pan. (If using only these fruits, do not add any water.) Cook for 10 minutes until all the fruit is just tender.

5 Using the back of a spoon, crush one-third of the fruit to release the pectin. If using a high proportion of strawberries or cherries, do a pectin test at this stage.

6 Add the sugar to the pan and stir over a low heat until it has dissolved completely. Increase the heat and bring to the boil. Continue to boil rapidly for about 10 minutes, stirring occasionally, until setting point is reached (105°C/220°F). Skim off any froth that rises to the surface.

IS IT A JAM, CONSERVE OR SPREAD?

Understanding the labels on store-bought preserves can be difficult. Here's a brief guide:

Jam This contains a minimum of 30g/1¼oz fruit and 60g/2¼oz/generous ¼ cup sugar per 100g/3¾oz jam. It may contain colourings, preservatives and gelling agents.

Extra jam This must contain at least 45g/1¾oz whole fruit per 100g/3¾oz jam. It contains no colourings, preservatives or flavourings.

Reduced-sugar jam This has a minimum of 35g/1½oz fruit and 30–55g/1¼–2¼oz sugar per 100g/3¾oz jam.

Conserve This implies a quality jam with a high fruit content, but check the label. Usually, the fruit is whole and steeped in sugar before cooking, giving a softer set.

Fruit spreads These are made from fruit pulps sweetened with fruit juice.

7 Remove the pan from the heat and leave to stand for 5 minutes. If necessary, skim off any froth, then stir to distribute larger pieces of fruit. Pot, seal and label.

making seedless raspberry jam

Some fruits, notably raspberries and blackberries, contain a large number of pips (seeds), which result in a very "pippy" jam or conserve. If you prefer a smooth jam without pips, they can be removed after initial cooking by pressing the fruit through a nylon or stainless steel sieve.

Makes about 750g/1⅔lb

INGREDIENTS
450g/1lb/2⅔ cups raspberries
about 450g/1lb/2¼ cups preserving or granulated sugar

1 Use a mixture of just-ripe and a few slightly underripe berries to ensure a good set. Put the fruit in a large heavy pan and gently crush to release the juices using the back of a wooden spoon.

2 Gently heat the fruit mixture to boiling point, then simmer for about 10 minutes, stirring now and then, until the fruit is really soft.

3 Tip the mixture into a fine nylon or stainless steel sieve (sifter) placed over a bowl and push through the fruit purée using the back of the wooden spoon. Discard the pips left in the sieve.

4 Measure the fruit pulp into the cleaned pan, adding 450g/1lb/ 2¼ cups sugar for each 600ml/ 1 pint/2½ cups purée. Heat gently, stirring, until the sugar dissolves, then boil rapidly until setting point is reached (105°C/220°F).

5 Using a slotted spoon, skim any froth from the surface, then pot the jam, cover and seal.

making cherry jam with commercial pectin

Fruits with a low pectin content require additional pectin to achieve a good set. Adding commercial pectin is an easy way to do this. Jams made in this way need only short boiling and require little or no water and a smaller proportion of fruit to sugar.

Makes about 1.8kg/4lb

INGREDIENTS
1.2kg/2½lb/6 cups pitted cherries
150ml/¼ pint/⅔ cup water
45ml/3 tbsp lemon juice
1.3kg/3lb/generous 6¾ cups granulated sugar
250ml/8fl oz/1 cup liquid pectin

1 Put the cherries, water and lemon juice in a large pan. Cover and cook for 15 minutes, stirring, until the cherries are tender.

2 Add the sugar to the pan and stir over a low heat until dissolved completely. Bring to the boil and boil rapidly for 1 minute.

3 Stir the liquid pectin into the jam, return to the boil and cook for 1 minute.

4 Remove the pan from the heat and, using a slotted spoon, skim off any froth from the surface. Set the jam aside and leave to stand for 5 minutes.

5 Stir the jam briefly to distribute the fruit evenly, then pot and seal. Use within 6 months.

PECTIN CONTENT OF FRUIT
Although the pectin content of fruits can vary depending on variety, growing conditions and when the fruits were picked, the list below can be used as a good basic guide to the set that will be achieved.

High Apples, blackcurrants, cranberries, damsons, gooseberries, grapefruit, lemons, limes, loganberries, redcurrants, quinces

Medium Apricots (fresh), apples (eating), bilberries, blackberries (early), grapes, greengages, mulberries, peaches, plums, raspberries

Low Bananas, blackberries (late), cherries, elderberries, figs, guavas, japonica, melons, nectarines, pears, pineapples, rhubarb, strawberries

MAKING CONSERVES

These are very similar to jams, but they have a slightly softer set and contain whole or large pieces of fruit. The fruit is first mixed with sugar and sometimes a little liquid, then allowed to stand for several hours or even days. The sugar draws out the juices from the fruit, making it firmer and minimizing the cooking time needed. The fruit should be just ripe and even in size. Not all fruit is suitable for making conserves; tough fruit skins do not soften when sugar is added, so fruit such as gooseberries are no good for making conserves.

making strawberry conserve

This preserve takes several days to make, so be sure to leave plenty of time for preparation.

Makes about 1.3kg/3lb

INGREDIENTS
1.3kg/3lb small or medium strawberries, hulled

1.3kg/3lb/generous 6¾ cups granulated sugar

1 Layer the hulled strawberries in a large bowl with the sugar. Cover with clear film (plastic wrap) and chill for 24 hours.

2 Transfer the strawberries, sugar and juices to a large heavy pan. Heat gently, stirring occasionally, until the sugar has dissolved. Bring to the boil and cook steadily (not rapidly) for 5 minutes.

3 Leave the mixture to cool, then place in a bowl, cover with clear film and chill for 2 days.

4 Pour the strawberry mixture into a large pan, bring to the boil and cook steadily for 10 minutes, then remove from the heat and set aside for 10 minutes. Stir, then ladle into warmed sterilized jars and seal.

flavouring conserves

Conserves are more luxurious than jams and often include dried fruit, nuts and spirits or liqueurs. These extra ingredients should be added after setting point is reached.

When adding dried fruit or nuts, chop them evenly and allow about 50g/2oz/½ cup fruit or nuts per 750g/1¾lb conserve.

Choose spirits or liqueurs that complement the flavour of the chosen fruit. For example, add apricot brandy or amaretto liqueur to apricot conserve, kirsch to cherry conserve and ginger wine to melon conserve; allow 30ml/2 tbsp to every 750g/1¾lb conserve.

TOP TIPS FOR SUCCESSFUL JAM-MAKING
• Always use the freshest fruit possible and avoid overripe fruit.

• If you wash the fruit, dry it well and use promptly because it will deteriorate on standing.

• Cook the fruit very slowly at first over a low heat to extract the maximum amount of juice and pectin. Stir the fruit frequently until very tender, but do not overcook. (Fruit skins toughen once sugar is added.)

• Warm the sugar in a low oven for about 10 minutes before adding it to the fruit. This will help it to dissolve.

• Stir the preserve to ensure the sugar is completely dissolved before boiling.

• Do not stir frequently when boiling. This lowers the temperature and delays reaching setting point.

• It is wasteful to remove scum too often. To help prevent scum from forming, add a small amount of unsalted (sweet) butter (about 15g/½oz/1 tbsp for every 450g/1lb fruit) when you add the sugar.

• Do not move freshly potted preserves until they are cool and have set completely.

Jellies are made using the juice strained from simmered fruit, which is then boiled with sugar to setting point. There is very little preparation of fruit, other than giving it a quick rinse and roughly chopping larger fruit, but you do need to allow plenty of time to make the jelly itself. The secret to a beautifully clear jelly lies in straining the fruit pulp through a jelly bag, drip by drip, which takes several hours.

The basic principles of jelly-making are the same as those for jam and the same three substances – pectin, sugar and acid – are needed for the jelly to set. A perfectly set jelly should retain its shape and quiver when spooned out of the jar. Fruits that are low in pectin such as strawberries, cherries and pears are not suitable on their own for making jellies, so are usually combined with high-pectin fruit.

Because the fruit pulp is discarded in jelly-making, the yield is not as large as in jam-making. For this reason many jelly recipes have evolved to make the most of wild fruits, which are free, or gluts of home-grown fruit.

Jellies can be served both as sweet and savoury preserves. Some, such as redcurrant, rowan and cranberry jellies, are classic accompaniments for hot or cold roasted meat or game, or are added to gravy for flavour and give an attractive glossy finish. Savoury jellies often contain chopped herbs and sometimes wine vinegar or cider vinegar to give it a sharper flavour. Sweet jellies may be eaten as a spread.

yield of jelly

The final yield of jelly depends on how juicy the fruit is, and this can vary depending on the time of the year, the weather during growth and its ripeness when harvested. Because of this, the juice, rather than the fruit, is measured and the amount of sugar is calculated accordingly. As a general rule, 450g/1lb/2¼ cups sugar is added for each 600ml/1 pint/2½ cups juice. (If the fruit is very rich in pectin, the recipe may suggest adding slightly less sugar.) As a rough guide, recipes containing 450g/1lb/2¼ cups sugar will make about 675–800g/1½–1¾lb jelly.

making redcurrant jelly

Makes about 1.3kg/3lb

INGREDIENTS

1.3kg/3lb just-ripe redcurrants
600ml/1 pint/2½ cups water
about 900g/2lb/4½ cups preserving
   or granulated sugar

1 Check the fruit is clean. If necessary, rinse in cold water and use a little less water in the recipe.

2 Remove the currants from the stalks. There is no need to top and tail the fruit.

3 Place the redcurrants in a large heavy pan with the water and simmer gently for about 30 minutes, or until the fruit is very soft and pulpy. Stir occasionally during cooking to prevent the fruit from catching and burning.

4 Pour the cooked fruit and juices into a sterilized jelly bag suspended over a large bowl. Leave to drain for about 4 hours, or until the juice stops dripping. (Do not press or squeeze the fruit in the bag because this will result in a cloudy jelly.)

5 Discard the pulp remaining in the bag (unless you plan to boil the pulp a second time – see page 54). Pour the juice into the cleaned pan and add 450g/1lb/2¼ cups warmed sugar for each 600ml/1 pint/2½ cups of juice. (When making jellies with low-pectin fruit or vegetables, stir in a little lemon juice or vinegar to improve the set. This will also help to offset the sweetness of the jelly.)

6 Heat the mixture gently, stirring frequently, until the sugar has completely dissolved, then increase the heat and bring to the boil.

7 Boil the jelly rapidly for about 10 minutes, or until setting point is reached. You can check this using the flake test or wrinkle test, or you can use a jam thermometer. The jelly should be heated to 105°C/220°F.

8 Remove the pan from the heat, then skim any froth from the surface of the jelly using a slotted spoon.

9 Carefully remove the last traces of froth using a piece of kitchen paper. Pot the jelly immediately because it will start to set fairly quickly.

10 Cover and seal the jelly while it is hot, then leave to cool completely. (Do not move or tilt the jars until the jelly is completely cold and set.) Label the jars and store in a cool, dark place.

USING A JELLY BAG

Jelly bags, which are made from heavy-duty calico, cotton flannel or close-weave nylon, allow only the juice from the fruit to flow through, leaving the skins, pulp and pips (seeds) inside the bag. The fruit pulp and juices are very heavy, so strong tape or loops are positioned on the corners for hanging the bag securely on a stand, upturned stool or chair.

1 Before use, sterilize the jelly bag by scalding in boiling water. This process also helps the juices to run through the bag, rather than being absorbed into it.

2 If you don't have a jelly bag, you can use three or four layers of sterilized muslin (cheesecloth) or a piece of fine linen cloth instead. Simply line a large nylon or stainless-steel sieve with the muslin or linen.

3 Carefully suspend the jelly bag or lined sieve over a large bowl to catch the juice. Make sure the bag or sieve is secure before spooning some of the simmered fruit and juices into it. (Don't add too much to start with.)

4 Leave the fruit to drain for a while, then spoon in more fruit. Continue gradually adding fruit in this way until it has all been placed in the bag or sieve, then leave to drain until it stops dripping completely. Some fruits will take 2–3 hours to release all their juice, while others may take as long as 12 hours.

5 Immediately after use, wash the jelly bag thoroughly, then rinse several times to remove all traces of detergent. Ensure the bag is completely dry before storing. The jelly bag may be reused many times, but be sure to sterilize it before every use.

boiling fruit twice

Rather than discarding the fruit pulp from the jelly bag after draining, you can boil it again to extract more liquid and flavour. This should be done only with pectin-rich fruits such as sharp apples, damsons or currants. The resulting jelly may have a slightly less concentrated flavour than jelly made from juice obtained from fruit that has been boiled once.

To boil the fruit a second time, return the fruit pulp to the pan and add just enough cold water to cover, using no more than half the amount of water used for the first boiling. Simmer the fruit gently for about 20 minutes, then drain through the jelly bag as before. Add the juice to the first batch.

flavouring jelly

Savoury jellies are often flavoured with fresh herbs such as thyme, mint, sage and rosemary. In some, such as mint jelly, the herb is most important and the fruit provides a base in which to suspend the herb; in others, herbs are used in small quantities to impart a subtle flavour.

1 To simply add flavour, add sprigs of herbs at the beginning of cooking. Woody herbs should be removed before draining because stems may damage the jelly bag.

2 When adding finely chopped herbs to the finished jelly, even distribution can be difficult and, if the jelly is too hot, the pieces may float to the top. To overcome this problem, put the herbs in a sieve and sprinkle with a little water to dampen them.

3 Leave the jelly to stand until it just starts to form a thin skin on top, then quickly stir in the chopped herbs. Pot straight away in very warm, but not hot, sterilized jars and seal. Cool before labelling.

4 Herb sprigs and aromatic leaves, such as lemon verbena or geranium leaves, can look stunning set in jelly. Pour the jelly into sterilized jars, then leave until semi-set and insert the herb sprigs or leaves.

TOP TIPS FOR SUCCESSFUL JELLY-MAKING

• There is no need to peel or stone (pit) fruit before cooking because all the debris will be removed during straining. However, it is important to discard any bruised or mouldy parts of the fruit because these will spoil the flavour. Rinse the fruit only if dusty or dirty.

• If using fruits such as apples that require longer cooking, chop the fruit very finely to reduce the cooking time required. Cooking the fruit for a shorter time also helps to give the jelly an intense, fresh flavour.

• Simmer the fruit very gently to extract the maximum amount of pectin and to avoid evaporating too much liquid. When cooking hard fruits that take a long time to soften, cover the pan for the first half of the cooking time to reduce the amount of liquid lost.

• Some fruits such as redcurrants or blackcurrants can be cooked in the oven to make highly flavoured jellies. Place the fruit in an oven-proof dish with about 75ml/5 tbsp water, cover tightly and cook at 140°C/275°F/Gas 1 for about 50 minutes, stirring occasionally, until pulpy. Drain through a jelly bag, then add 425g/15oz/generous 2 cups sugar for every 600ml/1 pint/2½ cups strained juice.

• Jellies set very quickly, so pot immediately. Warm a stainless steel funnel in the oven, or rinse a plastic one under hot water and dry it, then use to pot the jelly. If the jelly starts to set in the pan, warm it briefly until liquid again.

• Gently tap the jars as you fill with jelly to remove air bubbles.

• Although you can add a little butter to jam to disperse any scum, do not do this with jelly – it will make it cloudy.

MAKING MARMALADE

This preserve consists of a jelly base, usually with small pieces of fruit suspended in it. The name marmalade is derived from the Portuguese word *marmelo*, meaning quince, and it was from this fruit that marmalades were first made.

Modern marmalades are usually made from citrus fruits, or citrus fruits combined with other fruits such as pineapple, or flavoured with aromatic spices. Marmalades can range from thick and dark to light and translucent.

The citrus peel is shredded and cooked with the fruit juices and water until soft and tender, then boiled with sugar to make the marmalade. Citrus peel requires long, slow cooking in a large amount of water to become soft. The pith of Seville oranges, lemons and grapefruits becomes clear when cooked, but that of sweet oranges does not, so the pith should be scraped off the rind before shredding and cooking.

As well as classic marmalade, there is also jelly marmalade. This is perfect for people who enjoy the flavour of marmalade but do not like the peel that is suspended in the jelly. Rather than adding the shredded rind to the juices and water in the pan, the rind is tied in a muslin (cheesecloth) bag to keep it separate. The juices are then strained and boiled to setting point. The jelly may be left plain and potted as it is, or a little of the shredded rind can be stirred into the jelly just before potting. As with any jelly, it is difficult to give an exact yield for jelly marmalade.

making seville orange marmalade

Bitter Seville oranges are very popular for marmalade-making.

Makes about 2.5kg/5½lb

INGREDIENTS
900g/2lb Seville oranges
1 large lemon
2.4 litres/4 pints/2 quarts water
1.8kg/4lb/generous 9 cups preserving or granulated sugar

1 Wash and dry the fruits. If you are using waxed oranges and lemons, scrub the skins gently.

2 Halve the fruits and squeeze out the juice and pips (seeds), then pour into a muslin- (cheesecloth-) lined sieve set over a bowl.

3 Remove some of the pith from the citrus peels and reserve, then cut the peel into narrow strips.

4 Add the reserved pith to the pips in the muslin and tie together to make a loose bag. Allow plenty of room so that the water can bubble through the bag and extract the pectin from the pith and pips.

5 Place the shredded peel, juices and the muslin bag in a large preserving pan and pour in the water. Using a clean ruler, measure the depth of the contents in the pan and make a note of it.

6 Slowly bring the mixture to the boil and simmer for 1½–2 hours, or until the peel is very soft and the contents have reduced by about half their depth.

COOK'S TIPS
• To save time, shred the citrus peel in a food processor rather than by hand. Use either the fine or coarse cutting attachment.
• If you can't find Seville oranges, use Temple oranges instead.

7 To check that the peel is cooked, remove a piece from the pan and leave for a few minutes to cool. Once cooled, press the peel between finger and thumb; it should feel very soft.

8 Using a slotted spoon, remove the muslin bag from the pan and set it aside until cool enough to handle. Squeeze as much liquid as possible back into the pan to extract all the pectin from the pips and pith.

9 Add the sugar to the pan and stir over a low heat until the sugar has completely dissolved.

10 Bring the marmalade to the boil, then boil rapidly for about 10 minutes until setting point is reached (105°C/220°F). You may also use the flake or wrinkle test to check the set.

11 Using a slotted spoon, remove any scum from the surface of the marmalade, then leave to cool until a thin skin starts to form on the surface of the preserve.

12 Leave the marmalade to stand for about 5 minutes, then stir gently to distribute the peel evenly. Ladle into hot sterilized jars, then cover and seal.

making orange jelly marmalade

This recipe uses Seville oranges, and may be made as a plain jelly marmalade, or a few fine shreds of peel can be added before potting, which can look very pretty and adds an interesting texture. Any marmalade can be made in the same way; use exactly the same ingredients listed in the recipe but use the method below.

Makes about 2kg/4½lb

INGREDIENTS

450g/1lb Seville (Temple) oranges
1.75 litres/3 pints/7½ cups water
1.3kg/3lb/generous 6¾ cups preserving or granulated sugar
60ml/4 tbsp lemon juice

1 Wash and dry the oranges; gently scrub them with a soft brush if they have waxed skins.

2 If you want to add a little peel to the jelly marmalade, thinly pare and finely shred the rind from 2 or 3 of the oranges. Place the shreds in a square of muslin (cheesecloth) and tie it into a neat bag.

3 Halve the oranges and squeeze out the juice and pips (seeds), then tip the juice and pips into a large preserving pan.

4 Roughly chop the orange peel, including all the pith, and add it to the pan. Add the bag of shredded rind, if using, and pour over the water. Cover the pan with a lid and leave to soak for at least 4 hours, or overnight.

5 Bring the mixture to the boil, then reduce the heat and simmer gently for 1½ hours. Using a slotted spoon, remove the bag of peel, and carefully remove a piece of peel to check that it is tender. If not, re-tie the bag and simmer for a further 15–20 minutes. Remove the bag of peel and set aside.

6 Line a large nylon or stainless steel sieve with a double layer of muslin and place over a large bowl. Pour boiling water through the muslin to scald it. Discard the scalding water from the bowl. Alternatively, use a scalded jelly bag suspended over a bowl instead of the muslin-lined sieve.

7 Pour the fruit and juices into the sieve or jelly bag and leave to drain for at least 1 hour. Pour the juices into the cleaned pan.

8 Add the sugar, lemon juice and shredded orange rind, if using, to the pan. Stir over a low heat until the sugar has dissolved, then bring to the boil and boil rapidly for about 10 minutes until setting point is reached (105°C/220°F).

9 Remove any scum from the surface. Leave to cool until a thin skin starts to form on the surface. Stir, then pot, cover and seal.

TOP TIPS FOR SUCCESSFUL MARMALADE-MAKING

• Always wash citrus fruit well. Most citrus fruits have a wax coating that helps to prolong the life of the fruit, which should be removed before making the fruit into marmalade. Alternatively, buy unwaxed fruit, but always rinse before use.

• When shredding peel, always slice it slightly thinner than required in the finished preserve because the rind will swell slightly during cooking.

• Coarse-cut peel will take longer to soften than finely shredded peel. To reduce cooking time, soak the peel for a few hours in the water and juices before cooking.

• If the fruit needs to be peeled, put it in a bowl of boiling water and leave to stand for a couple of minutes. This will help to loosen the skins and make peeling easier. The rind's flavour will leach into the water, so use the soaking water in place of some of the measured water.

• If using small, thin-skinned fruit such as limes, cut the fruit into quarters lengthways, then slice flesh and rind into thin or thick shreds. If using larger, thick-skinned fruit such as grapefruit, pare off the peel, including some white pith, and shred. Cut the fruit into quarters, remove the remaining white pith and roughly chop the flesh.

• To make a coarse-cut preserve, boil the whole fruit for 2 hours until soft; pierce with a skewer to test. Lift out the fruit, halve, prise out the pips, then tie them loosely in muslin (cheesecloth) and add to the hot water. Boil rapidly for 10 minutes, then remove the bag. Slice the fruit and return to the pan. Stir in the sugar until dissolved, then boil to setting point.

• Shredded peel should be simmered gently; fierce cooking can give a tough result. Check that the peel is really soft before adding the sugar because it will not tenderize further after this.

• For easy removal, tie the muslin bag of pith and pips with string and attach it to the pan handle. It can then be lifted out of the boiling mixture easily.

• If the fruit contains a lot of pith, put only a small amount in the muslin bag with the pips. Put the remaining pith in a small pan, cover with water and boil for 10 minutes. Strain the liquid and use in place of some of the measured water for the recipe.

• To flavour marmalade with liqueur or spirits, add 15–30ml/ 1–2 tbsp for every 450g/1lb/ 2¼ cups sugar – stir it in just before potting. Unsweetened apple juice or dry (hard) cider may be used to replace up to half the water to add flavour to marmalades made with sharper fruits such as kumquats.

FRUIT CURDS, BUTTERS AND CHEESES

These rich, creamy preserves were once the highlight of an English tea during Edwardian and Victorian times. Curds and butters are delicious spread on slices of fresh bread and butter, or used as fillings for cakes; firmer fruit cheeses are usually sliced and can be enjoyed in similar ways. Fruit cheeses and butters are also very good served with roast meat, game or cheese.

Curds are made from fruit juice or purée cooked with eggs and butter. They have a soft texture and short keeping qualities. Fruit butters and cheeses are made from fruit purée boiled with sugar and are good if you have a glut of fruit because they require a relatively high proportion of fruit. Butters are lower in sugar and cooked for a shorter time, producing a soft, fruity preserve with a short shelf-life. Cheeses have a firm texture and may be set in moulds and turned out to serve.

MAKING FRUIT CURDS

Fruit curds are usually made with the juice of citrus fruits, but other acidic fruits such as passion fruit may be used. Smooth purées made from, for example, cooking apples or gooseberries can also be used.

The juice or purée is heated with eggs, butter and sugar until thick. The mixture is always cooked in a double boiler or a bowl set over a pan of simmering water to prevent the eggs curdling. Whole eggs are generally used, but if there is a lot of juice, egg yolks or a combination of whole eggs and yolks give a thicker result.

making lime curd

Makes about 675g/1½lb

INGREDIENTS
5 large, ripe juicy limes
115g/4oz/½ cup butter, cubed, at room temperature
350g/12oz/scant 1¾ cups caster (superfine) sugar
4 eggs, at room temperature

1 Finely grate the lime rind, ensuring you do not include any of the bitter white pith. Halve the limes and squeeze out the juice.

2 Place the lime rind in a large heatproof bowl set over a pan of barely simmering water, then strain in the lime juice to remove any bits of fruit or pips (seeds).

3 Add the cubed butter and the sugar to the bowl. Heat gently, stirring frequently, until the butter melts; the mixture should be barely warm, not hot.

4 Lightly beat the eggs with a fork, then strain through a fine sieve into the warm fruit mixture.

5 Keeping the water at a very gentle simmer, stir the fruit mixture continuously until the curd is thick enough to coat the back of a wooden spoon. Do not overcook because the curd will thicken on cooling.

6 Spoon the curd into warmed sterilized jars, then cover and seal when cold. Store in a cool, dark place, ideally in the refrigerator. Use within 2 months.

MAKING FRUIT BUTTERS

Smoother and thicker than jam, fruit butters have a spreadable quality not unlike dairy butter. Many recipes also contain a small amount of butter.

making apricot butter

Makes about 1.3kg/3lb

INGREDIENTS
1.3kg/3lb fresh ripe apricots
1 large orange
about 450ml/¾ pint/scant 2 cups water
about 675g/1½lb/scant 3½ cups caster (superfine) sugar
15g/½oz/1 tbsp butter (optional)

1 Rinse the apricots, then halve, stone (pit) and roughly chop. Remove the skins, unless you are going to purée the fruit by pressing through a sieve.

2 Scrub the orange and thinly pare 2–3 large strips of rind, avoiding any pith. Squeeze out the juice and put the apricots and the orange rind and juice in a large heavy pan.

3 Pour over enough of the water to cover the fruit. Bring to the boil, half-cover, then reduce the heat and simmer for 45 minutes.

4 Remove the orange rind, then blend the apricot mixture in a food processor until very smooth. Alternatively, press through a fine nylon or stainless steel sieve.

5 Measure the apricot purée and return it to the cleaned pan, adding 375g/13oz/1¾ cups sugar for each 600ml/1 pint/2½ cups purée.

6 Heat the mixture gently, stirring, until the sugar has dissolved, then bring to the boil and boil for about 20 minutes, stirring frequently, until thick and creamy. Remove the pan from the heat.

7 If using, stir the butter into the mixture until melted. (The butter gives a glossy finish.) Spoon into warmed sterilized jars and cover. Store in the refrigerator and use within 6 months.

FRUIT CHEESES

These sweet, firm preserves are known as cheeses because they are stiff enough to be cut into slices or wedges rather like their dairy counterparts. This name is particularly appropriate when the cheeses are set in moulds and turned out. They may be made either from fresh fruit, or from the pulp left from making jellies.

making cranberry and apple cheese

Makes about 900g/2lb

INGREDIENTS
450g/1lb/4 cups fresh cranberries
225g/8oz cooking apples
600ml/1 pint/2½ cups water
10ml/2 tsp lemon juice
about 450g/1lb/2¼ cups
  granulated sugar
glycerine, for greasing (optional)

1 Rinse the cranberries and place in a large heavy pan. Wash the apples and cut into small pieces (there is no need to peel or core). Add the water and lemon juice.

2 Cover the pan with a lid and bring the mixture to the boil; do not lift the lid until the cranberries stop popping because they often jump out of the pan and can be very hot. Simmer gently for 1 hour, or until the fruit is soft and pulpy.

3 Press the cranberry and apple mixture through a fine nylon or stainless steel sieve into a bowl.

4 Weigh the purée, then return it to the cleaned pan, adding 450g/1lb/ 2¼ cups sugar for every 450g/1lb purée. Gently heat the mixture over a low heat, stirring, until the sugar has dissolved completely.

5 Increase the heat a little and simmer the mixture until it is so thick that the spoon leaves a clean line through the mixture when drawn across the pan. It may take as long as 30 minutes to reduce the purée to this consistency. Stir frequently to stop the mixture burning on the base of the pan.

6 Spoon the fruit cheese into warmed sterilized jars and seal. Alternatively, spoon the mixture into moulds or jars greased with a little glycerine and cover with clear film (plastic wrap) when cool. In sealed jars, the cheese will keep for up to 1 year; in covered moulds, it should be kept in the refrigerator until you are ready to turn it out; eat within 1 month of making.

USING LEFTOVER PULP
The fruit pulp left from jelly-making is perfect for making into fruit cheeses. Remove the pulp from the jelly bag, stir in enough hot water to make a soft purée, then push through a sieve. Place the purée in a clean pan, adding 450g/1lb/2¼ cups sugar for every 450g/1lb purée and cook following the instructions for making fruit cheese above.

MODERN PRESERVING TECHNIQUES

With the advent of new kitchen equipment such as microwaves, pressure cookers and freezers, new ways to make fruit preserves have developed. The increased concern over healthy eating has also led to new types of preserves such as reduced-sugar jams.

PRESERVING IN A MICROWAVE

Preserves can be made using a microwave, but only using specific recipes intended for the appliance. It is difficult to adapt conventional recipes because many rely on the evaporation of liquid to achieve a set or to thicken the preserve.

Make sure the ingredients are at room temperature; if they are not, it will affect cooking times. Frozen fruit and vegetables can be used to make microwave preserves, but they must be defrosted first.

Chop fruit and vegetables into equal-size pieces so that they cook at the same speed, and stir the preserve frequently during cooking to distribute the heat evenly and avoid hot spots. Use a suitable microwave-proof bowl that will withstand very hot temperatures, and that is large enough to hold twice the volume of the ingredients.

When the preserve has finished cooking, leave it to stand for several minutes until it has stopped bubbling. It is essential to protect your hands with oven gloves when lifting the bowl; take care not to place it on a cold surface because this may cause the glass to crack – a wooden board is ideal for protecting the surface and bowl.

making microwave lemon curd

This recipe is based on an 800 watt microwave. For microwaves with a different wattage, adjust cooking times as follows – for a 900 watt oven: subtract 10 seconds per minute; for a 850 watt oven: subtract 5 seconds per minute; for a 750 watt oven: add 5 seconds per minute; for a 700 watt oven: add 10 seconds per minute.

Makes about 450g/1lb

INGREDIENTS
115g/4oz/½ cup butter, cubed
finely grated rind and juice
  of 3 large lemons
225g/8oz/generous 1 cup caster
  (superfine) sugar
3 eggs plus 1 egg yolk

1 Put the butter, lemon rind and juice in a large microwave-proof bowl. Cook on high for 3 minutes.

2 Add the sugar to the bowl and stir for 1 minute until it has almost dissolved. Return to the microwave and cook on 100% power for 2 minutes, stirring every 1 minute.

3 Beat the eggs and the yolk together, then whisk into the lemon mixture, a little at a time.

4 Cook on 40% power, for 10–12 minutes, whisking every 2 minutes, until the curd thickens. Ladle into hot sterilized jars, cover and seal. When cool, store in the refrigerator. Use within 2 months.

PRESERVING USING A PRESSURE COOKER

Preserves can be made very quickly using a pressure cooker. They are particularly useful for marmalades and for softening whole or hard fruits. Never fill the pan more than half full and always check the manufacturer's instructions.

making pressure-cooker orange marmalade

Makes about 2.5kg/5½lb

INGREDIENTS
900g/2lb Seville (Temple) oranges
1 large lemon
1.2 litres/2 pints/5 cups water
1.8kg/4lb/generous 9 cups preserving
  or granulated sugar

1 Scrub the fruit, then halve and squeeze out the juice. Quarter the oranges, scrape off the pulp and membranes and tie in a piece of muslin (cheesecloth) with the lemon halves and any pips.

2 Place the orange peel in the pressure cooker with the muslin bag and 900ml/1½ pints/3¾ cups of the water. Bring to medium (4.5kg/10lb) pressure and cook for 10 minutes.

3 Reduce the pressure and leave until the fruit is cool enough to handle. Remove the muslin bag and squeeze it over the pan.

4 Cut the orange peel into fine shreds and return to the pan with the remaining water and the fruit juice. Add the sugar and heat gently until the sugar has dissolved. Bring to the boil, then boil rapidly for about 10 minutes until setting point is reached (105°C/220°F).

5 Remove any scum from the surface using a slotted spoon, then leave the marmalade to cool until a thin skin starts to form on the surface. Stir gently to distribute the peel evenly, then ladle into hot sterilized jars, cover and seal.

MAKING FREEZER JAMS

This type of jam is not cooked, so it has a fresher, fruitier flavour and a brighter colour than cooked jam. Once thawed, it does not keep as well as traditional jam. Commercial pectin is used as a setting agent.

making strawberry freezer jam

Makes about 1.3kg/3lb

INGREDIENTS
800g/1¾lb/7 cups strawberries
900g/2lb/4½ cups caster (superfine) sugar
30ml/2 tbsp lemon juice
120ml/4fl oz/½ cup commercial liquid pectin

1 Wipe the fruit. (Only wash if necessary, then pat dry on kitchen paper.) Hull and cut into quarters, then put in a bowl with the sugar.

2 Lightly mash the fruit with a fork, leaving plenty of lumps of fruit. Cover and leave to stand for 1 hour, stirring once or twice.

3 Add the lemon juice and pectin to the fruit and stir for 4 minutes until thoroughly combined. Ladle the jam into small freezer-proof containers, cover and leave to stand for about 4 hours.

4 Put the jam in the refrigerator and chill for 24–48 hours, or until the jam sets. Freeze the jam for up to 6 months, or until ready to use.

5 To serve, remove the jam from the freezer and leave at room temperature for about 1 hour, or until defrosted. Keep any leftover defrosted jam in the refrigerator and use quickly.

MAKING REDUCED-SUGAR PRESERVES

Sugar is the vital preserving agent in sweet fruit preserves. It helps to prevent fermentation and spoilage, as well as adding sweetness and flavour, and improving the set. The proportion of sugar required for this is about 60 per cent of the final weight of preserve. Although it is possible to make reduced-sugar preserves, the yield is smaller and they will not keep for as long. In most recipes, the sugar content can be reduced by up to half. The jam should be stored in the refrigerator and used within 4 months.

USING FROZEN FRUIT
Freezing is a quick and convenient way to preserve fruit when it is at its best and cheapest. It is especially useful for fruit with a very short season, such as Seville or Temple oranges. Freezing does destroy some of the pectin content, so to compensate for this, an extra 10 per cent of fruit should be used in the recipe. Do a pectin test during cooking to check the set.

BOTTLED FRUITS

This is a traditional method of preserving fruit in syrup. The jars or bottles of fruit and syrup are heated to destroy micro-organisms. Although superseded by freezing, bottling is more suitable for some fruits such as peaches, pears, grapes and oranges; the method is less suitable for preserving soft berries such as raspberries.

making bottled fresh fruit salad

Makes about 1.8kg/4lb

INGREDIENTS
250g/9oz/generous 1¼ cups
  granulated sugar
350ml/12fl oz/1½ cups water
1 lemon
450g/1lb each eating apples, pears,
  peaches or nectarines
350g/12oz seedless green grapes
4 oranges

1 Put the sugar and water in a pan. Pare off a small strip of lemon rind, avoiding the pith, and add to the pan. Heat gently, stirring, until the sugar has dissolved. Bring to the boil and simmer for 1 minute. Cover and leave to stand.

2 Halve the lemon, then squeeze out the juice and strain.

3 Prepare the fruit, allowing 275g/10oz fruit for each 450g/1lb jar. Peel, core and slice the apples and pears and toss in lemon juice. Peel, halve, stone (pit) and slice the peaches or nectarines; halve the grapes; and segment the oranges.

4 Rinse hot sterilized jars with boiling water. Pack the fruit into the jars tightly, pressing down gently with a wooden spoon.

5 Strain the syrup through a fine sieve and return it to the cleaned pan. Bring to the boil, then pour over the fruit, filling the jars to within 1cm/½in of the top. Cover and heat-treat.

making poached pears

Fruit is often poached in syrup until just tender before bottling.

Makes about 1.8kg/4lb

INGREDIENTS
225g/8oz/scant 1¼ cups
  granulated sugar
1.2 litres/2 pints/5 cups water
1 orange
1 cinnamon stick
2kg/4½ lb cooking pears

1 Put the sugar and water in a large, wide pan and add a thinly pared strip of orange rind and the cinnamon. Heat gently until the sugar has dissolved, then bring to the boil and simmer for 1 minute.

2 Squeeze the juice from the orange, then strain. Peel and core the pears, then toss in lemon juice as soon as each one is prepared.

3 Add the pears to the syrup in a single layer. Place greaseproof (waxed) paper over the pears to keep them immersed. Poach for 15 minutes until just tender and slightly transluscent; the syrup should hardly bubble so that the fruit holds its shape. Once cooked, bottle and heat-treat.

MAKING SUGAR SYRUPS
Poach whole and slightly hard fruits such as pears and plums in a light syrup; poach figs, peaches, nectarines and apricots in a medium syrup; and poach soft fruits such as strawberries and raspberries in a heavy syrup.

To make a light syrup, use 115g/4oz/generous ½ cup sugar to 600ml/1 pint/2½ cups water; to make a medium syrup, use 175g/6oz/scant 1 cup sugar to 600ml/1 pint/2½ cups water; to make a heavy syrup, use 350g/12oz/1¾ cups sugar to 600ml/1 pint/2½ cups water.

Put the sugar and water in a pan and heat gently, stirring, until the sugar has dissolved. Bring to the boil and simmer for 1 minute. Use hot or cool.

HEAT TREATMENT

There are several ways to heat-treat bottled fruit. The filled jars may be heated in hot water, in the oven, or in a pressure cooker. As the fruit cools, a vacuum is created.

Use jars specifically designed for heat treatment. Preserving jars with clamp tops should be sealed once filled; the clamps expand slightly to allow steam to escape. Screw tops on preserving jars should not be tightened until after heating because the steam will not be able to escape and the jars may burst. Heat-treated preserves may be kept for up to 2 years.

water bath method

This is suitable for fruits bottled in either hot or cold syrup; the latter will take a little longer to process.

1 Wrap folded newspaper or cloth around each filled container, then stand them on a metal trivet or a thick layer of paper or cloth in a large heavy pan. (Containers placed directly on the pan may crack.)

2 Pour tepid water around the jars, right up to the neck, then cover the pan. Bring slowly to the boil (this should take 25–30 minutes), then simmer for the required time.

3 Turn off the heat and ladle out some of the hot water. Using tongs or oven gloves, lift the containers out of the pan and place on a wooden board. If they have screw-band lids, tighten immediately.

4 Leave the containers to cool for 24 hours, then remove the screw bands or clips. Holding the rim of the lid, carefully lift the container; it should hold its own weight. Containers with one-piece lids should have a very slight dip in the lid to indicate that they are sealed. If a jar is not sealed properly, it should be stored in the refrigerator and used as soon as possible.

HEATING TIMES FOR THE WATER BATH METHOD
The following times are for fruit packed in hot syrup after boiling. Allow 5 minutes more for fruit packed in cold syrup.

Fruit	Minutes
Soft berries and redcurrants	2
Blackcurrants, gooseberries, rhubarb, cherries, apricots and plums	10
Peaches and nectarines	20
Figs and pears	35

---

moderate oven method

This is only suitable for fruits covered with hot syrup; cold-filled jars may crack in the warm oven.

1 Preheat the oven to 150°C/300°F/Gas 2. Put the rubber rings and lids on the filled jars, but do not seal. Place in a roasting pan lined with newspaper or cloth, spacing the jars about 5cm/2in apart. Pour 1cm/½in boiling water into the pan.

2 Place the pan in the middle of the oven. Cook 500–600ml/17–20fl oz jars for 30–35 minutes and 1 litre/1¾ pint jars for 35–55 minutes. If there are more than four jars, allow a little extra time.

3 Remove from the oven and seal the lids immediately. Cool on a wooden board. Test the seals as for the water bath method.

pressure cooker method

If using clip-top jars, move the clips slightly to the side of the lid to reduce the pressure. Check the instructions for the pressure cooker.

1 Stand the jars on the trivet in the pressure cooker, ensuring they do not touch each other or the pan.

2 Pour in 600ml/1 pint/2½ cups hot water. Put on the lid with a low (2.25kg/5lb) weight and slowly bring to pressure. Maintain this pressure for 4 minutes. Leave to stand until the pressure drops.

3 Transfer the jars to a board and seal. Leave for 12 hours, then test as for the water bath method.

PICKLES

These can be sharp or sweet or a combination of the two. They are made by preserving raw or lightly cooked fruit or vegetables in spiced vinegar. They may be eaten alone or as a condiment with cheese or cold meat. There are two types of pickles: clear pickles or sweet pickles. To make clear pickles such as pickled onions, salt or brine is used to extract water from the vegetables to give them a crisp texture before they are bottled in vinegar. To make sweet pickles, fruit or vegetables are usually cooked until tender, then bottled in a sweet vinegar syrup.

Fruit and vegetables used for pickling should be firm and young. Small varieties such as baby (pearl) onions, beetroot (beets), gherkins, plums and cherries, which can be pickled whole, are particularly good. Large vegetables such as cucumbers, marrows (large zucchini), cabbage and cauliflower should be sliced or chopped.

Most pickles have to be matured in a cool dark place for a minimum of 3 weeks and preferably for at least 2 months to develop and mellow their flavour before eating. Pickled cabbage loses its crisp texture after 2–3 months, so it should be eaten within 2 months of making.

Take care when packing the fruit or vegetables into jars – they should be well packed, but not too tightly because the vinegar must surround each piece. It is important to fill jars to the brim and avoid trapping air in the pickles because this will cause discoloration and may encourage the growth of bacteria and moulds.

Large, wide-necked jars are recommended for pickling. Screw-top jars with lids that have plastic-coated linings such as those used for commercial pickles are an ideal choice. Vinegar reacts with metal, causing it to corrode and flavour the pickle, so metal tops should always be avoided when pickling.

CLEAR PICKLES

When making clear pickles, the ingredients are usually prepared first by soaking them in a brine. The salt draws out the moisture from the vegetables, making them more receptive to vinegar and preventing vegetable juices from diluting the preserving vinegar. Pure or kosher salt should always be used because iodized salt will taint the pickle with an iodine flavour and the additives in table salt will make it cloudy. There are two types of brine: dry brine, where the salt is sprinkled over the vegetables; and wet brine, where the salt is dissolved in water first.

making pickled peppers using dry brine

For this method, salt is rubbed into the vegetables or, more simply, sprinkled between layers of vegetables to draw out the juices. This then produces a brine. Salting vegetables makes them firmer and crunchier. It is particularly suitable for vegetables with a high water content such as (bell) peppers. Other vegetables that suit this method include cucumbers and courgettes (zucchini).

Makes about 1.8kg/4lb

INGREDIENTS

1.3kg/3lb red and yellow (bell) peppers
60ml/4 tbsp salt
750ml/1¼ pints/3 cups distilled malt vinegar
2 fresh bay leaves
2 thyme sprigs
5ml/1 tsp black peppercorns

1 Wash the peppers and pat them dry on kitchen paper. Cut each one into quarters lengthways, remove the seeds and cores, then cut each quarter in half to make long wide strips. If the peppers are very large, cut each quarter into three strips rather than two.

2 Layer the peppers in a large, non-corrosive bowl, fleshy side up, lightly sprinkling salt between each layer. Cover the bowl with clear film (plastic wrap) and leave to stand in a cool place for 8 hours or overnight to extract the moisture. If the weather is warm, place the bowl in the refrigerator.

3 Tip the peppers into a colander or large sieve and rinse thoroughly in cold water to remove the salt. The easiest way to check for salt is to taste one of the peppers: if it is too salty, rinse again.

4 Drain the peppers well and pat dry with kitchen paper. This is important because excess water will dilute the vinegar.

5 Pour the vinegar into a pan and add the herbs and peppercorns. Slowly bring to the boil, then simmer for 2 minutes.

6 Meanwhile, pack the peppers into hot sterilized jars. Remove the herbs from the pickling vinegar and tuck them into the jars.

7 Pour the vinegar and peppercorns over the peppers, filling the jars almost up to the brim. (To make an even crunchier pickle, allow the vinegar to cool first.)

8 Gently tap the jars on the work surface to release any trapped air bubbles, then seal with vinegar-proof lids. Store in a cool, dark place for 4 weeks before eating. Use within 1 year.

making vegetable pickle using wet brine

For this method, salt is mixed with water to make a brine solution. The ingredients are then immersed in the brine, sometimes for several days before pickling in vinegar. Wet brine may be used hot but it is more often used cold. For most pickles, a 10 per cent salt solution is used; this requires 50g/2oz/¼ cup salt to every 600ml/1 pint/2½ cups water. In some preserves where vinegar is used with sugar, this may be reduced to a 5 per cent solution.

Pickling using wet brine is suitable for ingredients with a very dense texture or thick skin such as whole lemons, watermelon rind and green walnuts, or where a softer result is required.

Makes about 1.3kg/3lb

INGREDIENTS
1.3kg/3lb mixed vegetables such as baby (pearl) onions, carrots, cauliflower and green beans
175g/6oz/¾ cup salt
1.75 litres/3 pints/7½ cups water
2 bay leaves
0.75–1 litre/1¼–1¾ pints/3–4 cups spiced vinegar

1 Prepare the vegetables: skin, peel, and trim as necessary. Leave the onions whole, thickly slice the carrots, break the cauliflower into small florets and cut the beans into 2.5cm/1in lengths. Place the vegetables in a large glass bowl.

2 Put the salt and water in a large pan and warm over a low heat until the salt has dissolved completely. Leave to cool, then pour enough over the prepared vegetables to cover completely.

3 Place a plate, slightly smaller than the diameter of the bowl, on top of the vegetables to keep them submerged in the brine. Leave to stand for 24 hours.

4 Tip the vegetables into a colander or sieve to drain, then rinse well in cold water to remove the excess brine. Drain again and pat dry using kitchen paper.

5 Put the bay leaves and vinegar in a pan and slowly bring to the boil over a low heat.

6 Meanwhile, pack the brined vegetables into hot sterilized jars. Tuck in the bay leaves and pour in the hot vinegar, filling the jars almost to the top.

7 Gently tap the jars to release any trapped air bubbles, cover and seal. Store the vegetables in a cool, dark place for 4 weeks before eating. Use within 1 year.

making unbrined pickled mushrooms

Not all clear pickles are brined before bottling in vinegar. The moisture can be removed from mushrooms by simmering them gently in water with a little salt until just tender. This method is also suitable for beetroot (beets).

Makes about 450g/1lb

INGREDIENTS

1 small onion
1 garlic clove
300ml/½ pint/1¼ cups
  white wine vinegar
6 black peppercorns
sprig of fresh thyme
275g/10oz/3¼ cups small button
  (white) mushrooms
600ml/1 pint/2½ cups water
10ml/2 tsp salt

1 Thinly slice the onion and bruise the garlic clove and place in a pan with the vinegar, peppercorns and thyme. Bring the mixture slowly to the boil over a low heat, then half cover the pan with a lid. Simmer for 15 minutes. Remove from the heat, cover completely with the lid and leave to cool.

2 Meanwhile, wipe the mushrooms clean with damp kitchen paper and trim the stems if necessary.

3 Place the mushrooms in a pan with the water and salt. Bring to the boil and simmer for 1 minute. Remove from the heat, cover and leave to cool for 4 minutes, stirring a couple of times, so that all sides of the mushrooms are immersed in the hot water.

4 Tip the mushrooms into a colander or sieve, leave to drain, then pat dry using kitchen paper.

5 Pack the mushrooms into clean sterilized jars, then strain the vinegar mixture into the jars, covering the mushrooms and filling the jars almost to the top.

6 Seal the jars and store in a cool dark place for at least 3 weeks before eating. Use within 1 year.

PICKLING GREEN VEGETABLES
The colour of green vegetables tends to be lost if stored for more than a few months, although their flavour remains the same. Blanching them in boiling water mixed with 5ml/ 1 tsp bicarbonate of soda (baking soda) for 30 seconds helps to retain their colour, but destroys the vitamin C content.

SPICED PICKLING VINEGAR

Ready-spiced pickling vinegar and jars or packets of mixed pickling spices are readily available from supermarkets. However, you can make your own, adapting the combination of spices according to personal preference and the ingredients to be preserved. You can use any variety of vinegar, but make sure that it has an acetic acid content of at least 5 per cent.

making basic spiced pickling vinegar

Makes 1.2 litres/2 pints/5 cups

INGREDIENTS

15ml/1 tbsp allspice berries
15ml/1 tbsp cloves
5cm/2in piece fresh root ginger, peeled
  and sliced
1 cinnamon stick
12 whole black peppercorns
1.2 litres/2 pints/5 cups vinegar

1 Put all the spices in a jar and pour over the vinegar. Cover the jar and leave to steep for 1–2 months, shaking occasionally.

2 After this time, strain the vinegar and return it to the cleaned jar and store it in a cool dark place until ready to use.

COOK'S TIP
To make quick pickling vinegar for immediate use, put all the ingredients in a pan and heat gently to boiling point. Simmer for about 1 minute, then remove from the heat, cover and leave to infuse (steep) for 1 hour. Strain and use.

SWEET PICKLES

For these pickles, fruit and some vegetables such as cucumbers are preserved in sweetened vinegar. They are excellent served as an accompaniment to cold meats, poultry and cheeses. Pickled apples or pears are also delicious served with hot baked ham or grilled (broiled) meat such as lamb chops. Sweet pickles are always made with distilled malt, wine or cider vinegar rather than brown malt vinegar, which would overpower the flavour and affect the colour of the fruit.

To offset the sharpness of the vinegar, a fairly large amount of sugar is added, usually between 350g/12oz/scant 1¾ cups and 450g/1lb/2¼ cups to every 300ml/ ½ pint/1¼ cups vinegar. Unlike vegetables, fruits do not need to be brined before pickling. Fruits that are pickled whole such as plums and cherries should be pricked before the initial cooking to allow the vinegar syrup to penetrate the skin and stop the fruit shrivelling. Some fruits such as berries become very soft when pickled and are therefore better preserved in sugar syrup or alcohol.

Spices and flavourings add zest to sweet pickles. They are best infused in the vinegar at the start of cooking, but also look attractive added to the bottle when packing the preserve. Use whole spices such as cinnamon, cloves, allspice, ginger, nutmeg and mace; ground spices will make the pickle murky. Citrus rind and vanilla pods (beans) also add a wonderful taste and aroma. Robustly flavoured herbs such as rosemary and bay leaves work well in sweet pickles.

making pickled apples

Makes about 1.3kg/3lb

INGREDIENTS
750ml/1¼ pints/3 cups raspberry, cider or white wine vinegar

1 cinnamon stick

5cm/2in piece fresh root ginger, peeled and sliced

6 whole cloves

1.3kg/3lb eating apples, peeled, cored and halved

800g/1¾lb/4 cups granulated sugar

1 Put the vinegar in a stainless steel pan with the cinnamon, ginger and cloves, and bring to the boil. Reduce the heat and simmer gently for about 5 minutes.

2 Add the apples to the vinegar and simmer for 5–10 minutes until they are almost tender. Be careful not to overcook the fruit; it will continue to cook in the hot syrup and should still be firm when packed into the jars.

3 Using a slotted spoon, lift the apples out of the vinegar and pack them into hot sterilized jars, adding the cloves and the cinnamon stick, if you like.

4 Add the sugar to the vinegar and heat gently over a low heat, stirring until dissolved completely.

5 Increase the heat and boil the syrup rapidly for 5 minutes, or until the syrup has reduced and thickened slightly.

6 Strain the syrup through a sieve into a jug (pitcher), then pour it over the apples to cover them completely. Seal and label. Store the jars in a cool dark place and use within 1 year.

RASPBERRY VINEGAR
Fruit vinegars are perfect for making sweet pickles and are very easy to make at home.

To make about 750ml/ 1¼ pints/3 cups raspberry vinegar, put 450g/1lb/generous 2½ cups fresh raspberries in a bowl with 600ml/1 pint/ 2½ cups white wine or cider vinegar. Cover the bowl with a cloth and leave in a cool place for 4–5 days, stirring each day.

Strain the vinegar through a nylon or stainless-steel sieve and discard the raspberries. Pour the liquid into a jelly bag suspended over a large bowl or jug (pitcher). Leave to drain, then pour the vinegar into sterilized bottles and seal. Store in a cool dark place and use within 1 year.

PICKLING DRIED FRUITS

All sorts of dried fruits can be made into excellent pickles. The fruits soak up the pickling syrup, becoming soft, succulent and juicy. Dried apricots, peaches, pears, figs, prunes and mango slices are all perfect for pickling.

Pickles made with dried fruit do not need as much sugar as pickles made with fresh fruit; dried fruits are already packed with sugar. A small amount of liquid such as apple juice or water may be used to rehydrate the fruit before pickling. This prevents the fruit soaking up too much vinegar and the flavour becoming overpowering.

When pickling light-coloured dried fruits such as apricots, pears or apples, use light-coloured sugars and vinegars. Dark-coloured fruits such as figs and prunes can be pickled using malt or red wine vinegar and darker sugars.

SWEET PICKLING VINEGAR

When choosing vinegar for sweet pickles, it is important to think about the colour as well as the flavour of the vinegar. For green fruits such as green figs or red fruits such as plums, choose a light-coloured vinegar and spices or flavourings that won't alter the colour. Using a dark vinegar will turn the fruits a sludgy brown colour. Yellow fruits such as nectarines and apricots, and white or creamy fruits such as pears look stunning pickled in a coloured vinegar such as raspberry.

making pickled prunes

Makes about 1.3kg/3lb

INGREDIENTS

675g/1½lb/3 cups prunes
150ml/¼ pint/⅔ cup clear apple juice
750ml/1¼ pints/3 cups pickling
  malt vinegar
strip of pared orange rind
350g/12oz/1½ cups light
  muscovado (brown) sugar

1 Put the prunes in a non-corrosive pan, pour over the apple juice and cover. Leave to soak for 2 hours, or until the prunes have absorbed most of the juice.

2 Uncover the pan, add the vinegar and orange rind and bring slowly to the boil over a gentle heat. Reduce the heat and simmer gently for 10–15 minutes until the prunes are plump and juicy.

3 Remove the strip of orange rind from the pan and discard. Using a slotted spoon, lift the prunes out of the vinegar and pack well into hot sterilized jars.

4 Add the sugar to the vinegar and heat gently, stirring, until the sugar has dissolved completely. Bring the mixture to a rapid boil and cook for about 5 minutes, or until slightly reduced and thickened.

5 Carefully pour the hot vinegar syrup over the prunes and seal. Store in a cool dark place for at least 2 weeks before eating. Use within 1 year.

USING DRIED FRUITS IN PRESERVES

Dried fruits can be used in many types of preserve. They absorb liquid readily, so are often added to chutneys to help thicken the mixture. Raisins and sultanas (golden raisins) are particularly popular for this. Chopped dried apricots, peaches, dates and figs can also be used and contribute a substantial texture as well as a lovely sweet flavour.

Dried fruit is widely used to impart a full, fruity flavour to cooked relishes and savoury preserves made with mildly flavoured vegetables such as pumpkin, squash and green (unripe) tomatoes.

When choosing dried fruit for pickling, select the fully dried type, rather than the softer ready-to-eat variety that is popular for general cooking. The former has a better texture when soaked for a long time in pickling vinegar.

FRUITS PRESERVED IN ALCOHOL

Fruits preserved in alcohol make luxurious instant desserts, served with crème fraîche or ice cream. One of the best-known fruit and alcohol preserves is German *rumtopf*, which means rum pot. It consists of summer and early autumn fruits bottled in alcohol, usually rum, but not always, with a little sugar. Traditionally, this preserve is made in a large jar with a wide neck and tight-fitting lid.

Pure alcohol is the best preservative because bacteria and moulds are unable to grow in it. Clear liqueurs, such as eau de vie, orange liqueur, Kirsch and Amaretto, or spirits such as brandy, rum and vodka, which are at least 40% ABV, may be used.

The alcohol content of table wine and dry (hard) cider is too low and so these are not effective preservatives on their own unless the bottles are heat-treated. Fruits preserved in wine or cider should be stored in the refrigerator and used within 1 month of making.

When using alcohol to preserve, it is usually best to combine it with sugar syrup because high-alcohol liqueurs and spirits tend to shrink the fruit. Most fruits are first simmered in syrup, which helps to tenderize the fruit and kills the bad enzymes.

The type of syrup used for preserving fruits in alcohol varies depending on the sweetness and juiciness of the fruit, as well as the desired result. A typical syrup would be 600ml/1 pint/2½ cups alcohol, blended with a syrup of 150ml/¼ pint/⅔ cup water and 150g/5oz/¾ cup sugar.

making nectarines in brandy syrup

For extra flavour, you can add whole spices such as vanilla or cinnamon to the syrup.

Makes about 900g/2lb

INGREDIENTS

350g/12oz/1¾ cups preserving or granulated sugar
150ml/¼ pint/⅔ cup water
450g/1lb firm, ripe nectarines
2 bay leaves
150ml/¼ pint/⅔ cup brandy

1 Put the sugar in a large heavy pan with the water and heat gently, stirring until dissolved completely. Bring to the boil, then reduce the heat and simmer for 10 minutes.

2 Halve and stone (pit) the nectarines. (If liked, you may also peel them.) Add them to the syrup.

3 Reduce the heat so that the syrup is barely simmering and poach the nectarines until almost tender. Add the bay leaves 1 minute before the end of the cooking. Turn off the heat and leave them to stand for 5 minutes; they will cook a little more as it cools.

4 Using a slotted spoon, lift the fruit out of the pan and pack into hot sterilized jars.

5 Bring the syrup to a rapid boil and cook for 3–4 minutes. Leave to cool for a few minutes, then stir in the brandy. (Do not add the brandy to the boiling syrup because the alcohol will evaporate and the syrup will lose its preserving qualities.) Pour the syrup into the jars, covering the fruit completely. Tap the jars to release any air and seal. Store in a cool dark place and use within 1 year.

CHUTNEYS

These are made from finely cut ingredients, cooked slowly with vinegar, a sweetener and frequently spices or other flavourings to make a thick, savoury jam-like mixture. Onions and apples are often included in chutneys, but almost any fruits and vegetables can be used. Chutneys should be matured in a cool dark place for at least 2 months before eating.

making tomato chutney

Makes about 2.25kg/5lb

INGREDIENTS

450g/1lb onions, chopped

900ml/1½ pints/3¾ cups malt vinegar

50g/2oz whole pickling spices, such as peppercorns, allspice berries, dried chillies, dried ginger and celery seeds

1kg/2¼lb ripe tomatoes, skinned and chopped

450g/1lb cooking apples, peeled, cored and chopped

350g/12oz/1½ cups soft light brown sugar

10ml/2 tsp salt

225g/8oz/1 cup sultanas (golden raisins)

1 Put the onions and vinegar in a large pan. Tie the pickling spices in a muslin (cheesecloth) bag and add to the pan. Bring slowly to the boil, then simmer gently for 30 minutes until the onions are almost tender.

2 Add the tomatoes and apples to the pan, and simmer for 10 minutes until the fruit is softened and starts to break down slightly.

3 Add the sugar and salt to the pan, and stir over a low heat until the sugar has dissolved completely, then stir in the sultanas.

4 Gently simmer the chutney for 1½–2 hours, stirring occasionally to prevent the mixture sticking. The chutney is ready when it is thick and there is no liquid on the surface. Draw a wooden spoon across the base of the pan: it should leave a clear line in the mixture.

5 Remove the pan from the heat and leave to cool for 5 minutes. Remove the spice bag and discard. Stir the mixture to ensure the chutney is evenly mixed, then spoon into warmed, sterilized jars.

6 Use the handle of a wooden spoon to release any trapped air bubbles and ensure the chutney is packed down well. Seal the jars immediately and leave to cool. Store the chutney in a cool, dark place and leave to mature for at least 1 month before eating. Use within 2 years.

TOP TIPS FOR SUCCESSFUL CHUTNEY-MAKING

• Use malt vinegar for its intense flavour. Wine vinegar or cider vinegar are better for preserving colourful or light-coloured vegetables because they will not spoil the colour of the vegetables.

• The choice of sugar will affect the end result: brown sugar gives the richest flavour and colour; demerara (raw) sugar and golden granulated sugar give a caramel flavour; and white sugar helps to retain the colour of light ingredients.

• Never cover the pan when making chutney. Cooking the preserve uncovered allows the liquid to evaporate and the chutney to thicken. Towards the end, stir the chutney frequently to prevent it from catching and burning on the base of the pan.

• Always store chutney in a cool dark place: warmth can cause it to ferment, and bright sunlight can affect the colour.

RELISHES

These are similar to chutneys, but are cooked for a shorter length of time to give a crisper, fresher result. The fruits and vegetables are usually cut into slightly smaller, neater pieces, and wine or cider vinegar is more frequently used than malt vinegar. Relishes contain a low proportion of vinegar and sugar, so do not keep for long. They can be eaten immediately or chilled and used within 2–3 months.

making hot pepper relish

Makes about 1.3kg/3lb

INGREDIENTS

900g/2lb red (bell) peppers, quartered, cored and seeded
10ml/2 tsp salt
4 fresh red chillies, seeded
450g/1lb red (Italian) onions, finely chopped
400ml/14fl oz/1⅔ cups red wine vinegar
5ml/1 tsp celery seeds
6 black peppercorns
200g/7oz/1 cup granulated sugar

1 Cut the peppers into 1cm/½in pieces and layer them in a colander or sieve placed over a large bowl, sprinkling salt between each layer. Leave the peppers to drain for at least 30 minutes.

2 Tip the red peppers into a large heavy pan and add the chillies, onions and vinegar.

3 Tie the celery seeds and black peppercorns in a square of muslin (cheesecloth) and add to the pan. Slowly bring to the boil over a low heat. Reduce the heat and simmer for about 25 minutes, or until the peppers are just tender.

4 Add the sugar and stir over a low heat until dissolved. Bring to the boil and simmer for 15 minutes, or until the relish is thick.

5 Remove the spice bag from the pan and discard. Spoon the relish into warmed, sterilized jars and seal. Store in the refrigerator and use within 3 months.

RELISHES WITH THICKENED SAUCES

Some relishes have a sauce base thickened with flour or cornflour (cornstarch). Mustard or turmeric may be added to the relish to give it a yellow colour. Corn relish, piccalilli and chow-chow are examples. The vegetables should retain their shape and be slightly crunchy, rather than soft.

making mustard relish

Makes about 1.3kg/3lb

INGREDIENTS

900g/2lb mixed vegetables, such as cauliflower, green beans, courgettes (zucchini), carrots, (bell) peppers and green tomatoes
225g/8oz shallots, finely sliced
750ml/1¼ pints/3 cups malt vinegar
1 garlic clove, crushed
50g/2oz/½ cup plain (all-purpose) flour
25g/1oz/¼ cup English mustard powder
200g/7oz/1 cup caster (superfine) sugar
2.5ml/½ tsp ground coriander
5ml/1 tsp salt

1 Break the cauliflower into small florets, cut the beans into 2.5cm/1in lengths and dice the courgettes, carrots, peppers and tomatoes.

2 Put the shallots in a large heavy pan with 600ml/1 pint/2½ cups of the vinegar. Simmer, uncovered, for 10 minutes. Add the vegetables and garlic and simmer for 10 minutes.

3 Mix together the flour, mustard, sugar, coriander, salt and remaining vinegar to make a smooth paste, then stir into the vegetables. Simmer for 10 minutes, stirring. Pot and store for 2 weeks before eating. Use within 6 months.

SALSAS

These fresh sauces and relishes originated in Mexico. They are made from fresh raw fruit and vegetables and usually flavoured with spices such as chilli and aromatic herbs such as coriander (cilantro). They may be hot and fiery or cool and refreshing.

Many salsas are meant to be eaten on the day of making. Some, however, are lightly cooked and will keep for a short time in the refrigerator. They can also be frozen and stored in the freezer for up to 2 months.

Vinegar and sugar may be included in salsas, but only as flavouring ingredients and not as preservatives. Like relishes, they are ready for eating immediately.

making sweet pepper and tomato salsa

This light and refreshing salsa uses similar ingredients to a relish, but the result is completely different due to the very short cooking time.

Makes about 900g/2lb

INGREDIENTS

450g/1lb firm ripe tomatoes
7.5ml/1½ tsp salt
675g/1½lb red, yellow and
  green (bell) peppers, quartered
  and seeded
1 onion
2 large fresh green
  chillies, seeded
1 garlic clove, crushed
45ml/3 tbsp olive oil
30ml/2 tbsp red wine vinegar
5ml/1 tsp caster (superfine) sugar
30ml/2 tbsp chopped fresh
  coriander (cilantro)

1 Cut a small cross in the base of each tomato and place in a large, heatproof bowl. Pour over boiling water to cover, then leave to stand for about 30 seconds. Drain the tomatoes and peel off the skins.

2 Cut the tomatoes into quarters and use a teaspoon to scoop out the seeds. (This gives a more attractive result and prevents the salsa becoming too wet.)

3 Cut the tomato flesh into 5mm/¼in pieces and layer them up in a nylon or stainless-steel sieve set over a bowl, sprinkling a little salt between each layer. Leave to drain for about 20 minutes.

4 Meanwhile, cut the peppers and onion into 5mm/¼in pieces and finely slice the chillies, ensuring all the white membrane has been discarded. Put in a large pan.

5 Add the chopped tomatoes to the pan and add the crushed garlic, olive oil, vinegar, sugar and fresh coriander. Bring the mixture to the boil and simmer for 5 minutes, stirring frequently.

6 If you are going to use the salsa quickly, spoon into clean jars, packing it down well, then seal. Store in the refrigerator and use within 2–3 days.

7 Alternatively, pack the salsa into freezerproof containers and freeze for up to 2 months. Before serving, remove the salsa from the freezer and place in the refrigerator. Leave to defrost overnight.

COOK'S TIPS

• It is important to lightly cook all the ingredients, including the coriander, because this kills enzymes that would otherwise cause the salsa to deteriorate more quickly.

• The oily substance, capsaicin, which is found in chillies, can cause intense irritation to the skin and eyes. Always wash your hands with soap and water immediately after handling chillies. Alternatively, protect your hands by wearing a pair of rubber (latex) gloves when chopping the chillies.

SAUCES

Made with similar ingredients to chutneys, sauces have a thinner consistency and are sieved to a smooth purée. Those made with vegetables low in acid must either be stored in the refrigerator and consumed quickly, or heat-treated.

making tomato ketchup

Makes about 600ml/1 pint/2½ cups

INGREDIENTS

900g/2lb ripe tomatoes
225g/8oz shallots, peeled
2cm/¾in piece fresh root ginger, peeled
2 garlic cloves, peeled
150ml/¼ pint/⅔ cup cider vinegar
about 40g/1½oz/scant ¼ cup granulated or soft light brown sugar
5ml/1 tsp paprika
5ml/1 tsp salt

1 Roughly chop the tomatoes, shallots, ginger and garlic. Make the pieces fairly small, so that the mixture cooks quickly and retains its fresh flavour.

2 Put the chopped vegetables in a large heavy pan and slowly bring to the boil, stirring frequently until the juices start to run. Reduce the heat, cover and simmer for about 20 minutes, stirring frequently, until the shallots are tender.

3 Spoon the tomato mixture into a sieve placed over a clean pan and press through using the back of a spoon. Alternatively, push the mixture through a food mill.

4 Bring the tomato purée to the boil, then reduce the heat and simmer gently for 45 minutes, or until reduced by half.

5 Add the vinegar, sugar, paprika and salt to the pan and stir to combine. Simmer the sauce for a further 45 minutes, stirring frequently, until well reduced and thickened. (The hot sauce should be a slightly thinner consistency at this stage than is required for the final ketchup; it will thicken as it cools.)

6 Using a funnel, carefully pour the hot sauce into hot sterilized bottles, then seal with corks and heat-treat. (If the bottles are not going to be heat-treated, plastic screw caps can be used instead of corks.)

7 Store the ketchup in a cool dark place, preferably the refrigerator. If it has been heat-treated, it will keep for up to 2 years; if it has simply been bottled, it will keep for up to 2 months in the refrigerator.

HEAT-TREATING BOTTLES

Bottles must have a ridge on the neck, so that the cork can be secured with string.

1 Press a cork into the neck of a filled bottle and make a shallow cut across the top of the cork. Cut a 40cm/16in length of string. Keeping one end about 20cm/8in longer than the other, wedge the string into the cut.

2 Loop the longest end of string around the bottle neck, then pull the end through the front of the loop. Pull both ends down to tighten. Securely tie the loose ends of the string on the top of the cork. Repeat with the other bottles.

3 Wrap cloth around each bottle, then stand on a thick layer of cloth in a deep pan. Pour water up to the bottle necks and heat for 20 minutes for 600ml/1 pint/2½ cup hot-packed bottles; 25 minutes for 1 litre/1¾ pint/4 cup hot-packed and 600ml/1 pint/2½ cup cold-packed bottles; and 30 minutes for 1 litre/1¾ pint/4 cup cold-packed bottles.

DRIED FRUITS AND VEGETABLES

Removing moisture from foods is one of the oldest methods of preserving. Traditional techniques depend on the correct proportions of sunlight, heat and humidity for successful results. If food is dried too fast, moisture can get trapped and spoil it; if it is dried too slowly, micro-organisms may start to grow. Most commercially dried fruits and vegetables, such as apricots, figs and tomatoes, which are high both in sugar and acid, are still wind- and sun-dried in the way they have been for centuries.

To re-create these conditions, an airy place with a steady temperature is needed. A very warm room or cupboard may be used if the temperature is constant, but the most efficient way is to use an oven on the lowest setting.

A fan oven is ideal because of the constant circulation of air. If using a conventional oven, leave the door open with the tiniest possible gap, or open frequently during the drying process to let steam escape. Be careful that the temperature does not become too high, or the fruit or vegetables will cook and shrivel. If necessary, turn off the oven occasionally and leave it to cool down.

Choose firm, fresh and ripe fruit and vegetables for drying. Citrus fruits and melons consist mainly of water, so do not dry well, nor do berry fruits because they discolour and become very seedy. To help preserve the dried fruit and prevent discoloration, the prepared pieces should be dipped into a very weak brine solution, or acidulated water, before drying.

making dried apple rings

INGREDIENTS

15ml/1 tbsp salt, or 90ml/6 tbsp lemon juice, or 30ml/2 tbsp ascorbic acid (vitamin C) powder

1.2 litres/2 pints/5 cups water

900g/2lb firm, ripe apples

1 Put the salt, lemon juice or ascorbic acid powder in a large bowl and pour in the water. Stir until dissolved.

2 Peel and core the apples, then cut into rings slightly thicker than 5mm/¼in. As soon as each apple is cut, put the rings in the bowl of water and leave for 1 minute before lifting out. Pat the rings dry using kitchen paper.

3 Thread the apple rings on to wooden skewers, leaving a small space between each ring, or spread the apple rings out on wire racks. (Baking sheets are not suitable because air needs to circulate around the fruit.)

4 If using skewers, rest them on the oven shelves, allowing the apple rings to hang between the gaps. If using wire racks, simply place the racks in the oven. Leave the door very slightly ajar.

5 Dry the apples at 110°C/225°F/ Gas ¼ for about 5 hours, or until the apple rings resemble soft, pliable leather.

6 Remove the fruit from the oven and leave to cool completely. Very crisp fruits and vegetables should be stored in airtight containers, but leathery, pliable fruits are better stored in paper bags or cardboard boxes; storing them in plastic bags may make them go mouldy.

7 To reconstitute the dried apple slices, put them in a bowl and pour over boiling water. Leave to soak for at least 5 minutes, then place in a pan and gently cook in the soaking liquid.

COOK'S TIPS

• Dried apple slices make a healthy snack and are popular with children.
• They are also good chopped and added to desserts and bakes.

PREPARING FRUITS AND VEGETABLES FOR DRYING

The time taken for fruit and vegetables to dry depends greatly on their size, so cut them into equal-size pieces.

Apples and pears Peel and core. Cut apples into 5mm/¼in slices; halve or quarter pears, depending on size.

Apricots, plums and figs These may be dried whole, but are better if halved and stoned (pitted). Place on the racks with the cut sides uppermost, so that the juices do not run out. If the oven has a lower setting, dry on this for 1 hour, before turning up to 110°C/225°C/Gas ¼, to prevent the skins from bursting.

Grapes Use seedless grapes. These can be dried whole: prick a tiny hole in each one to stop the skins bursting.

Onions and leeks Slice thinly crossways. The pieces may fall through wire racks, so cover the racks with muslin (cheesecloth) first.

Mushrooms and chillies Tie these up on to fine string or cotton thread and hang up to air-dry in the sun or in an airy room for 2–3 weeks until dry and shrivelled. The dried strings of mushrooms and chillies can look very pretty hung in the kitchen.

Plum tomatoes Split these lengthways and arrange cut side up. Sprinkle lightly with salt before placing in the oven to dry out.

FRUIT LEATHER

This unusual delicacy is made from slightly sweetened fruit pulp that has been spread out thinly and dried. The final result is a sweet, chewy fruit "leather" that can be eaten as confectionery or a snack. Most ripe fruits can be used; mangoes, peaches and apricots work particularly well and produce an intensely flavoured, orange-coloured confection.

making apricot leather

Makes about 115g/4oz

INGREDIENTS

900g/2lb ripe apricots
10ml/2 tsp lemon juice
45ml/3 tbsp caster
  (superfine) sugar

1 Put the apricots in a bowl and pour over boiling water. Leave to stand for about 30 seconds, then drain and peel off the skins. Halve the fruits and remove the stones (pits). Using a sharp knife, roughly chop the flesh.

2 Put the chopped apricots, lemon juice and sugar in a food processor or blender and process for about 3 minutes, or until the fruit has formed a smooth purée.

3 Line a large baking sheet with a piece of baking parchment. Pour the purée on to the middle of the baking parchment, then, using a palette knife (metal spatula), spread the purée out to a thickness of 5mm/¼in, leaving a 2cm/¾in margin. Tap the baking sheet on the work surface to level the purée.

4 Put the baking sheet in the oven, leaving the door slightly ajar, and dry at 110°C/225°F/Gas ¼ for about 8 hours, or until the purée is dry, but still pliable.

5 Leave the apricot leather to cool on the baking sheet, then roll it up, still on the baking parchment, and store in an airtight container for up to 3 months.

6 To eat, carefully unroll the fruit leather and cut into squares or 5cm/2in lengths while still on the baking parchment, then peel off the baking parchment.

CANDIED FRUIT

Sugar is an excellent preservative. Candying is a method by which fruit or citrus peel is preserved by steeping in syrup. The fruit or peel becomes so saturated in sugar that natural deterioration is virtually halted. The process works by gradually replacing the fruit's moisture with a saturated sugar solution. This has to be done slowly and takes at least 15 days, but is well worth it. Candied fruit is expensive to buy and, although you need to plan ahead when making candied fruit or peel, it requires only a little time each day.

making candied fruit

You can candy as much or as little fruit as you like, working with the basic proportions of fruit to sugar given in the recipe below. Always candy different fruits separately, so that each type retains its own flavour. Choose firm, fresh fruits that are free of blemishes.

INGREDIENTS

fresh, firm, just-ripe fruit, such as
  pineapples, peaches, pears, apples,
  plums, apricots, kiwi fruit or cherries
granulated sugar
caster (superfine) sugar, for sprinkling

Day 1

1 Prepare the fruit. Thickly peel and core pineapples, then slice into rings; peel, stone (pit) or core peaches, pears and apples, then halve or cut into thick slices; plums and apricots can be left whole (prick them all over with a fine skewer) or halve and stone; skin and quarter kiwi fruit, or thickly slice; stone cherries.

2 Weigh the fruit, then put in a pan and just cover with water. Bring to the boil and simmer until just tender. Do not overcook because the flavour and shape will be lost; do not undercook because the fruit will be tough when candied.

3 Using a slotted spoon, lift the cooked fruit into a large wide bowl; avoid piling the fruit up high. Retain the cooking liquid.

4 For every 450g/1lb prepared (uncooked) fruit, use 300ml/½ pint/1¼ cups of the cooking liquid and 175g/6oz/scant 1 cup sugar. Gently heat the sugar and liquid in a pan, stirring, until the sugar has dissolved, then bring to the boil.

5 Pour the boiling syrup over the fruit, making sure that the fruit is completely immersed. Cover and leave to stand for 24 hours.

Day 2

1 Drain the syrup from the fruit back into a pan, being careful not to damage the fruit as you do so. Return the fruit to the bowl.

2 Add 50g/2oz/¼ cup granulated sugar to the syrup and heat gently, stirring until dissolved completely, then bring to the boil.

3 Pour the hot syrup over the fruit. Allow to cool, then cover and leave to stand for 24 hours.

Days 3–7

Repeat the instructions for day 2 every day for the next 5 days. The concentration of sugar will become much stronger.

Days 8–9

1 Drain the syrup from the fruit into a large wide pan and add 90g/3½oz/½ cup sugar. Heat gently, stirring, until dissolved.

2 Carefully add the fruit to the syrup and simmer gently for about 3 minutes. Return the fruit and syrup to the bowl, cool, then cover and leave to stand for 48 hours.

Days 10–13

Repeat the instructions for days 8–9, leaving the fruit to soak for 4 days rather than 2.

COOK'S TIP

The final soaking stage from days 10–13 can be extended another 6 days, if you like – to a total of 10 days. The longer the fruit is left to soak in the syrup, the sweeter and more intense its flavour will become.

Days 14–15

1 Drain the fruit, discarding the syrup. Carefully spread the fruit out, spacing each piece slightly apart, on a wire rack placed over a baking sheet.

2 Cut a sheet of baking parchment or foil slightly larger than the baking sheet. Using a fine skewer, prick about 12 tiny holes at equal intervals in the sheet.

3 Cover the fruit with the baking parchment or foil, being very careful not to touch the fruit. The parchment or foil is simply to keep off any dust; some air should still be able to circulate around the fruit.

4 Leave the fruit in a warm place such as a sunny windowsill or airing cupboard for 2 days, turning each piece of fruit occasionally until all the fruit is thoroughly dry.

5 Sprinkle the fruit with a little caster sugar, then store in an airtight container in single layers between sheets of greaseproof (waxed) paper. Eat within 1 year.

COOK'S TIP

Candied fruits are very pretty, retaining the colour of the original fruits. They make great sweetmeats for serving after a meal, particularly at Christmas.

making candied peel

Citrus peel contains less moisture than the fruit, making candying simpler and less time-consuming.

INGREDIENTS

5 small oranges, 6 lemons or 7 limes, or a combination

granulated sugar

caster (superfine) sugar, for sprinkling

1 Scrub the fruit. Remove the peel in quarters, scraping away the pith. Place in a pan, cover with cold water and simmer for 1¼–1½ hours. Drain, reserving 300ml/½ pint/ 1¼ cups of the cooking water.

2 Pour the reserved water into the pan and add 200g/7oz/1 cup sugar. Heat gently, stirring until dissolved, then bring to the boil. Add the peel and simmer for 1 minute. Leave to cool, tip into a bowl, cover and leave for 48 hours.

3 Remove the peel and tip the syrup back into the pan. Add 150g/5oz/ ¾ cup sugar and heat gently, stirring until dissolved. Add the peel, bring to the boil, then simmer until the peel is transparent. Cool, tip into a bowl, cover and leave for 2 weeks.

4 Drain the peel, then dry, sprinkle and store in the same way as candied fruit.

making glacé fruit

Glacé, or crystallized, fruit is made from candied fruit, dipped in heavy syrup to give it a glossy coating.

INGREDIENTS

candied fruit

400g/14oz/2 cups granulated sugar

120ml/4fl oz/½ cup water

1 Make sure the candied fruit is dry and dust off any sugar coating. Put the sugar and water in a pan and heat gently, stirring, until the sugar has completely dissolved. Bring to the boil and simmer for 2 minutes.

2 Pour one-third of the syrup into a small bowl. Fill a second bowl with boiling water. Using a slotted spoon or fork, first dip the fruit into the boiling water for 15 seconds, then shake and dip into the syrup for 15 seconds. Place on a wire rack.

3 Repeat with the remaining fruit, topping up the bowl of syrup when necessary (return the syrup to the boil before doing this); replace the bowl of boiling water once or twice.

4 Dry the fruit on wire racks placed over baking sheets in a very warm place for 2–3 days, turning the fruit occasionally. Store in the same way as candied fruit.

jams and conserves

Preserving fruits in jams and conserves is one of the best ways of enjoying their delicious flavour all year round. In summer, with its long, warm days, there is an abundance of sweet juicy berries, while the autumn harvest offers a fabulous choice of stone and hedgerow fruits. All of these can be made into irresistible jams that can be enjoyed at any time of day – spread on toast, used as a filling or topping for plain cakes, or spooned over ice cream for a treat. All the recipes in this chapter will keep for at least 6 months.

seedless raspberry and passion fruit jam

The pips in raspberry jam can often put people off this wonderful preserve. This version has none of the pips and all of the flavour, and is enhanced by the tangy addition of passion fruit.

Makes about 1.3kg/3lb

INGREDIENTS

1.6kg/3½lb/14 cups raspberries

4 passion fruit, halved

1.3kg/3lb/6½ cups preserving sugar
  with pectin, warmed

juice of 1 lemon

COOK'S TIPS

• Check the instructions on the sugar packet for details of the boiling time.

• If you cannot find preserving sugar with pectin, use the same quantity of regular sugar and add powdered or liquid pectin. Check the instructions on the packet for quantities.

1 Place the raspberries in a large pan, then scoop out the passion fruit seeds and pulp and add to the raspberries. Cover and cook over a low heat for 20 minutes, or until the juices begin to run.

2 Remove the pan from the heat and leave to cool slightly, then, using the back of a spoon, press the fruit through a coarse sieve into a preserving pan.

3 Add the sugar and lemon juice to the pan and stir over a low heat until the sugar has dissolved. Bring to the boil and cook for 4 minutes, or until the jam reaches setting point (105°C/220°F).

4 Remove the pan from the heat and skim off any scum. Leave to cool slightly, then pour into warmed sterilized jars. Seal and label, then store in a cool place.

wild strawberry and rose petal conserve

This fragrant jam is ideal served with summer cream teas. Rose water complements the strawberries beautifully, but only add a few drops because the flavour can easily become over-powering.

Makes about 900g/2lb

INGREDIENTS

900g/2lb/8 cups wild Alpine strawberries

450g/1lb/4 cups strawberries, hulled and mashed

2 dark pink rose buds, petals only

juice of 2 lemons

1.3kg/3lb/6½ cups granulated sugar, warmed

a few drops of rose water

1 Put all the strawberries in a non-metallic bowl with the rose petals, lemon juice and warmed sugar. Cover and leave overnight.

2 The next day, tip the fruit into a preserving pan and heat gently, stirring, until all the sugar has dissolved. Boil for 10–15 minutes, or to setting point (105°C/220°F).

3 Stir the rose water into the jam, then remove the pan from the heat. Skim off any scum and leave to cool for 5 minutes, then stir and pour into warmed sterilized jars. Seal and label, then store.

COOK'S TIPS

• If you are unable to find wild berries, use ordinary strawberries instead. Leave the smaller berries whole but mash any large ones.

• To make plain strawberry jam, make in the same way but leave out the rose petals and rose water.

cherry-berry conserve

Tart cranberries enliven the taste of cherries and also add an essential dose of pectin to this pretty conserve, which is fabulous spread on crumpets or toast. It is also delicious stirred into meaty gravies and sauces served with roast duck, poultry or pork.

2 Add the water to the pan. Cover and bring to the boil, then simmer for 20–30 minutes, or until the cranberries are very tender.

3 Add the sugar to the pan and heat gently, stirring, until the sugar has dissolved. Bring to the boil, then cook for 10 minutes, or to setting point (105°C/220°F).

4 Remove the pan from the heat and skim off any scum using a slotted spoon. Leave to cool for 10 minutes, then stir gently and pour into warmed sterilized jars. Seal, label and store.

Makes about 1.3kg/3lb

INGREDIENTS

350g/12oz/3 cups fresh cranberries
1kg/2¼lb/5½ cups cherries, pitted
120ml/4fl oz/½ cup blackcurrant
  or raspberry syrup
juice of 2 lemons
250ml/8fl oz/1 cup water
1.3kg/3lb/6½ cups preserving
  or granulated sugar, warmed

COOK'S TIP

The cranberries must be cooked until very tender before the sugar is added, otherwise they will become tough.

1 Put the cranberries in a food processor and process until coarsely chopped. Scrape into a pan and add the cherries, fruit syrup and lemon juice.

summer berry and juniper jam

In late summer, there is a moment when all the different varieties of berries suddenly seem to be ripe at the same time. Combine them in jam as the flavours work well together, particularly when blended with juniper, which produces a taste reminiscent of gin.

Makes about 1.3kg/3lb

INGREDIENTS

675g/1½lb/6 cups raspberries
675g/1½lb/6 cups blackberries
10ml/2 tsp juniper berries,
  crushed
300ml/½ pint/1¼ cups water
1.3kg/3lb/6½ cups granulated
  sugar, warmed
juice of 2 lemons

COOK'S TIP

Juniper berries are quite soft and are easily broken down into coarsely crushed pieces. Put the berries in a mortar and crush with a pestle.

1 Put the raspberries, blackberries and juniper berries in a large heavy pan with the water. Set over a low heat, cover and cook gently for about 15 minutes, or until the juices begin to run.

2 Add the sugar and lemon juice to the pan and cook over a low heat, stirring frequently, until the sugar has dissolved. (Be careful not to break up the berries too much.)

3 Bring to the boil and cook for 5–10 minutes, or until the jam reaches setting point (105°C/220°F). Remove the pan from the heat and skim off any scum from the surface using a slotted spoon. Leave to cool for about 5 minutes, then stir gently and pour into warmed sterilized jars. Seal and label, then store in a cool, dark place.

blueberry and lime jam

The subtle yet fragrant flavour of blueberries can be illusive on its own. Adding a generous quantity of tangy lime juice enhances their flavour and gives this jam a wonderful zesty taste.

Makes about 1.3kg/3lb

INGREDIENTS

1.3kg/3lb/12 cups blueberries
finely pared rind and juice
  of 4 limes
1kg/2¼lb/5 cups preserving sugar
  with pectin

COOK'S TIP
Blueberries are not naturally high in pectin, so extra pectin is needed for a good set. If you prefer, used granulated sugar and add pectin according to the instruction on the packet in place of the preserving sugar with pectin.

1 Put the blueberries, lime juice and half the sugar in a large, non-metallic bowl and lightly crush the berries using a potato masher. Set aside for about 4 hours.

2 Tip the crushed berry mixture into a pan and stir in the finely pared lime rind and the remaining preserving sugar. Heat slowly, stirring continuously, until the sugar has completely dissolved.

3 Increase the heat and bring to the boil. Boil rapidly for about 4 minutes, or until the jam reaches setting point (105°C/220°F).

4 Remove the pan from the heat and set aside for 5 minutes. Stir the jam gently, then pour into warmed sterilized jars. Seal the jars, then label when completely cool. Store in a cool, dark place.

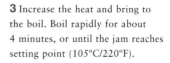

blackcurrant jam

This jam has a rich, fruity flavour and a wonderfully strong dark colour. It is punchy and delicious with scones for tea or spread on croissants for a continental-style breakfast.

Makes about 1.3kg/3lb

INGREDIENTS

1.3kg/3lb/12 cups blackcurrants

grated rind and juice of 1 orange

475ml/16fl oz/2 cups water

1.3kg/3lb/6½ cups granulated sugar, warmed

30ml/2 tbsp cassis (optional)

1 Place the blackcurrants, orange rind and juice and water in a large heavy pan. Bring to the boil, reduce the heat and simmer for 30 minutes.

2 Add the warmed sugar to the pan and stir over a low heat until the sugar has dissolved.

3 Bring the mixture to the boil and cook for about 8 minutes, or until the jam reaches setting point (105°C/220°F).

4 Remove the pan from the heat and skim off any scum from the surface using a slotted spoon. Leave to cool for 5 minutes, then stir in the cassis, if using.

5 Pour the jam into warmed sterilized jars and seal. Leave the jars to cool completely, then label and store in a cool, dark place.

dried apricot jam

This richly flavoured jam can be made at any time of year, so even if you miss the short apricot season, you can still enjoy the delicious taste of sweet, tangy apricot jam all year round.

Makes about 2kg/4½lb

INGREDIENTS

675g/1½lb dried apricots
900ml/1½ pints/3¾ cups apple juice
juice and grated rind of
  2 unwaxed lemons
675g/1½lb/scant 3½ cups preserving
  or granulated sugar, warmed
50g/2oz/½ cup blanched almonds,
  coarsely chopped

COOK'S TIP

Use the best quality traditional dried apricots to make this jam. They have a more suitable texture than the soft ready-to-eat dried apricots and will produce a better end result.

1 Put the apricots in a bowl, pour over the apple juice and leave to soak overnight.

2 Pour the soaked apricots and juice into a preserving pan and add the lemon juice and rind. Bring to the boil, then lower the heat and simmer for 15–20 minutes until the apricots are soft.

3 Add the warmed sugar to the pan and bring to the boil, stirring until the sugar has completely dissolved. Boil for 15–20 minutes, or until setting point is reached (105°C/220°F).

4 Stir the chopped almonds into the jam and leave to stand for about 15 minutes, then pour the jam into warmed, sterilized jars. Seal, then leave to cool completely before labelling. Store in a cool, dark place.

peach and amaretto jam

Adding amaretto (almond liqueur) produces a luxurious jam that's perfect served on warm buttered toast or English muffins. You can use peach schnapps in place of the amaretto if you prefer.

Makes about 1.3kg/3lb

INGREDIENTS

1.3kg/3lb peaches
250ml/8fl oz/1 cup water
juice of 2 lemons
1.3kg/3lb/6½ cups granulated
 sugar, warmed
45ml/3 tbsp amaretto liqueur

1 Carefully peel the peaches using a vegetable peeler, or blanch briefly in boiling water, then peel with a knife. Reserve the skins.

2 Halve and stone the fruit, dice the flesh and put in a pan with the water. Place the peach skins in a small pan with water to cover. Boil until the liquid is reduced to 30ml/2 tbsp. Press the skins and liquid through a sieve into the peaches. Cover and simmer for 20 minutes, or until soft.

3 Add the lemon juice and sugar to the pan. Heat, stirring, until the sugar has dissolved completely. Bring to the boil and cook for 10–15 minutes, or to setting point (105°C/220°F). Remove from the heat and skim off any scum from the surface using a slotted spoon.

4 Leave the jam to cool for about 10 minutes, then stir in the amaretto and pour into warmed sterilized jars. Seal, then leave to cool completely before labelling. Store in a cool, dark place.

gooseberry and elderflower jam

Pale green gooseberries and fragrant elderflowers make perfect partners in this sharp, aromatic, intensely flavoured jam. The jam turns an unexpected pink colour during cooking.

Makes about 2kg/4½lb

INGREDIENTS

1.3kg/3lb/12 cups firm gooseberries,
   topped and tailed

300ml/½ pint/1¼ cups water

1.3kg/3lb/6½ cups granulated
   sugar, warmed

juice of 1 lemon

2 handfuls of elderflowers removed
   from their stalks

COOK'S TIP

The time taken to reach setting point will vary depending on the ripeness of the gooseberries. The riper the fruit, the longer the jam will need to be cooked to reach setting point.

1 Put the gooseberries into a large preserving pan, add the water and bring the mixture to the boil.

2 Cover the pan with a lid and simmer gently for 20 minutes until the fruit is soft. Using a potato masher, gently mash the fruit to crush it lightly.

3 Add the sugar, lemon juice and elderflowers to the pan and stir over a low heat until the sugar has dissolved. Boil for 10 minutes, or to setting point (105°C/220°F). Remove from the heat, skim off any scum and cool for 5 minutes, then stir. Pot and seal, then leave to cool before labelling.

damson jam

Dark, plump damsons used to only be found growing in the wild, but today they are available commercially. They produce a deeply coloured and richly flavoured jam that makes a delicious treat spread on toasted English muffins or warm crumpets at tea time.

Makes about 2kg/4½lb

INGREDIENTS

1kg/2¼lb damsons or wild plums

1.4 litres/2½ pints/6 cups water

1kg/2¼lb/5 cups preserving
   or granulated sugar, warmed

COOK'S TIP

It is important to seal the jars as soon as you have filled them to ensure the jam remains sterile. However, you should then leave the jars to cool completely before labelling and storing them to avoid the risk of burns.

1 Put the damsons in a preserving pan and pour in the water. Bring to the boil. Reduce the heat and simmer gently until the damsons are soft, then stir in the sugar.

2 Bring the mixture to the boil, skimming off stones as they rise. Boil to setting point (105°C/220°F). Leave to cool for 10 minutes, then pot. Seal, then label and store when cool.

greengage and almond jam

This is the perfect preserve to make when greengages are readily available in stores, or if you find you have a glut of the fruit. It has a gloriously rich, golden honey colour and a smooth texture that contrasts wonderfully with the little slivers of almond.

Makes about 1.3kg/3lb

INGREDIENTS

1.3kg/3lb greengages, stoned (pitted)
350ml/12fl oz/1½ cups water
juice of 1 lemon
50g/2oz/½ cup blanched almonds,
  cut into thin slivers
1.3kg/3lb/6½ cups granulated
  sugar, warmed

COOK'S TIP

Greengages look like unripened plums. However, despite their appearance, they have a wonderfully aromatic flavour that is captured perfectly in this delicious jam.

1 Put the greengages and water in a preserving pan with the lemon juice and almond slivers. Bring to the boil, then cover and simmer for 15–20 minutes, or until the greengages are really soft.

2 Add the sugar to the pan and stir over a low heat until the sugar has dissolved. Bring to the boil and cook for 10–15 minutes, or until the jam reaches setting point (105°C/220°F).

3 Remove the pan from the heat and skim off any scum from the surface using a slotted spoon.

4 Leave to cool for 10 minutes, then stir gently and pour into warmed sterilized jars. Seal, then leave to cool completely before labelling. Store in a cool place.

rhubarb and ginger jam

Late summer is the time to make this preserve, when rhubarb leaves are enormous and the stalks thick and green. It has a wonderfully tart, tangy flavour and is delicious spooned over plain cake, or used as a filling with whipped cream.

Makes about 2kg/4½lb

INGREDIENTS

1kg/2¼lb rhubarb
1kg/2¼lb/5 cups preserving
  or granulated sugar
25g/1oz fresh root ginger, bruised
115g/4oz crystallized ginger
50g/2oz/¼ cup candied orange
  peel, chopped

COOK'S TIP

The young, slender rhubarb stems that are available in the spring are more suitable for making tarts and pies. Their delicate flavour does not shine through in preserves, so it is worth waiting until later in the season for mature rhubarb.

1 Cut the rhubarb into short pieces and layer with the sugar in a glass bowl. Leave to stand overnight.

2 The next day, scrape the rhubarb and sugar mixture into a large, heavy preserving pan.

3 Tie the bruised ginger root in a piece of muslin (cheesecloth) and add it to the rhubarb. Cook gently for 30 minutes, or until the rhubarb has softened.

4 Remove the root ginger from the pan and stir in the crystallized ginger and candied orange peel.

5 Bring the mixture to the boil, then cook over a high heat until setting point is reached (105°C/220°F). Leave to cool for a few minutes, then pour into warmed sterilized jars and seal. When completely cool, label and store.

papaya and apricot jam

Apricots and papaya make perfect partners in this tantalizing jam. However, if you prefer plain apricot jam, simply replace the papaya with the same weight of apricots.

2 Slice the apricots and place in a preserving pan with the kernels, papaya, grated lemon rind and juice and the water. Bring to the boil then cover and simmer for 20–30 minutes, or until the fruit is really tender.

3 Add the sugar to the pan and stir continuously over a low heat until the sugar has dissolved. Bring to the boil and cook for about 15 minutes, or until the jam reaches setting point (105°C/220°F).

Makes about 1.3kg/3lb

INGREDIENTS

900g/2lb stoned (pitted) apricots, 6 stones (pits) reserved

450g/1lb papaya, peeled, seeded and cut into small chunks

grated rind and juice of 2 lemons

250ml/8fl oz/1 cup water

1.3kg/3lb/6½ cups granulated sugar, warmed

COOK'S TIP

The bitter kernels from apricot stones contribute an almond-like flavour to the jam. Only a few should be used as they have a strong flavour. They are blanched to remove natural toxins.

1 Using a nut cracker or wooden mallet, crack the reserved apricot stones and remove the kernels inside. Put the kernels in a pan, pour over boiling water and cook for 2 minutes, then drain and slide off their skins.

4 Remove the pan from the heat and skim off any scum from the surface using a slotted spoon. Cool for 5 minutes, then stir gently and pour into warmed sterilized jars and seal. When cool, label the jars, then store in a cool, dark place.

melon and star anise jam

The delicate flavour of melon is brought out by spicy ginger and perfectly complemented by aromatic star-anise. Once opened, store this delicious jam in the refrigerator.

Makes about 1.3kg/3lb

INGREDIENTS

2 Charentais or cantaloupe melons, peeled and seeded

450g/1lb/2¼ cups granulated sugar

2 star anise

4 pieces preserved stem ginger in syrup, drained and finely chopped

finely grated rind and juice of 2 lemons

1 Cut the melons into small cubes and layer with the granulated sugar in a large non-metallic bowl. Cover with clear film (plastic wrap) and leave overnight, or until the melons release their juices.

2 Tip the melon and sugar mixture into a large pan and add the star anise, chopped ginger, lemon rind and juice and stir to combine.

3 Bring the mixture to the boil, then lower the heat. Simmer for 25 minutes, or until the melon has become transparent and the setting point reached (105°C/220°F).

4 Spoon the jam into hot sterilized jars and seal. Leave to cool, then label and store in a cool, dark place.

COOK'S TIP

To test for the set, spoon a little jam on to a chilled plate. It should wrinkle when pushed with a finger.

sweet fruit jellies

Sparkling, jewel-like sweet fruit jellies make a wonderful alternative to jams and conserves, spread on toast or crumpets, or spooned over ice cream in place of a sauce. The fruit is cooked gently for as short a time as possible, then strained through muslin to obtain the clear liquid. Jellies give a lower yield than jam but they really capture the true flavour of fruits and are a lovely way to preserve. All the recipes in this chapter will keep for up to 1 year.

hedgerow jelly

In the autumn, hedgerows are laden with damsons, blackberries and elderberries and it is well worth spending an afternoon in the countryside picking fruit to make into this delightful jelly.

2 Mash the fruit and leave to cool slightly. Pour into a scalded jelly bag suspended over a non-metallic bowl and leave to drain overnight.

3 Measure the strained juice into a preserving pan. Add 450g/1lb/ 2¼ cups sugar for every 600ml/ 1 pint/2½ cups strained fruit juice.

4 Heat the mixture, stirring, over a low heat until the sugar has dissolved. Increase the heat and boil rapidly without stirring for 10–15 minutes, or until the jelly reaches setting point (105°C/220°F).

Makes about 1.3kg/3lb

INGREDIENTS

450g/1lb damsons, washed
450g/1lb/4 cups blackberries, washed
225g/8oz/2 cups raspberries
225g/8oz/2 cups elderberries, washed
juice and pips (seeds) of 2 large lemons
about 1.3kg/3lb/6½ cups preserving
  or granulated sugar, warmed

COOK'S TIP

If you do not have enough of one fruit, you can vary the quantities as long as the total weight of fruit is the same.

1 Put the fruit, lemon juice and pips in a large pan. Add water to just below the level of the fruit. Cover and simmer for 1 hour.

5 Remove the pan from the heat and skim off any scum using a slotted spoon. Ladle into warmed, sterilized jars and seal. Leave to cool, then label and store.

mulberry jelly

Deep red mulberries are not often available but if you have access to a tree you will find they make the most wonderful jellies and jams. For a good set, pick the fruits when they are red.

Makes about 900g/2lb

INGREDIENTS

900g/2lb/8 cups unripe red mulberries
grated rind and juice of 1 lemon
600ml/1 pint/2½ cups water
about 900g/2lb/4½ cups preserving
 or granulated sugar, warmed

1 Put the mulberries in a pan with the lemon rind and juice and the water. Bring to the boil, cover and simmer for 1 hour, then remove from the heat and leave to cool.

2 Pour the fruit into a scalded jelly bag suspended over a non-metallic bowl and leave to drain overnight.

3 Measure the strained juice into a preserving pan. Add 450g/1lb/ 2¼ cups sugar for every 600ml/ 1 pint/2½ cups fruit juice.

4 Heat the mixture over a low heat, stirring, until the sugar has completely dissolved. Increase the heat and boil rapidly, without stirring, for 5–10 minutes, or to setting point (105°C/220°F).

5 Skim off any scum from the surface of the jelly using a slotted spoon. Ladle into warmed, sterilized jars, cover and seal. When the jars are completely cool, label, then store in a cool, dark place.

COOK'S TIPS
• To test for the set, spoon a little jelly on to a chilled saucer. Chill for about 3 minutes, then gently push the jelly with your finger; if the surface wrinkles, the jelly has reached setting point and it is ready to bottle.
• To make redcurrant jelly using the method here, measure the same quantity of fruit, but add slightly less sugar to the strained juice: 450g/ 1lb/1¼ cups sugar for every 600ml/ 1 pint/2½ cups juice.

cranberry jelly

This clear, well-flavoured preserve has a tart flavour and is absolutely delicious served with freshly baked scones, toasted tea cakes and crumpets, or as a glaze for fruit tarts. It can also be served at Christmas with a festive roast turkey, pheasant or guinea fowl.

Makes about 900g/2lb

INGREDIENTS

900g/2lb/8 cups cranberries

450g/1lb sweet eating apples, washed and chopped with skins and cores intact

grated rind and juice of 1 orange

600ml/1 pint/2½ cups water

about 900g/2lb/4½ cups preserving or granulated sugar, warmed

COOK'S TIP

Do not be tempted to squeeze the jelly bag while it is draining or the jelly will become cloudy.

1 Put the cranberries and apples in a pan with the orange rind, juice and water. Bring to the boil then cover and simmer for 1 hour.

2 Remove the pan from the heat and set aside to cool slightly. Pour the fruit and juices into a scalded jelly bag suspended over a non-metallic bowl and leave to drain overnight.

3 Measure the strained juice into a preserving pan. Add 450g/1lb/ 2¼ cups sugar for every 600ml/ 1 pint/2½ cups strained juice.

4 Heat, stirring, over a low heat until the sugar has dissolved completely. Increase the heat and boil rapidly, without stirring, for 5–10 minutes, or until the jelly reaches setting point (105°C/220°F).

5 Remove the pan from the heat and skim off any scum from the surface using a slotted spoon. Ladle into warmed, sterilized jars, cover and seal. Leave to cool, then label and store in a cool, dark place.

red plum and cardamom jelly

The fragrance of warm, spicy cardamom combines wonderfully with all varieties of plum – red plums with a good tart flavour are perfect for making into this sweet, fruity, aromatic jelly. Serve it with plain rich ice creams and custards or spread it on toast for breakfast.

Makes about 1.8kg/4lb

INGREDIENTS

1.8kg/4lb red plums, stoned (pitted)
10ml/2 tsp crushed green
  cardamom pods
600ml/1 pint/2½ cups red grape juice
150ml/¼ pint/⅔ cup water
about 1.3kg/3lb/6½ cups preserving
  or granulated sugar, warmed

1 Put the plums, cardamom pods, grape juice and water in a large pan. Bring to the boil, then cover and simmer gently for 1 hour. Leave to cool slightly, then pour into a scalded jelly bag suspended over a non-metallic bowl and leave to drain overnight.

2 Measure the strained juice into a preserving pan. Add 450g/1lb/ 2¼ cups sugar for every 600ml/ 1 pint/2½ cups strained juice.

3 Heat the mixture over a low heat, stirring constantly until the sugar has dissolved completely. Increase the heat and boil, without stirring, for 10–15 minutes, or until the jelly reaches setting point (105°C/220°F).

4 Remove the pan from the heat and skim off any scum. Spoon the jelly into warmed sterilized jars, cover and seal. When cool, label and store in a cool, dark place.

rhubarb and mint jelly

This delicious jelly is very pretty, specked with tiny pieces of chopped fresh mint. It has a sharp, tangy flavour and is fabulous spread on toast or crumpets at tea time.

Makes about 2kg/4½lb

INGREDIENTS
1kg/2¼lb rhubarb
about 1.3kg/3lb/6½ cups preserving
 or granulated sugar, warmed
large bunch fresh mint
30ml/2 tbsp finely chopped
 fresh mint

COOK'S TIPS
• This recipe is a good way to use up older dark red or green-stemmed rhubarb, which is usually too tough to use for desserts.
• As well as serving as a delightful sweet preserve, this jelly is also very good served with fatty roast meats such as lamb and goose.

1 Using a sharp knife, cut the rhubarb into chunks and place in a large, heavy pan. Pour in just enough water to cover, cover the pan with a lid and cook until the rhubarb is soft.

2 Remove the pan from the heat and leave to cool slightly. Pour the stewed fruit and juices into a scalded jelly bag suspended over a non-metallic bowl and leave to drain overnight.

3 Measure the strained juice into a preserving pan and add 450g/1lb/2¼ cups warmed sugar for each 600ml/1 pint/2½ cups strained juice.

4 Add the bunch of mint to the pan. Bring to the boil, stirring until the sugar has dissolved. Boil to setting point (105°C/220°F). Remove the mint.

5 Leave to stand for 10 minutes, stir in the chopped mint, then pot and seal. Label when cold.

red gooseberry jelly

This delicious jelly is a wonderfully rich, dark red colour and has a deliciously tangy flavour – perfect for spreading on toast at any time of the day. Choose small dark red gooseberries to produce a jelly with the best colour and flavour.

Makes about 2kg/4½lb

INGREDIENTS
1.3kg/3lb/12 cups red gooseberries
2 red-skinned eating apples, washed
 and chopped with skins and cores intact
2.5cm/1in piece fresh root ginger, sliced
about 1.3kg/3lb/6½ cups preserving
 or granulated sugar, warmed

COOK'S TIPS
The amount of pectin in gooseberries diminishes as the fruit ripens so select firm, just ripe fruit when making this jelly to achieve a really good set.

1 Put the fruit and ginger in a large pan and add water to just below the level of the fruit. Cover and simmer for 45 minutes.

2 Remove from the heat, cool slightly, then pour the fruit and juices into a scalded jelly bag suspended over a non-metallic bowl and leave to drain overnight.

3 Measure the strained juice into a preserving pan and add 450g/1lb/2¼ cups warmed sugar for every 600ml/1 pint/2½ cups juice.

4 Stir over a low heat until the sugar has dissolved. Boil for about 10 minutes, or to setting point (105°C/220°F). Skim off any scum, then pot, seal and label.

rosehip and apple jelly

*This economical jelly is made with windfall apples and wild rosehips. It is still rich in
vitamin C, full of flavour, and excellent spread on freshly toasted crumpets or scones.*

Makes about 2kg/4½lb

INGREDIENTS

1kg/2¼lb windfall apples, peeled,
  trimmed and quartered

450g/1lb firm, ripe rosehips

about 1.3kg/3lb/6½ cups preserving
  or granulated sugar, warmed

1 Place the quartered apples
in a large pan with just enough
water to cover, plus 300ml/½ pint/
1¼ cups of extra water.

COOK'S TIP

There is no need to remove all the peel
from the apples: simply cut out any
bruised, damaged or bad areas.

2 Bring the mixture to the boil
and cook gently until the apples
soften and turn to a pulp.
Meanwhile, chop the rosehips
coarsely. Add the rosehips to the
pan with the apple and simmer
for 10 minutes.

3 Remove from the heat and stand
for 10 minutes, then pour the
mixture into a scalded jelly bag
suspended over a non-metallic
bowl and leave to drain overnight.

4 Measure the juice into a
preserving pan and bring to the
boil. Add 400g/14oz/2 cups
warmed sugar for each 600ml/
1 pint/2½ cups of liquid. Stir until
the sugar has completely dissolved.
Boil to setting point (105°C/220°F).

5 Pour the jelly into warmed,
sterilized jars and seal. Label and
store when completely cold.

spiced cider and apple jelly

This wonderful spicy jelly has a rich, warming flavour, making it ideal to serve during the cold winter months. Serve as a spread or use it to sweeten apple pies and desserts.

Makes about 1.3kg/3lb

INGREDIENTS

900g/2lb tart cooking apples, washed and coarsely chopped with skins and cores intact

900ml/1¼ pints/3¾ cups sweet cider

juice and pips (seeds) of 2 oranges

1 cinnamon stick

6 whole cloves

150ml/½ pint/⅔ cup water

about 900g/2lb/4½ cups preserving or granulated sugar, warmed

2 Leave to cool slightly, then pour the fruit into a scalded jelly bag suspended over a non-metallic bowl and leave to drain overnight.

3 Measure the strained juice into a preserving pan. Add 450g/1lb/ 2¼ cups warmed sugar for every 600ml/1 pint/2½ cups juice.

4 Heat, stirring, over a low heat until the sugar has dissolved. Increase the heat and boil, without stirring, for 10 minutes, or until the jelly reaches setting point (105°C/220°F).

5 Remove from the heat and skim off any scum. Ladle into warmed sterilized jars. Cover, seal and label.

1 Put the apples, cider, juice and pips, cinnamon, cloves and water in a large pan. Bring to the boil, cover and simmer for about 1 hour.

quince and coriander jelly

When raw, quinces are inedible but once cooked and sweetened they become aromatic and have a wonderful flavour, which is enhanced here by the addition of warm, spicy coriander seeds.

2 Leave the fruit to cool slightly, then pour into a scalded jelly bag suspended over a non-metallic bowl and leave to drain overnight.

3 Measure the strained juice into a preserving pan. Add 450g/1lb/ 2¼ cups warmed sugar for every 600ml/1 pint/2½ cups juice.

4 Heat, stirring, over a low heat until the sugar has completely dissolved. Increase the heat and boil rapidly, without stirring, for 5–10 minutes or until the jelly reaches setting point (105°C/220°F).

Makes about 900g/2lb

INGREDIENTS

1kg/2¼lb quinces, washed and coarsely chopped with skins and cores intact
15ml/1 tbsp coriander seeds
juice and pips (seeds) of 2 large lemons
900ml/1½ pints/3¾ cups water
about 900g/2lb/4½ cups preserving or granulated sugar, warmed

VARIATION

If you don't have enough quinces, you can make up the quantity with apples. The flavour won't be quite the same but the jelly will still be delicious.

1 Put the quinces in a pan with the coriander seeds, lemon juice and pips, and the water. Bring to the boil, cover and simmer gently for about 1½ hours.

5 Remove the pan from the heat and skim off any scum from the surface using a slotted spoon. Ladle into warmed sterilized jars, cover and seal. When cold, label and store in a cool, dark place.

COOK'S TIP

Jellies can look very pretty served in decorative glasses. Bottle the jelly in jars as above, then, when ready to serve, gently heat the jelly in a pan with a very small amount of water until melted. Pour the jelly into a heatproof glass and leave to set before serving.

scented geranium and pear jelly

This jelly uses the leaves of scented geranium to give an aromatic lift to the pears. Use rose-scented leaves if you have them, otherwise add a couple of drops of rose water to the strained juice.

Makes about 900g/2lb

INGREDIENTS

900g/2lb Comice pears, washed and coarsely chopped with skins and cores intact

7 rose-scented geranium leaves, plus extra for storing

juice and pips (seeds) of 1 lemon

60ml/4 tbsp clear honey

900ml/1½ pints/3¾ cups water

about 900g/2lb/4½ cups preserving or granulated sugar, warmed

1 Put the pears, geranium leaves, lemon juice, honey and water in a large pan. Bring to the boil, then cover and simmer for 1 hour.

2 Remove the pan from the heat and leave to cool slightly. Pour the fruit into a scalded jelly bag suspended over a non-metallic bowl and leave to drain overnight.

3 Measure the strained juice into a preserving pan. Add 450g/1lb/ 2¼ cups warmed sugar for every 600ml/1 pint/2½ cups juice.

4 Heat, stirring, over a low heat until the sugar has dissolved. Increase the heat and boil rapidly, without stirring, for 10 minutes, or to setting point (105°C/220°F).

5 Remove the pan from the heat and skim off any scum using a slotted spoon. Place a blanched geranium leaf into each warmed sterilized jar, Then ladle in the jelly. Cover and seal, then label.

clementine and lemon balm jelly

This sweet, aromatic jelly make a delicious alternative to marmalade at breakfast. Clementines are the smallest of the tangerine family and have the most zesty skin and aromatic flesh.

Makes about 900g/2lb

INGREDIENTS

900g/2lb clementines, washed and coarsely chopped

450g/1lb tart cooking apples, coarsely chopped, with skins and cores intact

2 large sprigs of lemon balm or 1 lemon grass stalk, crushed

900ml/1½ pints/3¾ cups water

about 900g/2lb/4½ cups preserving or granulated sugar, warmed

COOK'S TIP

To prepare the lemon grass, you only need to crush the bulbous end of the stalk. Using the end of a rolling pin, gently bash the bulbous end of the stalk, then add to the pan. This helps to release its fragrant, zesty flavour into the jelly.

1 Put the fruit, lemon balm or lemon grass and water in a pan. Bring to the boil, cover and simmer for 1 hour until the fruit is soft. Cool slightly, then pour into a scalded jelly bag over a bowl and leave to drain overnight.

2 Measure the juice into a pan. Add 450g/1lb/2¼ cups sugar for every 600ml/1 pint/2½ cups juice.

3 Heat gently, stirring until the sugar has dissolved. Increase the heat and boil, without stirring, for 5–10 minutes, or until the jelly reaches setting point (105°C/220°F).

4 Remove the pan from the heat and skim off any scum using a slotted spoon. Pour into warmed sterilized jars, cover and seal. Label and store in a cool place.

muscat grape jelly

The wonderful perfumed flavour of Muscat grapes produces a deliciously fragrant, scented jelly. Do not be tempted to use other grapes because they will not give the same result.

Makes about 900g/2lb

INGREDIENTS

900g/2lb/6 cups Muscat grapes, washed and halved

juice and pips (seeds) of 2 lemons

600ml/1 pint/2½ cups water

30ml/2 tbsp elderflower cordial

about 900g/2lb/4½ cups preserving or granulated sugar, warmed

1 Place the grapes in a pan with the lemon juice and pips, and water. Bring to the boil, cover and simmer for 1½ hours. Cool slightly.

2 Mash the grapes, then pour the mixture into a scalded jelly bag suspended over a non-metallic bowl and leave to drain overnight.

3 Measure the juice into a pan and pour in the elderflower cordial. Add 450g/1lb/2¼ cups sugar for every 600ml/1 pint/2½ cups juice. Heat gently, stirring, until the sugar has dissolved. Increase the heat and boil, without stirring, for 5–10 minutes, or until the jelly reaches setting point (105°C/220°F).

4 Remove the pan from the heat and skim off any scum. Ladle into warmed sterilized jars. Cover, seal and label. Store in a cool place.

pineapple and passion fruit jelly

This exotic jelly has a wonderful warming glow to its taste and appearance. For the best-flavoured jelly, use a tart-tasting, not too ripe pineapple rather than a very ripe, sweet one.

Makes about 900g/2lb

INGREDIENTS

1 large pineapple, peeled, topped and tailed and coarsely chopped

4 passion fruit, halved, with seeds and pulp scooped out

900ml/1½ pints/3¾ cups water

about 900g/2lb/4½ cups preserving or granulated sugar, warmed

COOK'S TIP

For the best flavour, choose passion fruit with dark, wrinkled skins.

1 Place the pineapple and the passion fruit seeds and pulp in a large pan with the water.

2 Bring the mixture to the boil, cover and simmer for 1½ hours. Remove from the heat and leave to cool slightly. Transfer the fruit to a food processor and process briefly.

3 Tip the fruit pulp and any juices from the pan, into a scalded jelly bag suspended over a non-metallic bowl and leave to drain overnight.

4 Measure the strained juice into a preserving pan and add 450g/1lb/2¼ cups warmed sugar for every 600ml/1 pint/2½ cups juice.

5 Heat gently, stirring, until the sugar has dissolved. Increase the heat and boil rapidly, without stirring, for 10–15 minutes or to setting point (105°C/220°F).

6 Remove the pan from the heat and skim off any scum using a slotted spoon. Ladle the jelly into warmed sterilized jars, cover and seal. When cool, label and store in a cool, dark place.

pomegranate and grenadine jelly

The slightly tart flavoured, jewel-like flesh of the pomegranate makes the most wonderful jelly.
Be careful though, because pomegranate juice can stain indelibly when spilt on clothing.

Makes about 900g/2lb

INGREDIENTS

6 ripe red pomegranates, peeled and
  seeds removed from membranes
120ml/4fl oz/½ cup grenadine syrup
juice and pips (seeds) of 2 oranges
300ml/½ pint/1¼ cups water
about 900g/2lb/4½ cups preserving
  or granulated sugar, warmed

1 Put the pomegranate seeds in
bowl and crush to release their
juice. Transfer them to a pan and
add the grenadine, orange juice,
pips and water.

2 Bring the mixture to the boil,
cover and simmer for 1½ hours.
Mash the fruit and leave to cool
slightly, then pour into a scalded
jelly bag suspended over a bowl
and leave to drain overnight.

3 Measure the juice into a pan and
add 450g/1lb/2¼ cups sugar for
every 600ml/1 pint/2½ cups juice.

4 Heat, stirring, over a low heat
until the sugar has dissolved.
Increase the heat and boil rapidly,
without stirring, for 5–10 minutes,
or until the jelly reaches setting
point (105°C/220°F).

5 Remove the pan from the heat
and skim off any scum. Ladle into
warmed sterilized jars, cover, seal
and label. Store in a cool place.

marmalades

These classic preserves come somewhere between a jam and a jelly and are traditionally served for breakfast. Usually made of citrus fruits, marmalades have a jelly base with small pieces of fruit suspended in it. They can be tart and bitter with thick-cut shreds of peel, or sweet with thinly cut zest. The Seville orange is favoured because of its refreshing tang and high pectin content but any citrus fruit can be used, as long as its shredded rind is cooked until very tender. All the recipes in this chapter will keep for at least 1 year.

oxford marmalade

The characteristic caramel colour and rich flavour of a traditional Oxford marmalade is obtained by cutting the fruit coarsely and cooking it for several hours before adding the sugar.

Makes about 2.25kg/5lb

INGREDIENTS

900g/2lb Seville (Temple) oranges

1.75 litres/3 pints/7½ cups water

1.3kg/3lb/6½ cups granulated sugar, warmed

COOK'S TIP

Traditionalists say that only bitter oranges such as Seville should be used to make marmalade. Although this isn't always true, it is most certainly the case when making Oxford marmalade.

1 Scrub the orange skins, then remove the rind using a vegetable peeler. Thickly slice the rind and put in a large pan.

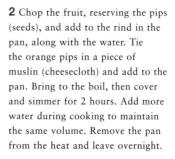

2 Chop the fruit, reserving the pips (seeds), and add to the rind in the pan, along with the water. Tie the orange pips in a piece of muslin (cheesecloth) and add to the pan. Bring to the boil, then cover and simmer for 2 hours. Add more water during cooking to maintain the same volume. Remove the pan from the heat and leave overnight.

3 The next day, remove the muslin bag from the oranges, squeezing well, and return the pan to the heat. Bring to the boil, then cover and simmer for 1 hour.

4 Add the warmed sugar to the pan, then slowly bring the mixture to the boil, stirring until the sugar has dissolved completely. Increase the heat and boil rapidly for about 15 minutes, or until setting point is reached (105°C/220°F).

5 Remove the pan from the heat and skim off any scum from the surface. Leave to cool for about 5 minutes, stir, then pour into warmed sterilized jars and seal. When cold, label, then store in a cool, dark place.

st clement's marmalade

This classic preserve made from oranges and lemons has a lovely citrus tang. It has a light, refreshing flavour and is perfect for serving for breakfast, spread on freshly toasted bread.

Makes about 2.25kg/5lb

INGREDIENTS
450g/1lb Seville (Temple) oranges
450g/1lb sweet oranges
4 lemons
1.5 litres/2½ pints/6¼ cups water
1.2kg/2½lb/5½ cups granulated sugar, warmed

1 Wash the oranges and lemons, then halve and squeeze the juice into a large pan. Tie the pips (seeds) and membranes in a muslin (cheesecloth) bag, shred the orange and lemon rind and add to the pan.

2 Add the water to the pan, bring to the boil, then cover and simmer for 2 hours. Remove the muslin bag, leave to cool, then squeeze any liquid back into the pan.

3 Add the warmed sugar to the pan and stir over a low heat until completely dissolved. Bring to the boil and boil rapidly for about 15 minutes or until the marmalade reaches setting point (105°C/220°F).

4 Remove the pan from the heat and skim off any scum from the surface. Leave to cool for about 5 minutes, stir, then pour into warmed sterilized jars and seal. When cold, label, then store in a cool, dark place.

pink grapefruit and cranberry marmalade

Cranberries give this glorious marmalade an extra tartness and a full fruit flavour, as well as an inimitable vibrant colour. The resulting preserve makes a lively choice for breakfast or a brilliant accompaniment for cold roast turkey during the festive season.

2 Tie the grapefruit and lemon pips in a muslin (cheesecloth) bag and place in a large pan with the grapefruit slices and lemon juice.

3 Add the water and bring to the boil. Cover and simmer gently for 1½–2 hours, or until the grapefruit rind is very tender. Remove the muslin bag, leave to cool, then squeeze over the pan.

4 Add the cranberries to the pan, then bring to the boil. Simmer for 15–20 minutes, or until the berries have popped and softened.

5 Add the sugar to the pan and stir over a low heat until the sugar has completely dissolved. Bring to the boil and boil rapidly for about 10 minutes, or until setting point is reached (105°C/220°F).

Makes about 2.25kg/5lb

INGREDIENTS

675g/1½lb pink grapefruit
juice and pips (seeds) of 2 lemons
900ml/1½ pints/3¾ cups water
225g/8oz/2 cups cranberries
1.3kg/3lb/6½ cups granulated sugar, warmed

6 Remove the pan from the heat and skim off any scum from the surface using a slotted spoon. Leave to cool for 5–10 minutes, then stir and pour into warmed sterilized jars. Seal, then label when the marmalade is cold.

COOK'S TIP

You can use fresh or frozen cranberries to make this marmalade. Either gives equally good results.

1 Wash, halve and quarter the grapefruit, then slice them thinly, reserving the pips (seeds) and any juice that runs out.

ruby red grapefruit marmalade

If you prefer a really tangy marmalade, grapefruit is the perfect choice. To achieve a wonderfully red-blushed preserve, look for the red variety rather than pink. They have a wonderful flavour and make a really delicious, sweet, jewel-coloured preserve.

Makes about 1.8kg/4lb

INGREDIENTS

900g/2lb ruby red grapefruit
1 lemon
1.2 litres/2 pints/5 cups water
1.3kg/3lb/6½ cups granulated sugar, warmed

1 Wash the grapefruit and lemon and remove the rind in thick pieces using a vegetable peeler. Cut the fruit in half and squeeze the juice into a preserving pan, reserving all the pips (seeds).

2 Put the pips and membranes from the fruit in a muslin (cheesecloth) bag and add to the pan. Discard the grapefruit and lemon shells.

3 Using a sharp knife, cut the grapefruit and lemon rind into thin or coarse shreds, as preferred, and place in the pan.

COOK'S TIP

Although you can use yellow grapefruit to make this marmalade, it tends to give a very pale result with more tang than the ruby red variety, but a much less fruity flavour.

4 Add the water to the pan and bring to the boil. Cover and simmer for 2 hours, or until the rind is very tender.

5 Remove the muslin bag from the pan, leave to cool, then squeeze it over the pan. Add the sugar and stir over a low heat until it has dissolved. Bring to the boil, then boil rapidly for 10–15 minutes, or to setting point (105°C/220°F).

6 Remove the pan from the heat and skim off any scum using a slotted spoon. Leave to cool for about 10 minutes, then stir and pour into warmed sterilized jars. Seal, then label when cold.

lemon and ginger marmalade

This combination of lemon and ginger produces a really zesty and versatile preserve, perfect served on toast at any time of day. It is also excellent added to meat glazes. Mix a few spoonfuls of the marmalade with a little soy sauce and brush over meat before grilling.

Makes about 1.8kg/4lb

INGREDIENTS

1.2kg/2½lb lemons

150g/5oz fresh root ginger, peeled and finely grated

1.2 litres/2 pints/5 cups water

900g/2lb/4½ cups granulated sugar, warmed

COOK'S TIP

When choosing fresh root ginger, select young, firm, fine-skinned pieces. For the best results, grate only the tender, juicy parts of the root and discard any tough, hairy parts.

1 Quarter and slice the lemons. Tie the pips (seeds) in a muslin (cheesecloth) bag and place in a preserving pan with the lemons, ginger and water. Bring to the boil, cover with a lid and simmer for 2 hours, or until the fruit is tender.

2 Remove the muslin bag from the pan, leave to cool then squeeze over the pan to release all the juice and pectin. Stir in the sugar over a low heat until dissolved, then increase the heat and boil for 5–10 minutes, or until setting point is reached (105°C/220°F).

3 Remove the pan from the heat and skim off any scum from the surface using a slotted spoon.

4 Leave to cool for 5 minutes, stir, then pour into warmed sterilized jars and seal. When cold, label and store in a cool place.

orange and coriander marmalade

This traditional marmalade made with bitter Seville oranges has the added zing of warm, spicy coriander. Cut the orange rind into thin or coarse shreds, according to taste.

Makes about 1.8kg/4lb

INGREDIENTS

675g/1½lb Seville (Temple) oranges

2 lemons

15ml/1 tbsp crushed coriander seeds

1.5 litres/2½ pints/6¼ cups water

900g/2lb/4½ cups granulated sugar, warmed

1 Cut the oranges and lemons in half and squeeze out all the juice. ̤e and lemon pips ̤slin (cheesecloth) ̤arp knife, cut the ̤ and place in a ̤ith the juice.

2 Put the coriander seeds in the muslin bag with the pips and place in the pan. Add the water and bring to the boil. Cover and simmer for 2 hours, or until the mixture has reduced by half and the peel is soft.

3 Remove the muslin bag from the pan. Set it aside to cool, then squeeze it over the pan to release all the juices and pectin.

4 Add the sugar to the pan and stir over a low heat until it has dissolved. Bring to the boil and boil rapidly for 5–10 minutes, or to setting point (105°C/220°F).

5 Remove the pan from the heat and skim off any scum from the surface using a slotted spoon. Leave to cool for 5 minutes, stir then pour into warmed sterilized jars. Seal, then label when cold.

orange and whisky marmalade

Adding whisky to orange marmalade gives it a fantastic warmth and flavour. The whisky is stirred in after the marmalade is cooked, to retain its strength and slightly bitter edge, which would be lost if boiled. Whisky marmalade is great spooned over a steamed sponge pudding.

3 Remove the muslin bag from the pan, leave to cool, then squeeze it over the pan to release any juice and pectin. Add the sugar, then stir over a low heat until the sugar has dissolved. Increase the heat and boil for 5–10 minutes until setting point is reached (105°C/220°F).

4 Remove the pan from the heat and skim off any scum from the surface using a slotted spoon. Stir in the whisky, then leave to cool for 5 minutes. Stir and pour the marmalade into warmed sterilized jars. Seal, then label when cold. Store in a cool dark place.

Makes about 2.25kg/5lb

INGREDIENTS

900g/2lb Seville (Temple) oranges
juice and pips (seeds) of 1 large lemon
1.2 litres/2 pints/5 cups water
1.5kg/3lb 6oz/7½ cups granulated sugar, warmed
60ml/4 tbsp whisky

1 Scrub the oranges and cut in half. Squeeze the juice into a large pan, reserving the pips (seeds) and any membranes. Place these in a muslin (cheesecloth) bag with the lemon pips and add to the juice.

2 Using a sharp knife, thinly slice the orange rind and put in the pan along with the water. Bring to the boil, then cover and simmer for 1½–2 hours, or until the citrus rind is very tender.

fine lime shred marmalade

There is something about lime marmalade that really captures the flavour and essence of the fruit. It is important to cut the slices very finely though, because lime skins tend to be tougher than those on any other citrus fruit and can result in a chewy marmalade if cut thickly.

Makes about 2.25kg/5lb

INGREDIENTS

12 limes
4 kaffir lime leaves
1.2 litres/2 pints/5 cups water
1.3kg/3lb/6½ cups granulated sugar, warmed

1 Halve the limes lengthways, then slice thinly, reserving any pips (seeds). Tie the pips and lime leaves in a muslin (cheesecloth) bag and place the bag in a large pan with the sliced fruit.

2 Add the water to the pan and bring to the boil. Cover and simmer gently for 1½–2 hours, or until the rind is very soft. Remove the muslin bag, leave to cool, then squeeze it over the pan to release any juice and pectin.

COOK'S TIP

To check whether the rind is cooked, remove a piece from the pan (before the sugar is added) and leave it to cool briefly. When cool enough to handle, press the rind between finger and thumb – it should be very soft.

3 Add the sugar to the pan, and stir over a low heat until the sugar has dissolved. Bring to the boil, then boil rapidly for 15 minutes, stirring occasionally, until setting point is reached (105°C/220°F).

4 Remove the pan from the heat and skim off any scum. Leave to cool for 5 minutes, stir, then pour into warmed sterilized jars. Seal, then label when cold. Store in a cool, dark place.

COOK'S TIPS

• To check for setting, spoon a little marmalade on to a chilled saucer and chill for 2 minutes. Push the surface with your finger; if wrinkles form, the marmalade is ready to bottle.

• Stirring marmalade after standing and before potting distributes the fruit rind evenly as the preserve begins to set.

spiced pumpkin marmalade

The bright orange colour and warm flavour of this marmalade is guaranteed to banish the winter blues. The addition of pumpkin gives the preserve more body and a lovely, satisfying texture. It's perfect for spreading on hot buttered toast or serving with warm croissants.

2 Thinly slice the orange rind and place in the pan, along with the sliced lemons. Tie the orange and lemon pips and membranes in a muslin (cheesecloth) bag with the spices and add to the pan with the water. Bring to the boil, then cover and simmer for 1 hour.

3 Add the pumpkin to the pan and continue cooking for 1–1½ hours. Remove the muslin bag, leave to cool, then squeeze over the pan.

4 Stir in the sugar over a low heat until completely dissolved. Bring to the boil, then boil rapidly for 15 minutes, or until the marmalade becomes thick and reaches setting point (105°C/220°F). Stir once or twice to ensure the marmalade does not stick to the pan.

5 Remove the pan from the heat and skim off any scum. Leave to cool for 5 minutes, then stir and pour into warmed sterilized jars. Cover the surface of the preserve with wax discs, then seal. Label when the marmalade is cold and store in a cool, dark place.

Makes about 2.75kg/6lb

INGREDIENTS

900g/2lb Seville (Temple) oranges,
  washed and halved

450g/1lb lemons, halved and
  thinly sliced, pips (seeds) reserved

2 cinnamon sticks

2.5cm/1in piece fresh root ginger,
  peeled and thinly sliced

1.5ml/¼ tsp grated nutmeg

1.75 litres/3 pints/7½ cups water

800g/1¾lb squash or pumpkin, peeled,
  seeds (pips) removed and thinly sliced

1.3kg/3lb/6½ cups granulated sugar,
  warmed

1 Squeeze the juice from the oranges and pour into a preserving pan. Remove the white membranes and reserve with the pips.

clementine and liqueur marmalade

Small, tart clementines make a particularly full-flavoured preserve, which can be put to a wide variety of culinary uses. Stir it into yogurt or warm it with a little water to make a zesty sauce for pancakes or crêpes. It is also superlative served with smooth ripe Brie and crisp crackers.

Makes about 1.8kg/4lb

INGREDIENTS

900g/2lb clementines, washed and halved

juice and pips (seeds) of 2 lemons

900ml/1½ pints/3¾ cups water

900g/2lb/4½ cups granulated sugar, warmed

60ml/4 tbsp Grand Marnier or Cointreau

COOK'S TIP

Any member of the mandarin family can be used to make this preserve, but clementines give the best result.

1 Slice the clementines, reserving any pips. Tie the pips in a muslin (cheesecloth) bag with the lemon pips and place in a large pan with the sliced fruit.

2 Add the lemon juice and water to the pan and bring to the boil, then cover and simmer for about 1½ hours, or until the rind is very tender. Remove the muslin bag, cool, then squeeze over the pan.

3 Stir in the sugar over a low heat until dissolved, then bring to the boil and cook 5–10 minutes, or to setting point (105°C/220°F).

4 Remove the pan from the heat and skim off any scum. Cool for 5 minutes, then stir in the liqueur and pour into warmed sterilized jars. Seal, then label when cold.

tangerine and lemon grass marmalade

The subtle flavours of lemon grass and kaffir lime leaves add an exotic edge to this marmalade. You can also stir in thinly shredded lime leaf before bottling, which gives a very pretty result.

Makes about 1.8kg/4lb

INGREDIENTS

900g/2lb tangerines, washed and halved

juice and pips (seeds) of 2 Seville (Temple) oranges

900ml/1½ pints/3¾ cups water

2 lemon grass sticks, halved and crushed

3 kaffir lime leaves

900g/2lb/4½ cups granulated sugar, warmed

COOK'S TIP

If you can't find kaffir lime leaves, you can substitute the finely pared rind of one lime.

1 Using a sharp knife, slice the tangerines thinly, reserving the pips. Place the sliced fruit in a preserving pan, along with juice from the Seville oranges and the measured water.

2 Tie all the pips, lemon grass and lime leaves in a piece of muslin (cheesecloth) and add to the pan. Boil, then simmer for 1½–2 hours, or until the tangerine rind is soft. Remove the bag, leave to cool, then squeeze over the pan.

3 Stir in the sugar over a low heat until completely dissolved, then boil for 5–10 minutes, or to setting point (105°C/220°F).

4 Remove the pan from the heat and skim off any scum. Leave to cool for 5 minutes, then stir and pour into warmed sterilized jars. Seal, then label when cold.

pomelo and pineapple marmalade

Slightly larger than a grapefruit, pomelos have lime-green skin and a sharp, refreshing flavour and are delicious combined with tangy pineapple. Serve as a spread or spoon over desserts.

Makes about 2.75kg/6lb

INGREDIENTS

2 pomelos

900ml/1½ pints/3¾ cups water

2 x 432g/14¼oz cans crushed pineapple in fruit juice

900g/2lb/4½ cups granulated sugar, warmed

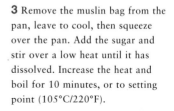

2 Cover the pan and simmer for 1½–2 hours, stirring occasionally, or until the fruit is soft. Add the pineapple and juice and simmer for a further 30 minutes.

3 Remove the muslin bag from the pan, leave to cool, then squeeze over the pan. Add the sugar and stir over a low heat until it has dissolved. Increase the heat and boil for 10 minutes, or to setting point (105°C/220°F).

4 Remove the pan from the heat and skim off any scum from the surface using a slotted spoon. Leave to cool for 10 minutes, then stir and pour into warmed sterilized jars. Seal, then label the jars when they are cold.

1 Wash and halve the pomelos. Squeeze out the juice, reserving any pips (seeds), and pour into a large pan. Remove the membranes and any excess pith and tie in muslin (cheesecloth) with the pips. Slice the peel thinly and add to the pan along with the muslin bag and water. Bring to the boil.

peach and kumquat marmalade

Combined with sweet, scented peaches, kumquats make a wonderful, fresh-tasting preserve. This lovely marmalade has a jam-like consistency and is great at any time of day.

Makes about 1.8kg/4lb

INGREDIENTS

675g/1½lb kumquats, sliced thinly, pips (seeds) and juice reserved

juice and pips of 1 lime

900g/2lb peaches, skinned and thinly sliced, skins reserved

900ml/1½ pints/3¾ cups water

900g/2lb/4½ cups granulated sugar, warmed

1 Tie the pips and the peach skins in a muslin (cheesecloth) bag and put in a pan with the kumquats, juices and water. Bring to the boil, then cover and simmer for 50 minutes.

2 Add the peaches to the pan, bring to the boil, then simmer for 40–50 minutes, or until the fruit has become very soft. Remove the muslin bag, leave to cool, then squeeze over the pan.

3 Add the sugar to the pan and stir over a low heat until it has dissolved. Bring the mixture to the boil, then boil rapidly for about 15 minutes, stirring occasionally, to setting point (105°C/220°F).

4 Remove the pan from the heat and skim off any scum from the surface using a slotted spoon.

5 Leave to cool for 5–10 minutes, then stir and pour into warmed sterilized jars. Seal, then label when the jars are cold. Store in a cool, dark place.

apricot and orange marmalade

Serve this sweet marmalade with warm croissants and strong coffee for a leisurely weekend breakfast. The combination of oranges and rich-tasting apricots is a winner.

Makes about 1.5kg/3lb 6oz

INGREDIENTS

2 Seville (Temple) oranges, washed and quartered

1 lemon, washed and quartered

1.2 litres/2 pints/5 cups water

900g/2lb apricots, stoned (pitted) and thinly sliced

900g/2lb/4½ cups granulated sugar, warmed

COOK'S TIP

It is important to use a food processor to chop the oranges and lemon for this recipe. Chopping them this finely gives the marmalade its wonderful consistency. Preparing the fruits by hand will not give the same result.

1 Remove the pips (seeds) from the citrus fruit and tie in a muslin (cheesecloth) bag. Finely chop the oranges and lemons in a food processor and put in a large pan with the muslin bag and water.

2 Bring the mixture to the boil, then simmer, covered, for 1 hour.

3 Add the apricots to the pan, bring to the boil, then simmer for 30–40 minutes, or until the fruits are very tender.

4 Add the sugar to the pan and stir over a low heat until the sugar has dissolved. Bring to the boil, then boil rapidly for 15 minutes, stirring occasionally, until setting point is reached (105°C/220°F).

5 Remove the pan from the heat and skim off any scum from the surface using a slotted spoon. Leave to cool for about 5 minutes, then stir and pour into warmed sterilized jars. Seal, then label when cold. Store in a cool place.

curds, butters and cheeses

These smooth, thick, luscious preserves capture the colours and flavours of the season. Butters and curds are thick and spreadable, delicious spooned on to toast or griddle cakes. In contrast, cheeses are firmer and can be cut into wedges or slices, or set in small individual moulds. Serve them as a delicious accompaniment to roast meats or dairy cheeses, or cut into wedges, dredge in sugar and serve as a sweetmeat after the meal.

lemon curd

This classic tangy, creamy curd is still one of the most popular of all the curds. It is delicious spread thickly over freshly baked white bread or served with American-style pancakes, and also makes a wonderfully rich, zesty sauce spooned over fresh fruit tarts.

Makes about 450g/1lb

INGREDIENTS

3 lemons

200g/7oz/1 cup caster (superfine) sugar

115g/4oz/8 tbsp unsalted (sweet) butter, diced

2 large (US extra large) eggs

2 large (US extra large) egg yolks

1 Wash the lemons, then finely grate the rind and place in a large heatproof bowl. Using a sharp knife, halve the lemons and squeeze the juice into the bowl. Set over a pan of gently simmering water and add the sugar and butter. Stir until the sugar has dissolved and the butter melted.

2 Put the eggs and yolks in a bowl and beat together with a fork. Pour the eggs through a sieve into the lemon mixture, and whisk well until thoroughly combined.

3 Stir the mixture constantly over the heat until the lemon curd thickens and lightly coats the back of a wooden spoon.

4 Remove the pan from the heat and pour the curd into small, warmed sterilized jars. Cover, seal and label. Store in a cool, dark place, ideally in the refrigerator. Use within 3 months. (Once opened, store in the refrigerator.)

COOK'S TIP

If you are really impatient when it comes to cooking, it is possible to cook the curd in a heavy pan directly over a low heat. However, you really need to watch it like a hawk to avoid the mixture curdling. If the curd looks as though it's beginning to curdle, plunge the base of the pan in cold water and beat vigorously.

seville orange curd

Using flavoursome Seville oranges gives this curd a fantastic orange flavour and a real citrus tang. It is perfect for spreading on toast for breakfast or at tea time, and is also superlative folded into whipped cream and used as a filling for cakes, roulades and scones.

Makes about 450g/1lb

INGREDIENTS

2 Seville (Temple) oranges

115g/4oz/8 tbsp unsalted (sweet) butter, diced

200g/7oz/1 cup caster (superfine) sugar

2 large (US extra large) eggs

2 large (US extra large) egg yolks

1 Wash the oranges, then finely grate the rind and place in a large heatproof bowl. Halve the oranges and squeeze the juice into the bowl with the rind.

2 Place the bowl over a pan of gently simmering water and add the butter and sugar. Stir until the sugar has completely dissolved and the butter melted.

3 Put the eggs and yolks in a small bowl and lightly whisk, then pour into the orange mixture through a sieve. Whisk them together until thoroughly combined.

4 Stir the orange and egg mixture constantly over the heat until the mixture thickens and lightly coats the back of a wooden spoon.

5 Pour the orange curd into small, warmed sterilized jars, cover and seal. Store in a cool, dark place, preferably in the refrigerator.

WATCHPOINTS

• The very young, the elderly, pregnant women, and those with a compromised immune system are advised against eating raw eggs or food containing raw eggs. Although the eggs in fruit curds are lightly cooked, they may still be unsuitable for these groups of people.

• Fruit curds do not have the shelf-life of many other preserves and should be used within 3 months of making.

• Once opened, always store fruit curds in the refrigerator.

grapefruit curd

If you favour tangy and refreshing preserves, this grapefruit curd is the one to try. Really fresh free-range eggs give the best results and flavour when making curd.

Makes about 675g/1½lb

INGREDIENTS

finely grated rind and juice of 1 grapefruit

115g/4oz/8 tbsp unsalted (sweet) butter, diced

200g/7oz/1 cup caster (superfine) sugar

4 large (US extra large) eggs, lightly beaten

1 Put the grapefruit rind and juice in a large heatproof bowl with the butter and sugar, and set over a pan of gently simmering water. Heat the mixture, stirring occasionally, until the sugar has dissolved and the butter melted.

2 Add the beaten eggs to the fruit mixture, straining them through a sieve. Whisk together, then stir constantly over the heat until the mixture thickens and lightly coats the back of a wooden spoon.

3 Pour the curd into small, warmed sterilized jars, cover and seal. Label when the jars are cold. Store in a cool, dark place, preferably in the refrigerator and use within 3 months. (Once opened, store the curd in the refrigerator.)

VARIATION

Tangy grapefruit and sweet orange marry particularly well in creamy fruit curds. Add the grated rind of a small orange to this grapefruit recipe for an extra zingy, zesty alternative.

passion fruit curd

The tropical flavour and aroma of passion fruit fills this curd with a gloriously sunny character. It is perfect spread on toasted English muffins or little American pancakes.

Makes about 675g/1½lb

INGREDIENTS

grated rind and juice of 2 lemons

115g/4oz/8 tbsp unsalted (sweet) butter, diced

275g/10oz/1⅓ cups caster (superfine) sugar

4 passion fruit

4 eggs

2 egg yolks

1 Place the lemon rind and juice in a large heatproof bowl and add the butter and sugar.

2 Halve the passion fruit and scoop the seeds into a sieve set over the bowl. Press out all the juice and discard the seeds.

3 Place the bowl over a pan of gently simmering water and stir occasionally until the sugar has dissolved and the butter melted.

4 Beat the eggs and yolks together and add to the bowl, pouring them through a sieve, then whisk well to combine. Stir constantly until the mixture thickens and lightly coats the back of a spoon.

5 Pour the curd into small, warmed sterilized jars, cover and seal. Store in a cool, dark place, preferably in the refrigerator and use within 3 months. (Once opened, store in the refrigerator.)

apple and cinnamon butter

Fans of apple pies and crumbles will love this luscious apple butter. Serve on toast or with warmed brioche for a breakfast treat or with pancakes and cream for tea.

Makes about 1.8kg/4lb

INGREDIENTS

475ml/16fl oz/2 cups dry (hard) cider
450g/1lb tart cooking apples, peeled, cored and sliced
450g/1lb eating apples, peeled, cored and sliced
grated rind and juice of 1 lemon
675g/1½lb/scant 3½ cups granulated sugar, warmed
5ml/1 tsp ground cinnamon

COOK'S TIP

Leaving the butter to stand for 2 days give the flavours a chance to develop.

1 Pour the cider into a large pan and bring to the boil. Boil hard until the volume is reduced by half, then add the apples and lemon rind and juice.

2 Cover the pan and cook for 10 minutes. Uncover and continue cooking for 20–30 minutes, or until the apples are very soft.

3 Leave the mixture to cool slightly, then pour into a food processor or blender and blend to a purée. Press through a fine sieve into a bowl.

4 Measure the purée into a large heavy pan, adding 275g/10oz/ 1⅓ cups warmed sugar for every 600ml/1 pint/2½ cups of purée. Add the ground cinnamon and stir well to combine.

5 Gently heat the mixture, stirring continuously, until the sugar has completely dissolved. Increase the heat and boil steadily for about 20 minutes, stirring frequently, until the mixture forms a thick purée that hold its shape when spooned on to a cold plate.

6 Spoon the apple and cinnamon butter into warmed sterilized jars. Seal and label, then store in a cool, dark place for 2 days to allow the flavours to develop before serving.

pear and vanilla butter

The delicate flavour of pears is enhanced by vanilla in this butter that really captures the essence of the fruit. It is well worth allowing it to mature for a few days before eating.

Makes about 675g/1½lb

INGREDIENTS

900g/2lb pears, peeled, cored
 and chopped

juice of 3 lemons

300ml/½ pint/1¼ cups water

1 vanilla pod (bean), split

675g/1½lb/scant 3½ cups granulated
 sugar, warmed

1 Place the pears in a large pan with the lemon juice, water and vanilla pod. Bring to the boil, then cover and simmer for 10 minutes. Uncover the pan and continue cooking for a further 15–20 minutes, or until the pears are very soft.

2 Remove the vanilla pod from the pan, then carefully scrape the seeds into the fruit mixture using the tip of a knife.

3 Tip the fruit and juices into a food processor or blender and blend to a purée. Press the purée through a fine sieve into a bowl.

4 Measure the purée into a large heavy pan, adding 275g/10oz/ 1⅓ cups warmed sugar for every 600ml/1 pint/2½ cups of purée.

5 Stir the mixture over a low heat until the sugar dissolves. Increase the heat and boil for 15 minutes, stirring, until the mixture forms a thick purée that holds its shape when spooned on to a cold plate.

6 Spoon the pear butter into small, warmed sterilized jars. Seal, label and store in a cool, dark place for at least 2 days before serving.

COOK'S TIPS

• Fruit butters have a soft spreading consistency – thicker than fruit curds, but softer than fruit cheeses. They make an excellent tea time preserve.

• Fruit butters keep well in sealed jars and can be stored for up to 3 months. Once opened, they should be stored in the refrigerator.

plum butter

Simmering plums down into a butter concentrates their tart, tangy flavour and creates a preserve with a wonderful rich, red colour and a really smooth, luxurious texture.

Makes about 900g/2lb

INGREDIENTS

900g/2lb red plums, stoned (pitted)
grated rind and juice of 1 orange
150ml/¼ pint/⅔ cup water
450g/1lb/2¼ cups granulated sugar,
  warmed

1 Place the plums in a large, heavy pan with the orange rind and juice and the water. Bring to the boil, then cover with a lid and cook for 20–30 minutes, or until the plums are very soft. Set aside to cool.

2 Press the fruit through a fine sieve. Measure the purée into a pan and add 350g/12oz/1¼ cups sugar for every 600ml/1 pint/2½ cups purée. Gently heat, stirring.

3 When the sugar has dissolved, increase the heat and boil for 10–15 minutes, stirring frequently, until the mixture holds its shape when spooned on to a cold plate.

4 Spoon the mixture into warmed sterilized jars. Seal and label, then store in a cool, dark place for 2 days to mature before serving.

COOK'S TIP

Serve the plum butter on toasted walnut and raisin bread for a delicious breakfast, at tea time or just as a snack.

golden peach butter

There is definitely something quite decadent about this subtle, aromatic butter. Its wonderfully rich, dark golden colour and delicate, spicy, fragrant flavour makes it a real treat every time.

Makes about 2.25kg/5lb

INGREDIENTS

1.3kg/3lb ripe peaches, stoned (pitted)
600ml/1 pint/2½ cups water
675g/1½lb/scant 3½ cups granulated
  sugar, warmed
grated rind and juice of 1 lemon
2.5ml/½ tsp ground cinnamon
2.5ml/½ tsp ground nutmeg

1 Slice the peaches and place in a large pan with the water. Bring to the boil, then cover and simmer for about 10 minutes.

2 Remove the lid from the pan and simmer gently for a further 45 minutes, or until the peaches are quite soft.

3 Leave the fruit mixture to cool slightly, then transfer to a food processor or blender and process to a purée. Press the purée through a fine sieve into a bowl.

4 Measure the purée into a large heavy pan, adding 275g/10oz/1⅓ cups warmed sugar for every 600ml/1 pint/2½ cups of purée.

5 Add the lemon rind and juice and spices to the pan and stir to combine. Gently heat, stirring, until the sugar has dissolved.

6 Bring the mixture to the boil and cook for 15–20 minutes, stirring frequently, until the mixture forms a thick purée that holds its shape when spooned on to a cold plate.

7 Spoon the butter into small, warmed sterilized jars. Seal and label, then store in a cool, dark place for 2 days before eating.

COOK'S TIP

For a really special treat, spoon this sweet, fragrant butter into tiny tart cases or on to bite-size brioches.

pumpkin and maple butter

This all-American butter has a lovely bright, autumnal colour and flavour. It is perfect served spread on little pancakes fresh from the griddle, or used as a filling or topping for cakes.

Makes about 675g/1½lb

INGREDIENTS

1.2kg/2½lb pumpkin or butternut squash, peeled, seeded and chopped
450ml/¾ pint/scant 2 cups water
grated rind and juice of 1 orange
5ml/1 tsp ground cinnamon
120ml/4fl oz/½ cup maple syrup
675g/1½lb/scant 3½ cups granulated sugar, warmed

VARIATION

This butter is also delicious made with clear honey instead of maple syrup. It adds a distinct flavour.

1 Put the pumpkin or squash in the pan with the water and cook for 30–40 minutes, or until it is very tender. Drain and, using the back of a spoon, press the cooked pumpkin or squash through a fine sieve into a bowl.

2 Stir the orange rind and juice, cinnamon and maple syrup into the purée, then measure the purée into a large pan, adding 275g/10oz/1⅓ cups warmed sugar for every 600ml/1 pint/2½ cups purée.

3 Gently heat the purée, stirring, until the sugar has dissolved. Increase the heat and boil for 10–20 minutes, stirring frequently, until the mixture forms a thick purée that holds its shape when spooned on to a cold plate.

4 Spoon the butter into small, warmed sterilized jars. Seal and label, then store in a cool, dark place for 2 days before eating.

mango and cardamom butter

You need to use really ripe mangoes for this recipe. If the mangoes are not ripe enough, they will need much longer cooking and will not produce such a richly flavoured, citrus butter.

Makes about 675g/1½lb

INGREDIENTS

900g/2lb ripe mangoes, peeled
6 green cardamom pods, split
120ml/4fl oz/½ cup freshly squeezed
  lemon juice
120ml/4fl oz/½ cup freshly squeezed
  orange juice
50ml/2fl oz/¼ cup water
675g/1½lb/scant 3½ cups granulated
  sugar, warmed

1 Cut the mango flesh away from the stones and chop, then place it in a pan with the cardamom pods, fruit juices and water.

2 Cover and simmer for 10 minutes. Remove the lid and simmer for a further 25 minutes, or until the mangoes are very soft and there is very little liquid left in the pan.

3 Remove the cardamom pods from the pan and discard. Transfer the fruit to a food processor and blend to a purée. Press the purée through a fine sieve into a bowl.

4 Measure the purée into a large, heavy pan, adding 275g/10oz/ 1⅓ cups warmed sugar for every 600ml/1 pint/2½ cups purée. Gently heat, stirring, until the sugar has dissolved. Increase the heat and boil for 10–20 minutes, stirring, until a thick butter forms that holds its shape when spooned on to a cold plate.

5 Spoon the mango and cardamom butter into small, warmed sterilized jars. Seal and label, then store in a cool, dark place for at least 2 days before eating. (The butter can be stored for up to 3 months.)

damson and vanilla cheese

You can use any type or variety of plum for this cheese, but damsons have the most intense flavour. This cheese is good with roast lamb, duck and game, or semi-soft cheese.

Makes about 900g/2lb

INGREDIENTS

1.5kg/3lb 6oz damsons
1 vanilla pod (bean), split
800g/1¾lb/4 cups granulated
sugar, warmed

COOK'S TIPS

• When the cheese is ready, you should be able to see the base of the pan when a wooden spoon is drawn through the mixture. To test the set, spoon a small amount of the damson mixture on to a chilled plate; it should form a firm jelly.

• To make cheese shapes, spoon the mixture into greased moulds, and leave to set before turning out and serving.

1 Wash the damsons and place in a large pan with the vanilla pod and pour in enough water to come halfway up the fruit. Cover and simmer for 30 minutes.

2 Remove the vanilla pod from the pan and scrape the seeds back into the pan using the point of a knife.

3 Press the fruit and juices through a sieve into a bowl. Measure the purée into a large, heavy pan, adding 400g/14oz/ 2 cups sugar for every 600ml/ 1 pint/2½ cups purée.

4 Gently heat the purée, stirring, until the sugar has dissolved. Increase the heat slightly and cook for about 45 minutes, stirring frequently with a wooden spoon, until very thick.

5 Spoon the damson cheese into warmed, sterilized jars. Seal and label, then store in a cool, dark place for 2–3 months to dry out slightly before eating.

quince cheese

This wonderfully fragrant fruit cheese is particularly good set in squares, dusted with sugar and served as a sweetmeat, but it is just as good bottled in jars and spooned out as required.

Makes about 900g/2lb

INGREDIENTS

1.3kg/3lb quinces
800g/1¾lb/4 cups granulated
sugar, warmed
caster (superfine) sugar, for dusting

COOK'S TIP

Rather than setting the cheese and cutting it into squares, simply spoon the mixture into warmed, sterilized, straight-sided jars. Seal and label, then store in a cool, dark place for 2–3 months to dry out slightly before eating.

1 Wash the quinces, then chop and place in a large pan. Pour in enough water to nearly cover the fruit, then cover with a lid and simmer for 45 minutes, or until the fruit is very tender. Cool slightly.

2 Press the mixture through a fine sieve into a bowl. Measure the purée into a large, heavy pan, adding 400g/14oz/2 cups sugar for every 600ml/1 pint/2½ cups purée. Heat gently, stirring, until the sugar has dissolved. Increase the heat and cook for 40–50 minutes, stirring frequently, until very thick (see Cook's Tip left).

3 Pour the mixture into a small oiled baking tin (pan) and leave to set for 24 hours. Cut into small squares, dust with sugar and store in an airtight container.

spiced cherry cheese

*For the best results, try to use cherries that have a good tart flavour and dark red flesh.
Serve as an accompaniment to strong cheese, or sliced with roast duck or pork.*

Makes about 900g/2lb

INGREDIENTS

1.5kg/3lb 6oz/8¼ cups cherries,
  stoned (pitted)

2 cinnamon sticks

800g/1¾lb/4 cups granulated
  sugar, warmed

COOK'S TIPS

• Store the cheese in a cool, dark
place for 2–3 months before eating.

• To serve a fruit cheese in slices, turn
it out of its container and slice using a
sharp knife. The slices may be cut into
smaller portions. Try to use a straight-
sided container so that the cheese can
slide out easily.

1 Place the cherries in a large pan
with the cinnamon sticks. Pour in
enough water to almost cover the
fruit. Bring to the boil, then cover
and simmer for 20–30 minutes, or
until the cherries are very tender.
Remove the cinnamon sticks from
the pan and discard.

2 Tip the fruit into a sieve and
press into a bowl, using the back
of a spoon. Measure the purée into
a large, heavy pan, adding 350g/
12oz/1¾ cups warmed sugar for
every 600ml/1 pint/2½ cups purée.

3 Gently heat the purée, stirring,
until the sugar dissolves. Increase
the heat and cook for 45 minutes,
stirring frequently, until very thick.
To test, spoon a little of the cheese
on to a cold plate; it should form
a firm jelly.

4 Spoon into warmed, sterilized
jars or oiled moulds. Seal, label,
and store in a cool, dark place.

blackberry and apple cheese

This rich, dark preserve has an incredibly intense flavour and fabulous colour. For a fragrant twist, add a few raspberries – or even strawberries – in place of some of the blackberries.

Makes about 900g/2lb

INGREDIENTS

900g/2lb/8 cups blackberries

450g/1lb tart cooking apples, cut into chunks, with skins and cores intact

grated rind and juice of 1 lemon

800g/1¾lb/4 cups granulated sugar, warmed

1 Put the blackberries, apples and lemon rind and juice in a pan and pour in enough water to come halfway up the fruit. Bring to the boil, then uncover and simmer for 15–20 minutes or until the fruit is very soft.

2 Leave the fruit to cool slightly, then tip the mixture into a sieve and press into a bowl, using the back of a spoon. Measure the purée into a large, heavy pan, adding 400g/14oz/2 cups warmed sugar for every 600ml/1 pint/ 2½ cups purée.

3 Gently heat the purée, stirring, until the sugar dissolves. Increase the heat slightly and cook for 40–50 minutes, stirring frequently, until very thick (see Cook's Tip).

4 Spoon the blackberry and apple cheese into warmed, sterilized straight-sided jars or oiled moulds. Seal and label the jars or moulds, then store in a cool, dark place for 2–3 months to dry out slightly.

COOK'S TIP

When the cheese is ready, you should be able to see the base of the pan when a wooden spoon is drawn through the mixture. Spoon a small amount of the mixture on to a chilled plate; it should form a firm jelly.

sweet fruit preserves

Seasonal fruits bottled in spirits or syrups look stunning stacked in your store cupboard and taste divine spooned over ice cream, cakes and desserts. Some fruits can even be enjoyed on their own with just a spoonful of cream. Preserving in syrups and alcohol helps to retain the colour, texture and flavour of the fruit, while ensuring that they do not ferment or spoil on keeping. Alcohol also adds extra flavour and body and can turn simple preserved fruits into an indulgent treat.

mulled pears

These pretty pears in a warming spiced syrup make a tempting dessert, particularly during the cold winter months. Serve them with crème fraîche or vanilla ice cream, or in open tarts.

Makes about 1.3kg/3lb

INGREDIENTS

1.8kg/4lb small firm pears

1 orange

1 lemon

2 cinnamon sticks, halved

12 whole cloves

5cm/2in piece fresh root ginger, peeled and sliced

300g/11oz/1½ cups granulated sugar

1 bottle fruity light red wine

COOK'S TIP

Pears have a delicate flavour, so use a light, fruity wine such as Beaujolais or Merlot to make the syrup.

1 Peel the pears leaving the stalks intact. Peel very thin strips of rind from the orange and lemon, using a vegetable peeler. Pack the pears and citrus rind into large sterilized preserving jars, dividing the spices evenly between the jars.

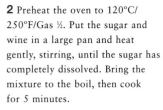

2 Preheat the oven to 120°C/250°F/Gas ½. Put the sugar and wine in a large pan and heat gently, stirring, until the sugar has completely dissolved. Bring the mixture to the boil, then cook for 5 minutes.

3 Pour the wine syrup over the pears, making sure that there are no air pockets and that the fruits are completely covered with the syrup.

4 Cover the jars with their lids, but do not seal. Place them in the oven and cook for 2½–3 hours.

5 Carefully remove the jars from the oven, place on a dry dishtowel and seal. Leave the jars to cool completely, then label and store in a cool, dark place.

COOK'S TIP

To check that jars are properly sealed, leave them to cool for 24 hours, then loosen the clasp. Very carefully, try lifting the jar by the lid alone: if the jar is sealed properly, the lid should be fixed firmly enough to take the weight of the pot. Replace the clasp and store until ready to use.

poached spiced plums in brandy

Bottling plums in a spicy syrup is a great way to preserve the flavours of autumn and provide a store of instant desserts during the winter months. Serve them with whipped cream.

Makes about 900g/2lb

INGREDIENTS

600ml/1 pint/2½ cups brandy
rind of 1 lemon, peeled in a long strip
350g/12oz/1¾ cups caster
  (superfine) sugar
1 cinnamon stick
900g/2lb plums

VARIATION

Any member of the plum family can be preserved using this recipe. Try bottling damsons or wild yellow plums as a delicious alternative. Cherries will also work very well.

1 Put the brandy, lemon rind, sugar and cinnamon in a large pan and heat gently until the sugar dissolves. Add the plums and poach for 15 minutes until soft. Remove the fruit and pack in sterilized jars.

2 Boil the syrup rapidly until reduced by a third, then strain over the plums to cover. Seal the jars tightly. Label when cold and store for up to 6 months in a cool, dark place.

apricots in amaretto syrup

Amaretto brings out the delicious flavour of apricots. Try serving the drained fruit on top of a tart filled with crème patissière, using some of the amaretto syrup to glaze the apricots.

2 Add the apricots to the syrup and bring almost to the boil. Cover and simmer gently for 5 minutes. Remove the apricots with a slotted spoon and drain in a colander.

3 Add the remaining sugar to the pan and heat gently, stirring until the sugar has dissolved, then boil rapidly until the syrup reaches 104°C/219°F. Cool slightly, then remove the vanilla pod and stir in the amaretto.

4 Pack the apricots loosely in large, warmed sterilized jars. Pour the syrup over, twisting and tapping the jars to expel any air. Seal and store in a cool, dark place for 2 weeks before eating.

Makes about 900g/2lb

INGREDIENTS

1.3kg/3lb firm apricots
1 litre/1¾ pints/4 cups water
800g/1¾lb/4 cups granulated sugar
1 vanilla pod (bean)
175ml/6fl oz/¾ cup amaretto liqueur

COOK'S TIP

For the best results, make this preserve when apricots are in season. Choose firm, unblemished fruits blushed with pink, that give slightly when squeezed gently in the palm of the hand.

1 Cut a slit in each apricot and remove the stone (pit), keeping the fruit intact. Put the water, half the sugar and the vanilla pod in a large pan, heat gently, stirring, until the sugar dissolves. Increase the heat and simmer for 5 minutes.

figs infused with earl grey

The aromatic flavour of Earl Grey tea in this syrup permeates the figs to create a sweet and intriguing flavour. They are delicious spooned over creamy Greek yogurt.

Makes about 1.8kg/4lb

INGREDIENTS

900g/2lb ready-to-eat dried figs
1.2 litres/2 pints/5 cups Earl Grey tea
pared rind of 1 orange
1 cinnamon stick
275g/10oz/1⅓ cups granulated sugar
250ml/8fl oz/1 cup brandy

VARIATION

Use Grand Marnier or Cointreau instead of brandy to emphasize the flavour of zesty orange in the syrup.

1 Put the figs in a pan and add the tea, orange rind and cinnamon stick. Bring to the boil, cover and simmer for 10–15 minutes, or until the figs are tender.

2 Using a slotted spoon, remove the figs from the pan and leave to drain. Add the sugar to the tea and heat gently, stirring, until the sugar has dissolved. Boil rapidly for 2 minutes until syrupy.

3 Remove the pan from the heat, then stir in the brandy. Pack the figs and orange rind into warmed sterilized jars and pour in the hot syrup to cover. Twist and gently tap the jars to expel any air bubbles, then seal and store in a cool, dark place for 1 month.

peaches in peach schnapps

The fragrant taste of peaches is complemented and intensified by the addition of the schnapps. Serve with whipped cream flavoured with some of the syrup and a squeeze of lemon juice.

Makes about 1.3kg/3lb

INGREDIENTS

1.3kg/3lb firm peaches

1 litre/1¾ pints/4 cups water

900g/2lb/4½ cups granulated sugar

8 green cardamom pods

50g/2oz/½ cup whole blanched almonds, toasted

120ml/4fl oz/½ cup peach schnapps

VARIATION

Amaretto, an Italian liqueur flavoured with almond and apricot kernels, can be used instead of peach schnapps.

1 Put the peaches in a bowl and pour over boiling water. Drain immediately and peel, then halve and remove the stones (pits).

2 Put the water and half the sugar in a large pan and heat gently until the sugar has dissolved. Increase the heat and boil for 5 minutes.

3 Add the peaches to the syrup and return to the boil. Reduce the heat, cover and simmer gently for 5–10 minutes, or until tender but not too soft. Using a slotted spoon, remove the peaches and set aside to drain.

4 Put the cardamom pods and almonds in a large pan, then add 900ml/1½ pints/3¾ cups of the syrup and the remaining sugar.

5 Gently heat the syrup, stirring until the sugar has dissolved. Bring to the boil and boil until the syrup reaches 104°C/219°F. Leave to cool slightly, remove the cardamom pods, then stir in the schnapps.

6 Pack the peaches loosely in warmed sterilized jars. Pour the syrup and almonds over the fruit, twisting and gently tapping the jars to release any air bubbles. Seal and store in a cool, dark place for 2 weeks before eating.

pineapple in coconut rum

The tropical flavour of pineapple is enhanced by the addition of coconut rum. For a really special treat, serve topped with whipped cream and grated bitter chocolate.

3 Add the remaining sugar to the syrup and heat, stirring, until the sugar has dissolved completely. Bring to the boil and boil for about 10 minutes, or until the syrup has thickened. Remove from the heat and set aside to cool slightly, then stir in the coconut rum.

4 Pack the drained pineapple loosely in warmed sterilized jars. Pour in the syrup until the fruit is covered, tapping and twisting the jars to release any air bubbles. Seal, label and store in a cool, dark place for 2 weeks before eating.

COOK'S TIP
Choose plump pineapples that feel heavy for their size, with fresh, stiff plumes. To test for ripeness, gently pull out one of the bottom leaves; it should come out easily.

Makes about 900g/2lb

INGREDIENTS

1 orange
1.2 litres/2 pints/5 cups water
900g/2lb/4½ cups granulated sugar
2 pineapples, peeled, cored and cut into small chunks
300ml/½ pint/1¼ cups coconut rum

1 Thinly pare strips of rind from the orange, then slice into thin matchsticks. Put the water and half the sugar in a large pan with the orange rind and heat gently until the sugar has dissolved. Increase the heat and boil for 5 minutes.

2 Carefully add the pineapple pieces to the syrup and return to the boil. Reduce the heat and simmer gently for 10 minutes. Using a slotted spoon, remove the pineapple from the pan and set aside to drain.

clementines in juniper syrup

Whole clementines preserved in spiced syrup make a lovely dessert served on their own, with just a spoonful of mascarpone or clotted cream. They also make an excellent addition to trifles.

Makes about 1.3kg/3lb

INGREDIENTS

5cm/2in piece fresh root ginger, sliced
6 whole cloves, plus extra for the jars
5ml/1 tsp juniper berries, crushed,
 plus extra for the jars
900g/2lb/4½ cups granulated sugar
1.2 litres/2 pints/5 cups water
1.3kg/3lb clementines, peeled

COOK'S TIPS

• These pretty spiced clementines look fabulous packed in attractive jars and make an excellent Christmas gift for friends and family.
• When peeling the clementines, try to remove as much of the white pith from the fruit as possible.

1 Tie the ginger, cloves and juniper berries together in a small muslin (cheesecloth) bag.

2 Put the sugar and water in a large pan and heat gently, stirring, until the sugar has dissolved. Add the spice bag to the pan, bring to the boil and cook for 5 minutes.

3 Add the clementines to the pan and simmer for 8–10 minutes, or until tender. Using a slotted spoon, remove the fruit from the syrup and drain well.

4 Pack the hot fruit into warmed sterilized jars and add a few cloves and juniper berries to each jar. Pour off any excess liquid.

5 Return the syrup to the boil and boil rapidly for 10 minutes. Leave the syrup to cool slightly, then pour over the fruit to cover completely. Twist and gently tap the jars to release any trapped air bubbles, then seal and store in a cool, dark place.

kumquats and limequats in brandy syrup

These yellow and green fruits are highly decorative and taste very good indeed, so make a few extra jars of this luxurious preserve to enjoy throughout the coming months. For a really indulgent dessert, serve with good-quality chocolate ice cream or a creamy baked custard.

Makes about 900g/2lb

INGREDIENTS

450g/1lb kumquats and limequats
175g/6oz/scant 1 cup granulated sugar
600ml/1 pint/2½ cups water
150ml/¼ pint/⅔ cup brandy
15ml/1 tbsp orange flower water

COOK'S TIP

Kumquats and limequats are unusual among the citrus family because they are eaten whole and do not need to be peeled. Their thin skins have a pleasantly bitter flavour.

1 Using a cocktail stick (toothpick), prick each individual kumquat and limequat several times.

2 Put the sugar and water in a large pan and heat, stirring, until the sugar has dissolved. Bring to the boil, add the fruit and simmer for 25 minutes, or until tender. Using a slotted spoon, remove the fruit to warmed, sterilized jars.

3 The syrup should be fairly thick: if not, boil for a few minutes, then leave to cool very slightly.

4 Stir the brandy and orange flower water into the syrup, then pour over the fruit and seal immediately. Store in a cool, dark place and use within 6 months.

forest berries in kirsch

This preserve captures the essence of the season in its rich, dark colour and flavour. Adding the sweet cherry liqueur Kirsch to the syrup intensifies the flavour of the bottled fruit.

Makes about 1.3kg/3lb

INGREDIENTS

1.3kg/3lb/12 cups mixed prepared
  summer berries, such as blackberries,
  raspberries, strawberries, redcurrants
  and cherries

225g/8oz/generous 1 cup
  granulated sugar

600ml/1 pint/2½ cups water

120ml/4fl oz/½ cup Kirsch

COOK'S TIP

Be careful not to overcook the fruits because they will lose their beautiful colour and fresh flavour.

1 Preheat the oven to 120°C/250°F/Gas ½. Pack the prepared fruit loosely into sterilized jars. Cover without sealing and place in the oven for 50–60 minutes, or until the juices start to run.

2 Meanwhile, put the sugar and water in a large pan and heat gently, stirring, until the sugar has dissolved. Increase the heat, bring to the boil and boil for 5 minutes. Stir in the Kirsch and set aside.

3 Carefully remove the jars from the oven and place on a dishtowel. Use the fruit from one of the jars to top up the rest.

4 Pour the boiling syrup into each jar, twisting and tapping each one to ensure that no air bubbles have been trapped. Seal, then store in a cool, dark place.

cherries in eau de vie

These potent cherries should be consumed with respect as they pack quite an alcoholic punch.
Serve them with rich, dark chocolate torte or as a wicked topping for creamy rice pudding.

2 Spoon the sugar over the fruit, then pour in the eau de vie to cover and seal tightly.

3 Store for at least 1 month before serving, shaking the bottle now and then to help dissolve the sugar.

COOK'S TIP

Eau de vie actually refers to all spirits distilled from fermented fruits. Eau de vie is always colourless, with a high alcohol content (sometimes 45% ABV) and a clean, pure scent and the flavour of the founding fruit. Popular eaux de vie are made from cherries and strawberries.

Makes about 1.3kg/3lb

INGREDIENTS

450g/1lb/generous 3 cups ripe cherries
8 blanched almonds
75g/3oz/6 tbsp granulated sugar
500ml/17fl oz/scant 2¼ cups eau de vie

VARIATIONS

Strawberries, raspberries and blackcurrants are all excellent preserved in eau de vie. They will all produce fine fruity liqueurs as well as the macerated fruit.

1 Wash and stone (pit) the cherries then pack them into a sterilized, wide-necked bottle along with the blanched almonds.

blackcurrant brandy

Spoon a little of the brandy into a wine glass and top up with chilled white wine or champagne for a special celebration drink. Alternatively serve in small liqueur glasses as a digestif.

Makes about 1 litre/1¾ pints/4 cups

INGREDIENTS

900g/2lb/8 cups blackcurrants, washed
600ml/1 pint/2½ cups brandy
350g/12oz/1¾ cups granulated sugar

COOK'S TIP

When you have strained off the brandy, reserve the blackcurrants and freeze for later use. They are great added to fruit salads and trifles, or make a delicious richly flavoured ice cream topping. Be careful though, because they pack quite a boozy punch.

1 Strip the blackcurrants off their stems and pack the fruit into a sterilized 1.5 litre/2½ pint/6¼ cup preserving jar. Using the back of a wooden spoon, crush the blackcurrants lightly.

2 Add the brandy and sugar to the jar, ensuring the fruit is completely covered by the brandy. Twist and gently tap the jar to ensure there are no trapped air bubbles.

3 Seal the jar, then store in a cool, dark place for about 2 months, shaking the jar occasionally.

4 Pour the liquor through a sieve lined with a double layer of muslin (cheesecloth) into a sterilized jug (pitcher). Pour into sterilized bottles, seal, label and store in a cool, dark place.

...ueberries in gin syrup

These aromatic berries preserved in a gin-laced syrup make a wonderful topping for vanilla ice cream. The syrup turns a fabulous blue colour and the distinctive flavour of the gin complements, rather than masks, the essence of the blueberries.

Makes about 1.8kg/4lb

INGREDIENTS

1.3kg/3lb/12 cups blueberries
225g/8oz/1 cup granulated sugar
600ml/1 pint/2½ cups water
120ml/4fl oz/½ cup gin

1 Preheat the oven to 120°C/250°F/Gas ½. Pack the blueberries into sterilized jars and cover, without sealing. Put the jars in the oven and bake for 50–60 minutes until the juices start to run.

2 Meanwhile, put the sugar and water in a pan and gently heat, stirring continuously, until the sugar has dissolved completely. Increase the heat and boil for 5 minutes. Stir in the gin.

3 Carefully remove the jars from the oven and place on a dry dishtowel. Use the fruit from one of the jars to top up the others.

4 Carefully pour the boiling gin syrup into the jars to completely cover the fruit. Twist and gently tap the jars to ensure that no air bubbles have been trapped.

5 Seal, then store in a cool, dark place until ready to serve.

rumtopf

This fruit preserve originated in Germany, where special earthenware rumtopf pots are traditionally filled with fruits as they come into season. It is not necessary to use the specific pot; you can use a large preserving jar instead. Store in a cool, dark place.

Makes about 3 litres/5 pints/12½ cups

INGREDIENTS

900g/2lb fruit, such as strawberries, blackberries, blackcurrants, redcurrants, peaches, apricots, cherries and plums

250g/9oz/1¼ cups granulated sugar

1 litre/1¾ pints/4 cups white rum

1 Prepare the fruit: remove stems, skins, cores and stones (pits) and cut larger fruit into bitesize pieces. Combine the fruit and sugar in a large non-metallic bowl, cover and leave to stand for 30 minutes.

2 Spoon the fruit and juices into a sterilized 3 litre/5 pint/12½ cup preserving or earthenware jar and pour in the white rum to cover.

3 Cover the jar with clear film (plastic wrap), then seal and store in a cool, dark place.

4 As space allows, and as different fruits come into season, add more fruit, sugar and rum in appropriate proportions, as described above.

5 When the jar is full, store in a cool, dark place for 2 months. Serve the fruit spooned over ice cream or other desserts and enjoy the rum in glasses as a liqueur.

spiced apple mincemeat

This fruity mincemeat is traditionally used to fill little pies at Christmas but it is great at any time. Try it as a filling for large tarts finished with a lattice top and served with custard. To make a lighter mincemeat, add some extra grated apple just before using.

Makes about 1.8kg/4lb

INGREDIENTS

500g/1¼lb tart cooking apples, peeled, cored and finely diced

115g/4oz/½ cup ready-to-eat dried apricots, coarsely chopped

900g/2lb/5⅓ cups luxury dried mixed fruit

115g/4oz/1 cup whole blanched almonds, chopped

175g/6oz/1 cup shredded beef or vegetarian suet (chilled, grated shortening)

225g/8oz/generous 1 cup dark muscovado (molasses) sugar

grated rind and juice of 1 orange

grated rind and juice of 1 lemon

5ml/1 tsp ground cinnamon

2.5ml/½ tsp grated nutmeg

2.5ml/½ tsp ground ginger

120ml/4fl oz/½ cup brandy

1 Put the apples, apricots, dried fruit, almonds, suet and sugar in a large non-metallic bowl and stir together until thoroughly combined.

2 Add the orange and lemon rind and juice, cinnamon, nutmeg, ginger and brandy and mix well. Cover the bowl with a clean dishtowel and leave to stand in a cool place for 2 days, stirring occasionally.

3 Spoon the mincemeat into cool sterilized jars, pressing down well, and being very careful not to trap any air bubbles. Cover and seal.

4 Store the jars in a cool, dark place for at least 4 weeks before using. Once opened, store in the refrigerator and use within 4 weeks. Unopened, the mincemeat will keep for 1 year.

COOK'S TIP

If, when opened, the mincemeat seems dry, pour a little extra brandy or orange juice into the jar and gently stir in. You may need to remove a spoonful or two of the mincemeat from the jar to do this.

pickles

Sharp and sweet, warm and mellow, or hot and piquant – pickles are the magical condiments that can transform simple foods into exhilarating meals. Fresh fruits and vegetables preserved in salt or vinegar and flavoured with spices and herbs make fabulously flavoursome and aromatic accompaniments to cold meats and cheeses, and go well with many roast meats too. They are simple to make and gloriously varied – each one with its own unique character and taste.

dill pickles

Redolent of garlic and piquant with fresh chilli, salty dill pickles can be supple and succulent or crisp and crunchy. Every pickle aficionado has a favourite type.

Makes about 900g/2lb

INGREDIENTS

20 small, ridged or knobbly pickling (small) cucumbers

2 litres/3½ pints/8 cups water

175g/6oz/¾ cup coarse sea salt

15–20 garlic cloves, unpeeled

2 bunches fresh dill

15ml/1 tbsp dill seeds

30ml/2 tbsp mixed pickling spice

1 or 2 hot fresh chillies

1 Scrub the cucumbers and rinse well in cold water. Leave to dry.

2 Put the measured water and salt in a large pan and bring to the boil. Turn off the heat and leave to cool to room temperature.

3 Using the flat side of a knife blade or a wooden mallet, lightly crush each garlic clove, breaking the papery skin.

4 Pack the cucumbers tightly into one or two wide-necked, sterilized jars, layering them with the garlic, fresh dill, dill seeds and pickling spice. Add one chilli to each jar. Pour over the cooled brine, making sure that the cucumbers are completely covered. Tap the jars on the work surface to dispel any trapped air bubbles.

5 Cover the jars with lids and then leave to stand at room temperature for 4–7 days before serving. Store in the refrigerator.

COOK'S TIP

If you cannot find ridged or knobbly pickling cucumbers, use any kind of small cucumbers instead.

pickled mushrooms with garlic

This method of preserving mushrooms is popular throughout Europe. The pickle is good made with cultivated mushrooms, but it is worth including a couple of sliced ceps for their flavour.

Makes about 900g/2lb

INGREDIENTS

500g/1¼lb/8 cups mixed mushrooms, such as small ceps, chestnut mushrooms, shiitake and girolles

300ml/½ pint/1¼ cups white wine vinegar or cider vinegar

15ml/1 tbsp sea salt

5ml/1 tsp caster (superfine) sugar

300ml/½ pint/1¼ cups water

4–5 fresh bay leaves

8 large fresh thyme sprigs

15 garlic cloves, peeled, halved, with any green shoots removed

1 small red onion, halved and thinly sliced

2–3 small dried red chillies

5ml/1 tsp coriander seeds, lightly crushed

5ml/1 tsp black peppercorns

a few strips of lemon rind

250–350ml/8–12fl oz/1–1½ cups extra virgin olive oil

1 Trim and wipe the mushrooms and cut any large ones in half.

2 Put the vinegar, salt, sugar and water in a pan and bring to the boil. Add the bay leaves, thyme, garlic, onion, chillies, coriander seeds, peppercorns and lemon rind and simmer for 2 minutes.

3 Add the mushrooms to the pan and simmer for 3–4 minutes. Drain the mushrooms through a seive, retaining all the herbs and spices, then set aside for a few minutes more until the mushrooms are thoroughly drained.

4 Fill one large or two small cool sterilized jars with the mushrooms. Distribute the garlic, onion, herbs and spices evenly among the layers of mushrooms, then add enough olive oil to cover by at least 1cm/½in. You may need to use extra oil if you are making two jars.

5 Leave the pickle to settle, then tap the jars on the work surface to dispel any air bubbles. Seal the jars, then store in the refrigerator. Use within 2 weeks.

pickled red cabbage

This delicately spiced and vibrant-coloured pickle is an old-fashioned favourite to serve with bread and cheese for an informal lunch, or to use to accompany cold ham, duck or goose.

Makes about 1–1.6kg/2¼–3½lb

INGREDIENTS

675g/1½lb/6 cups red
 cabbage, shredded
1 large Spanish onion, sliced
30ml/2 tbsp sea salt
600ml/1 pint/2½ cups red wine vinegar
75g/3oz/6 tbsp light muscovado
 (brown) sugar
15ml/1 tbsp coriander seeds
3 cloves
2.5cm/1in piece fresh root ginger
1 whole star anise
2 bay leaves
4 eating apples

1 Put the cabbage and onion in a bowl, add the salt and mix well until thoroughly combined. Tip the mixture into a colander over a bowl and leave to drain overnight.

2 The next day, rinse the salted vegetables, drain well and pat dry using kitchen paper.

3 Pour the vinegar into a pan, add the sugar, spices and bay leaves and bring to the boil. Remove from the heat and leave to cool.

4 Core and chop the apples, then layer with the cabbage and onions in sterilized preserving jars. Pour over the cooled spiced vinegar. (If you prefer a milder pickle, strain out the spices first). Seal the jars and store for 1 week before eating. Eat within 2 months. Once opened, store in the refrigerator.

pickled turnips and beetroot

This delicious pickle is a Middle Eastern speciality. The turnips turn a rich red in their beetroot-spiked brine and look gorgeous stacked on shelves in the storecupboard.

2 Put the salt and water in a bowl, stir and leave to stand until the salt has completely dissolved.

3 Sprinkle the beetroot with lemon juice and place in the bottom of four 1.2 litre/2 pint sterilized jars. Top with sliced turnip, packing them in very tightly, then pour over the brine, making sure that the vegetables are covered.

4 Seal the jars and leave in a cool place for 7 days before serving.

Makes about 1.6kg/3½lb

INGREDIENTS

1kg/2¼lb young turnips
3–4 raw beetroot (beets)
about 45ml/3 tbsp coarse sea salt
about 1.5 litres/2½ pints/6¼ cups water
juice of 1 lemon

COOK'S TIP

Be careful when preparing the beetroot because their bright red juice can stain clothing.

1 Wash the turnips and beetroot, but do not peel them, then cut into slices about 5mm/¼in thick.

shallots in balsamic vinegar

These whole shallots, cooked in balsamic vinegar and herbs, are a modern variation on traditional pickled onions. They have a much more gentle, smooth flavour and are delicious served with cold meats or robustly flavoured hard cheeses.

Makes one large jar

INGREDIENTS

500g/1¼lb shallots

30ml/2 tbsp muscovado (molasses) sugar

several bay leaves and/or fresh thyme sprigs

300ml/½ pint/1¼ cups balsamic vinegar

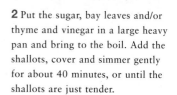

VARIATION

Use other robust herbs in place of the thyme sprigs. Rosemary, oregano or marjoram are all good choices.

1 Put the unpeeled shallots in a bowl. Pour over boiling water and leave to stand for 2 minutes to loosen the skins. Drain and peel the shallots, leaving them whole.

2 Put the sugar, bay leaves and/or thyme and vinegar in a large heavy pan and bring to the boil. Add the shallots, cover and simmer gently for about 40 minutes, or until the shallots are just tender.

3 Transfer the shallots and vinegar mixture to a warmed sterilized jar, packing the shallots down well. Seal and label the jar, then store in a cool, dark place for about 1 month before eating.

hot thai pickled shallots

Although they may be quite difficult to find and require lengthy preparation, Thai pink shallots look and taste exquisite in this spiced pickle. The shallots taste good finely sliced, and served as a condiment with a wide range of South-east Asian meals.

Makes about three jars

INGREDIENTS

5–6 fresh red or green bird's eye chillies, halved and seeded if liked

500g/1¼lb Thai pink shallots, peeled

2 large garlic cloves, peeled, halved and green shoots removed

600ml/1 pint/2½ cups cider vinegar

45ml/3 tbsp granulated sugar

10ml/2 tsp salt

5cm/2in piece fresh root ginger, sliced

15ml/1 tbsp coriander seeds

2 lemon grass stalks, cut in half lengthways

4 kaffir lime leaves or strips of lime rind

15ml/1 tbsp chopped fresh coriander (cilantro)

1 If leaving the chillies whole (they will be hotter), prick several times with a cocktail stick (toothpick).

2 Bring a large pan of water to the boil. Blanch the chillies, shallots and garlic for 1–2 minutes, then drain. Rinse the vegetables under cold water and leave to drain.

VARIATION
Ordinary shallots and pickling onions are widely available and can be preserved using the same method.

3 To prepare the vinegar, put the cider vinegar, sugar, salt, ginger, coriander seeds, lemon grass and lime leaves or lime rind in a large pan and bring to the boil. Simmer over a low heat for 3–4 minutes, then remove from the heat and set aside to cool.

4 Using a slotted spoon, remove the sliced ginger from the pan and discard. Return the vinegar to the boil, then add the fresh coriander, garlic and chillies, and cook for about 1 minute.

5 Pack the shallots, spices and aromatics into warmed sterilized jars and pour over the hot vinegar. Cool, then seal. Leave in a dark place for 2 months before eating.

english pickled onions

These powerful pickles are traditionally served with a plate of cold meats and bread and cheese. They should be made with malt vinegar and stored for at least 6 weeks before eating.

Makes about four jars

INGREDIENTS

1kg/2¼lb pickling onions

115g/4oz/½ cup salt

750ml/1¼ pints/3 cups malt vinegar

15ml/1 tbsp sugar

2–3 dried red chillies

5ml/1 tsp brown mustard seeds

15ml/1 tbsp coriander seeds

5ml/1 tsp allspice berries

5ml/1 tsp black peppercorns

5cm/2in piece fresh root ginger, sliced

2–3 blades mace

2–3 fresh bay leaves

1 To peel the onions, trim off the root ends, but leave the onion layers attached. Cut a thin slice off the top (neck) end of the onion. Place the onions in a bowl, then cover with boiling water. Leave to stand for about 4 minutes, then drain. The skin should then be easy to peel using a small, sharp knife.

2 Place the peeled onions in a bowl and cover with cold water, then drain the water into a large pan. Add the salt and heat slightly to dissolve it, then cool before pouring the brine over the onions.

3 Place a plate inside the top of the bowl and weigh it down slightly so that it keeps all the onions submerged in the brine. Leave to stand for 24 hours.

4 Meanwhile, place the vinegar in a large pan. Wrap all the remaining ingredients, except the bay leaves, in a piece of muslin (cheesecloth). Bring to the boil, simmer for about 5 minutes, then remove the pan from the heat. Set aside and leave to infuse overnight.

5 The next day, drain the onions, rinse and pat dry. Pack them into sterilized 450g/1lb jars. Add some or all of the spice from the vinegar, except the ginger slices. The pickle will become hotter if you add the chillies. Pour the vinegar over to cover and add the bay leaves. (Store leftover vinegar in a bottle for another batch of pickles.)

6 Seal the jars with non-metallic lids and store in a cool, dark place for at least 6 weeks before eating.

instant pickle of mixed vegetables

This fresh, salad-style pickle doesn't need lengthy storing so makes the perfect choice if you need a bowl of pickle immediately. However, it does not have good storing properties.

Makes about 450g/1lb

INGREDIENTS

½ cauliflower head, cut into florets

2 carrots, sliced

2 celery sticks, thinly sliced

¼–½ white cabbage, thinly sliced

115g/4oz/scant 1 cup runner (green) beans, cut into bitesize pieces

6 garlic cloves, sliced

1–4 fresh chillies, whole or sliced

5cm/2in piece fresh root ginger, sliced

1 red (bell) pepper, sliced

2.5ml/½ tsp turmeric

105ml/7 tbsp white wine vinegar

15–30ml/1–2 tbsp granulated sugar

60–90ml/4–6 tbsp olive oil

juice of 2 lemons

salt

1 Toss the cauliflower, carrots, celery, cabbage, beans, garlic, chillies, ginger and pepper with salt and leave them to stand in a colander over a bowl for 4 hours.

2 Shake the vegetables well to remove any excess juices.

3 Transfer the salted vegetables to a bowl. Add the turmeric, vinegar, sugar to taste, oil and lemon juice. Toss to combine, then add enough water to distribute the flavours. Cover the bowl and leave to chill for at least 1 hour, or until you are ready to serve.

stuffed baby aubergines

This Middle Eastern fermented pickle makes a succulent and spicy accompaniment to cold meats, but is equally good served with a few salad leaves and bread as a simple appetizer.

Makes about 3 jars

INGREDIENTS

1kg/2¼lb baby aubergines (eggplant)
2 fresh red chillies, halved lengthways
2 green chillies, halved lengthways
2 celery sticks, cut into matchstick strips
2 carrots, cut into matchstick strips
4 garlic cloves, peeled and finely chopped
20ml/4 tsp salt
4 small fresh vine leaves (optional)
750ml/1¼ pints/3 cups cooled boiled water
45ml/3 tbsp white wine vinegar

2 Steam the slit aubergines for 5–6 minutes or until they are just tender when tested with the tip of a sharp knife.

3 Put the aubergines in a colander set over a bowl, then place a plate on top. Place a few weights on the plate to press it down gently and leave for 4 hours to squeeze out the moisture from the vegetables.

6 Pour the water into a jug (pitcher) and add the remaining 15ml/1 tbsp salt and the vinegar. Stir together until the salt has dissolved. Pour enough brine into the jar to cover the aubergines, then weigh down the top.

7 Cover the jar with a clean dishtowel and leave in a warm, well-ventilated place to ferment. The brine will turn cloudy as fermentation starts, but will clear after 1–2 weeks when the pickle has finished fermenting. As soon as this happens, cover and seal the jar and store in the refrigerator. Eat the pickle within 2 months.

1 Trim the aubergine stems, but do not remove them completely. Cut a slit lengthways along each aubergine, almost through to the other side, to make a pocket.

COOK'S TIPS

• Aubergines come in a multitude of colours from a deep purple-black to yellow and creamy white. Whichever type you use, choose ones with taut, glossy skins.

• Steam the aubergines as soon as you have slit them open because their flesh discolours rapidly when exposed to air.

4 Finely chop two red and two green chilli halves and place in a bowl. Add the celery and carrots to the chillies with the garlic and 5ml/1 tsp of the salt. Mix and use to stuff the aubergine pockets.

5 Tightly pack the aubergines, remaining chillies and vine leaves, if using, into a large sterilized jar.

preserved lemons

These richly flavoured fruits are widely used in Middle Eastern cooking. Only the rind, which contains the essential flavour of the lemon is used in recipes. Traditionally whole lemons are preserved, but this recipe uses wedges, which can be packed into jars more easily.

2 Pack the salted lemon wedges into two 1.2 litre/2 pint/5 cup warmed sterilized jars. To each jar, add 30–45ml/2–3 tbsp sea salt and half the lemon juice, then top up with boiling water to cover the lemon wedges. Seal the jars and leave to stand for 2–4 weeks before using.

3 To use, rinse the preserved lemons well to remove some of the salty flavour, then pull off and discard the flesh. Cut the lemon rind into strips or leave in chunks and use as desired.

Makes about 2 jars

INGREDIENTS

10 unwaxed lemons

about 200ml/7fl oz/scant 1 cup fresh lemon juice or a combination of fresh and preserved juice

boiling water

sea salt

COOK'S TIP

The salty, well-flavoured juice that is used to preserve the lemons can be used to flavour salad dressings or added to hot sauces.

1 Wash the lemons well and cut each into six to eight wedges. Press a generous amount of salt on to the cut surface of each wedge.

pickled limes

This hot, pungent pickle comes from the Punjab in India. Salting softens the rind and intensifies the flavour of the limes, while they mature in the first month or two of storage. Pickled limes are extremely salty so are best served with slightly under-seasoned dishes.

Makes about 1kg/2¼lb

INGREDIENTS

1kg/2¼lb unwaxed limes

75g/3oz/⅓ cup salt

seeds from 6 green cardamom pods

6 whole cloves

5ml/1 tsp cumin seeds

4 fresh red chillies, seeded and sliced

5cm/2in piece fresh root ginger, peeled and finely shredded

450g/1lb/2¼ cups preserving or granulated sugar

1 Put the limes in a large bowl and pour over cold water to cover. Leave to soak for 8 hours, or overnight, if preferred.

2 The next day, remove the limes from the water. Using a sharp knife, cut each lime in half from end to end, then cut each half into 5mm/¼in-thick slices.

3 Place the lime slices in the bowl, sprinkling the salt between the layers. Cover and leave to stand for a further 8 hours.

4 Drain the limes, catching the juices in a preserving pan. Crush the cardamom seeds with the cumin seeds. Add to the pan with the chillies, ginger and sugar. Bring to the boil, stirring until the sugar dissolves. Simmer for 2 minutes and leave to cool.

5 Mix the limes in the syrup. Pack into sterilized jars, cover and seal. Store in a cool, dark place for at least 1 month before eating. Use within 1 year.

striped spiced oranges

These delightful sweet-sour spiced orange slices have a wonderfully warming flavour and look very pretty. Serve them with baked ham, rich terrines and gamey pâtés. They are also delicious with roasted red peppers and grilled halloumi cheese.

Makes about 1.2kg/2½lb

INGREDIENTS

6 small or medium oranges

750ml/1¼ pints/3 cups white wine vinegar

900g/2lb/4½ cups preserving or granulated sugar

7.5cm/3in cinnamon stick

5ml/1 tsp whole allspice

8 whole cloves

45ml/3 tbsp brandy (optional)

COOK'S TIP

These preserved oranges, with their bright colour and warming flavour, make them a perfect accompaniment during the festive season – delicious with leftover turkey or wafer thin slices of festive ham.

1 Scrub the oranges well, then cut strips of rind from each one using a canelle knife (zester) to achieve a striped effect. Reserve the strips of rind.

2 Using a sharp knife, cut the oranges across into slices slightly thicker than 5mm/¼in. Remove and discard any pips (seeds).

3 Put the orange slices into a preserving pan and pour over just enough cold water to cover the fruit. Bring to the boil, then reduce the heat and simmer gently for about 5 minutes, or until the oranges are tender. Using a slotted spoon, transfer the orange slices to a large bowl and discard the cooking liquid.

4 Put the vinegar and sugar in the cleaned pan. Tie the cinnamon, whole allspice and orange rind together in muslin (cheesecloth) and add to the pan. Slowly bring to the boil, stirring, until the sugar has dissolved. Simmer for 1 minute.

5 Return the orange slices to the pan and cook gently for about 30 minutes, or until the rind is translucent and the orange slices look glazed. Remove from the heat and discard the spice bag.

6 Using a slotted spoon, transfer the orange slices to hot sterilized jars, adding the cloves between the layers. Bring the syrup to a rapid boil and boil for about 10 minutes, or until slightly thickened.

7 Allow the syrup to cool for a few minutes, then stir in the brandy, if using. Pour the syrup into the jars, making sure that the fruit is completely immersed. Gently tap the jars on the work surface to release any air bubbles, then cover and seal. Store for at least 2 weeks before using. Use within 6 months.

pickled plums

This preserve is popular in Central Europe and works well for all varieties of plums, from small wild bullaces and astringent damsons to the more delicately flavoured yellow or red-flushed mirabelle. Plums soften easily, so make sure that you choose very firm fruit.

Makes about 900g/2lb

INGREDIENTS

900g/2lb firm plums

150ml/¼ pint/⅔ cup clear apple juice

450ml/¾ pint/scant 2 cups cider vinegar

2.5ml/½ tsp salt

8 allspice berries

2.5cm/1in piece fresh root ginger, peeled and cut into matchstick strips

4 bay leaves

675g/1½lb/scant 3½ cups preserving or granulated sugar

VARIATION

Juniper berries can be used instead of the allspice berries.

1 Wash the plums, then prick them once or twice using a wooden cocktail stick (toothpick). Put the apple juice, vinegar, salt, allspice berries, ginger and bay leaves in a preserving pan.

2 Add the plums to the pan and slowly bring to the boil. Reduce the heat and simmer gently for 10 minutes, or until the plums are just tender. Remove the plums with a slotted spoon and pack them into hot sterilized jars.

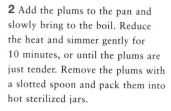

3 Add the sugar to the pan and stir over a low heat until dissolved. Boil steadily for 10 minutes, or until the mixture is syrupy.

4 Leave the syrup to cool for a few minutes, then pour over the plums. Cover and seal. Store for at least 1 month before using and use within 1 year of making.

italian mustard fruit pickles

This traditional and popular Italian preserve is made from late summer and autumn fruits, and then left to mature in time for Christmas when it is served with Italian steamed sausage. The fruits can be mixed together, or arranged in layers in the jars for a stunning effect.

2 Prepare the fruit. Wash and pat dry the peaches, nectarines, apricots and plums, then stone (pit) and thickly slice or halve. Cut the melon in half, discard the seeds (pips), then slice into 1cm/½in pieces or scoop into balls using a melon baller. Cut the figs into quarters and remove the stalks from the cherries.

3 Add the sugar to the mustard vinegar and heat gently, stirring occasionally, until the sugar has dissolved completely. Bring to the boil, reduce the heat and simmer for 5 minutes, or until syrupy.

Makes about 1.2kg/2½lb

INGREDIENTS

450ml/¾ pint/scant 2 cups white wine vinegar

30ml/2 tbsp mustard seeds

1kg/2¼lb mixed fruit, such as peaches, nectarines, apricots, plums, melon, figs and cherries

675g/1½lb/scant 3½ cups preserving or granulated sugar

4 Add the fruit to the syrup and poach it over a gentle heat for 5–10 minutes. Some fruit will be ready sooner than others, so lift out as soon as each variety is tender, using a slotted spoon.

1 Put the vinegar and mustard seeds in a pan, bring to the boil, then simmer for 5 minutes. Remove from the heat, cover and leave to infuse for 1 hour. Strain the vinegar into a clean pan and discard the mustard seeds.

5 Pack the fruit into hot sterilized jars. Ladle the hot mustard syrup over the fruit. Cover and seal. Allow the pickles to mature for at least 1 month before eating. Use within 6 months.

VARIATION

If you prefer a slightly less tangy pickle, use cider vinegar instead of the white wine vinegar used here.

sweet pickled watermelon rind

This unusual pickle has a slightly aromatic melon flavour and a crunchy texture. It's the perfect way to use up the part of the fruit that is normally discarded.

Makes about 900g/2lb

INGREDIENTS

900g/2lb watermelon rind
  (from 1 large fruit)
50g/2oz/¼ cup salt
900ml/1½ pints/3¾ cups water
450g/1lb/2¼ cups preserving or
  granulated sugar
300ml/½ pint/1¼ cups white wine vinegar
6 whole cloves
7.5cm/3in cinnamon stick

COOK'S TIP

Leave the watermelon rind to mature for at least 4 weeks before eating. This really helps the flavours to develop.

1 Remove the dark green skin from the watermelon rind, leaving a thin layer, no more than 3mm/⅛in thick, of the pink fruit. Cut the rind into slices about 5cm × 5mm/2 × ¼in thick, and place in a large bowl.

2 Dissolve the salt in 600ml/1 pint/2½ cups of the water. Pour over the watermelon rind, cover and leave for at least 6 hours or overnight.

3 Drain the watermelon rind and rinse under cold water. Put the rind in a pan and cover with fresh water. Bring the boil, reduce the heat and simmer for 10–15 minutes until just tender. Drain well.

4 Put the sugar, vinegar and remaining water in a clean pan. Tie the cloves and cinnamon in muslin (cheesecloth) and add to the pan. Heat gently, stirring occasionally, until the sugar has dissolved, then bring to the boil and simmer for 10 minutes. Turn off the heat. Add the rind, cover and leave to stand for about 2 hours.

5 Slowly bring the mixture back to the boil, then reduce the heat and simmer gently for 20 minutes, or until the rind has a translucent appearance. Remove and discard the spice bag. Place the rind in hot sterilized jars. Pour over the hot syrup, tapping the jar to release any trapped air. Cover and seal.

blushing pears

As this pickle matures, the fruits absorb the colour of the vinegar, giving them a glorious pink hue. They're especially good served with cold turkey, game pie, well-flavoured cheese or pâté.

Makes about 1.3kg/3lb

INGREDIENTS

1 small lemon
450g/1lb/2¼ cups golden granulated sugar
475ml/16fl oz/2 cups raspberry vinegar
7.5cm/3in cinnamon stick
6 whole cloves
6 allspice berries
150ml/¼ pint/⅔ cup water
900g/2lb firm pears

1 Using a sharp knife, thinly pare a few strips of rind from the lemon. Squeeze out 30ml/2 tbsp of the juice and put it in a large pan with the strips of rind.

2 Add the sugar, vinegar, spices and water to the pan. Heat gently, stirring occasionally, until the sugar has completely dissolved, then slowly bring to the boil.

VARIATION

Nectarines and peaches may be pickled using the same method. Blanch and skin the fruits, then halve and stone (pit). Add a strip of orange rind to the syrup instead of lemon rind.

3 Meanwhile, prepare the pears. Peel and halve the pears, then scoop out the cores using a melon baller or small teaspoon. If the pears are very large, cut them into quarters rather than halves.

4 Add the pears to the pan and simmer very gently for about 20 minutes, or until tender and translucent but still whole. Check the pears frequently towards the end of the cooking time. Using a slotted spoon, remove the pears from the pan and pack into hot sterilized jars, adding the spices and strips of lemon rind.

5 Boil the syrup for 5 minutes, or until slightly reduced. Skim off any scum, then ladle the syrup over the pears. Cover and seal. Store for at least 1 month before eating.

chutneys

Long, slow cooking produces the classic rich and intriguing flavours that epitomize thick, chunky chutneys. Fresh vegetables and fruits are combined with fresh herbs and spices, then simmered to perfection to created wonderfully mellow flavours. These versatile condiments are marvellous served with cold meats and cheeses, or spread thickly in sandwiches to enliven and enhance the simplest fillings.

green tomato chutney

This is a classic chutney for using the last tomatoes of summer that just never seem to ripen. Apples and onions contribute essential flavour, which is enhanced by the addition of spice.

Makes about 2.5kg/5½lb

INGREDIENTS

1.8kg/4lb green tomatoes,
  roughly chopped
450g/1lb cooking apples, peeled,
  cored and chopped
450g/1lb onions, chopped
2 large garlic cloves, crushed
15ml/1 tbsp salt
45ml/3 tbsp pickling spice
600ml/1 pint/2½ cups cider vinegar
450g/1lb/2¼ cups granulated sugar

COOK'S TIP

Allow the chutney to mature for at least 1 month before using.

1 Place the tomatoes, apples, onions and garlic in a large pan and add the salt.

2 Tie the pickling spice in a piece of muslin (cheesecloth) and add to the ingredients in the pan.

3 Add half the vinegar to the pan and bring to the boil. Reduce the heat and simmer for 1 hour, or until the chutney is reduced and thick, stirring frequently.

4 Put the sugar and remaining vinegar in a pan and heat gently until the sugar has dissolved, then add to the chutney. Simmer for 1½ hours until the chutney is thick, stirring it occasionally.

5 Remove the muslin bag from the chutney, then spoon the hot chutney into warmed sterilized jars. Cover and seal immediately.

COOK'S TIPS

• To avoid spillages and speed up the process of potting preserves, use a wide-necked jam funnel to transfer the chutney into the jars. Wipe the jars immediately, then label them when cold.
• Use a long-handled teaspoon to press and poke the chutney right down into the pots to exclude any trapped air pockets.
• Press wax discs on the surface of the chutney before sealing the jar.

tomato chutney

This spicy and dark, sweet-sour chutney is delicious served with a selection of well-flavoured cheeses and biscuits or bread, or with cold roast meats such as ham, turkey, tongue or lamb.

Makes about 1.8kg/4lb

INGREDIENTS

900g/2lb tomatoes, skinned
225g/8oz/1½ cups raisins
225g/8oz onions, chopped
225g/8oz/generous 1 cup caster
(superfine) sugar
600ml/1 pint/2½ cups malt vinegar

VARIATION

Dried dates may be used in place of the raisins, and red wine or sherry vinegar may be used in place of the malt vinegar. Stone (pit) and chop the dates, or buy stoned cooking dates that have been compressed in a block and chop them finely.

1 Chop the tomatoes roughly and place in a preserving pan. Add the raisins, onions and caster sugar.

2 Pour the vinegar into the pan and bring the mixture to the boil. Simmer for 2 hours, uncovered, until soft and thickened.

3 Transfer the chutney to warmed sterilized jars. Top with waxed discs and lids. Store in a cool, dark place and leave to mature for 1 month. The chutney will keep unopened for up to 1 year. Once the jars have been opened, store them in the refrigerator.

mediterranean chutney

Reminiscent of the warm Mediterranean climate, this mixed vegetable chutney is colourful, mild and warm in flavour and goes particularly well with grilled meats and sausages. For a hotter, spicier flavour, add a little cayenne pepper with the paprika.

Makes about 1.8kg/4lb

INGREDIENTS

450g/1lb Spanish onions, chopped

900g/2lb ripe tomatoes, skinned and chopped

1 aubergine (eggplant), weighing about 350g/12oz, trimmed and cut into 1cm/½in cubes

450g/1lb courgettes (zucchini), sliced

1 yellow (bell) pepper, quartered, seeded and sliced

1 red (bell) pepper, quartered, seeded and sliced

3 garlic cloves, crushed

1 small sprig of rosemary

1 small sprig of thyme

2 bay leaves

15ml/1 tbsp salt

15ml/1 tbsp paprika

300ml/½ pint/1¼ cups malt vinegar

400g/14oz/2 cups granulated sugar

1 Put the chopped onions, tomatoes, aubergine, courgettes, peppers and garlic in a preserving pan. Cover the pan with a lid and cook gently over a very low heat, stirring occasionally, for about 15 minutes, or until the juices start to run.

2 Tie the rosemary, thyme and bay leaves in a piece of muslin (cheesecloth). Add to the pan with the salt, paprika and half the malt vinegar. Simmer, uncovered, for 25 minutes, or until the vegetables are tender and the juices reduced.

3 Add the remaining vinegar and sugar to the pan and stir over a low heat until the sugar has dissolved. Simmer for 30 minutes, stirring the chutney frequently towards the end of cooking time.

4 When the chutney is reduced to a thick consistency and no excess liquid remains, discard the herbs, then spoon the chutney into warmed sterilized jars. Set aside until cool, then cover and seal with vinegar-proof lids.

5 Store the chutney in a cool, dark place and allow to mature for at least 2 months before eating. Use the chutney within 2 years. Once opened, store in the refrigerator and use within 2 months.

confit of slow-cooked onions

This jam of slow-cooked, caramelized onions in sweet-sour balsamic vinegar will keep for several days in a sealed jar in the refrigerator. You can make it with red, white or yellow onions, but yellow onions will produce the sweetest result.

Makes about 500g/1¼lb

INGREDIENTS

30ml/2 tbsp olive oil

15g/½oz/1 tbsp butter

500g/1¼lb onions, sliced

3–5 fresh thyme sprigs

1 fresh bay leaf

30ml/2 tbsp light muscovado (brown) sugar, plus a little extra

50g/2oz/¼ cup ready-to-eat prunes, chopped

30ml/2 tbsp balsamic vinegar, plus a little extra

120ml/4fl oz/½ cup red wine

salt and ground black pepper

3 Add the prunes, vinegar, wine and 60ml/4 tbsp water to the pan and cook over a low heat, stirring frequently, for 20 minutes, or until most of the liquid has evaporated. Add a little more water and reduce the heat if it looks dry. Remove from the heat.

4 Adjust the seasoning if necessary, adding more sugar and/or vinegar to taste. Leave the confit to cool then stir in the remaining 5ml/1 tsp olive oil and serve.

VARIATION

Gently brown 500g/1¼lb peeled pickling (pearl) onions in 60ml/4 tbsp olive oil. Sprinkle in 45ml/3 tbsp brown sugar and caramelize a little, then add 7.5ml/1½ tsp crushed coriander seeds, 250ml/8fl oz/1 cup red wine, 2 bay leaves, a few thyme sprigs, 3 strips orange rind, 45ml/3 tbsp tomato purée (paste) and the juice of 1 orange. Cook gently, covered, for 1 hour, stirring occasionally. Uncover for the last 20 minutes. Sharpen with 15–30ml/1–2 tbsp sherry vinegar.

1 Reserve 5ml/1 tsp of the oil, then heat the remaining oil with the butter in a large pan. Add the onions, cover and cook gently over a low heat for about 15 minutes, stirring occasionally.

2 Season the onions with salt and ground black pepper, then add the thyme, bay leaf and sugar. Cook slowly, uncovered, for a further 15–20 minutes until the onions are very soft and dark. Stir the onions occasionally during cooking to prevent them sticking or burning.

Kashmir chutney

In the true tradition of the Kashmiri country store, this is a typical family recipe passed down from generation to generation. It is wonderful served with plain or spicy grilled sausages.

Makes about 2.75kg/6lb

INGREDIENTS

1kg/2¼lb green eating apples
15g/½oz garlic cloves
1 litre/1¾ pints/4 cups malt vinegar
450g/1lb dates
115g/4oz preserved stem ginger
450g/1lb/3 cups raisins
450g/1lb/2 cups soft light brown sugar
2.5ml/½ tsp cayenne pepper
30ml/2 tbsp salt

COOK'S TIP

This sweet, chunky, spicy chutney is perfect served with cold meats for an informal buffet lunch.

1 Quarter the apples, remove the cores and chop coarsely. Peel and chop the garlic.

2 Place the apple and garlic in a pan with enough vinegar to cover. Bring to the boil and boil for 10 minutes.

3 Chop the dates and ginger and add them to the pan, together with the rest of the ingredients. Cook gently for 45 minutes.

4 Spoon the mixture into warmed sterilized jars and seal immediately.

fiery bengal chutney

Not for timid tastebuds, this fiery chutney is the perfect choice for lovers of hot and spicy food. Although it can be eaten a month after making, it is better matured for longer.

Makes about 2kg/4½lb

INGREDIENTS

115g/4oz fresh root ginger
1kg/2¼lb cooking apples
675g/1½lb onions
6 garlic cloves, finely chopped
225g/8oz/1½ cups raisins
450ml/¾ pint/scant 2 cups malt vinegar
400g/14oz/1¾ cups demerara
  (raw) sugar
2 fresh red chillies
2 fresh green chillies
15ml/1 tbsp salt
5ml/1 tsp turmeric

1 Peel and finely shred the fresh root ginger. Peel, core and roughly chop the apples. Peel and quarter the onions, then slice as thinly as possible. Place in a preserving pan with the garlic, raisins and vinegar.

2 Bring to the boil, then simmer steadily for 15–20 minutes, stirring occasionally, until the apples and onions are thoroughly softened. Add the sugar and stir over a low heat until the sugar has dissolved. Simmer the mixture for about 40 minutes, or until thick and pulpy, stirring frequently towards the end of the cooking time.

3 Halve the chillies and remove the seeds, then slice them finely. (Always wash your hands with soapy water immediately after handling chillies.)

4 Add the chillies to the pan and cook for a further 5–10 minutes, or until no excess liquid remains. Stir in the salt and turmeric.

5 Spoon the chutney into warmed sterilized jars, cover and seal them immediately, then label when cool.

6 Store the chutney in a cool, dark place and leave to mature for at least 2 months before eating. Use within 2 years of making. Once opened, store in the refrigerator and use within 1 month.

butternut, apricot and almond chutney

Coriander seeds and turmeric add a slightly spicy touch to this rich golden chutney. It is delicious in little canapés or with cubes of mozzarella cheese; it is also good in sandwiches.

Makes about 1.8kg/4lb

INGREDIENTS

1 small butternut squash, weighing about 800g/1¾lb

400g/14oz/2 cups golden granulated sugar

600ml/1 pint/2½ cups cider vinegar

2 onions, chopped

225g/8oz/1 cup ready-to-eat dried apricots, quartered

finely grated rind and juice of 1 orange

2.5ml/½ tsp turmeric

15ml/1 tbsp coriander seeds

15ml/1 tbsp salt

115g/4oz/1 cup flaked (sliced) almonds

1 Halve the butternut squash lengthways and scoop out the seeds. Peel off the skin, then cut the flesh into 2cm/¾in cubes.

2 Put the sugar and vinegar in a preserving pan and heat gently, stirring occasionally, until the sugar has dissolved.

3 Add the squash, onions, apricots, orange rind and juice, turmeric, coriander seeds and salt to the preserving pan. Bring the mixture slowly to the boil.

4 Reduce the heat and simmer gently for 45–50 minutes, stirring frequently towards the end of the cooking time, until the chutney is reduced to a thick consistency and no excess liquid remains. Stir in the flaked almonds.

5 Spoon the chutney into warmed sterilized jars, cover and seal. Store in a cool, dark place and allow to mature for at least 1 month before eating. Use within 2 years. Once opened, store in the refrigerator and use within 2 months.

VARIATION

If butternut squash is unavailable, use a wedge of pumpkin weighing about 500g/1¼lb instead.

sweet and hot dried fruit chutney

This rich, thick and slightly sticky preserve of spiced dried fruit is a wonderful way to enliven cold roast turkey left over from Christmas or Thanksgiving dinners.

Makes about 1.5kg/3lb 6oz

INGREDIENTS

350g/12oz/1½ cups ready-to-eat dried apricots

225g/8oz/1½ cups dried dates, stoned (pitted)

225g/8oz/1½ cups dried figs

50g/2oz/⅓ cup glacé (candied) citrus peel

150g/5oz/1 cup raisins

50g/2oz/½ cup dried cranberries

120ml/4fl oz/½ cup cranberry juice

400ml/14fl oz/1⅔ cups cider vinegar

225g/8oz/1 cup demerara (raw) sugar

finely grated rind and juice of 1 lemon

5ml/1 tsp mixed spice (apple pie spice)

5ml/1 tsp ground coriander

5ml/1 tsp cayenne pepper

5ml/1 tsp salt

1 Roughly chop the dried apricots, dates, figs and citrus peel, then put all the dried fruit in a preserving pan. Pour over the cranberry juice, stir, then cover and leave to soak for 2 hours, or until the fruit has absorbed most of the juice.

2 Add the cider vinegar and sugar to the pan. Stir over a low heat until the sugar has dissolved.

3 Bring the mixture to the boil, then reduce the heat and simmer for about 30 minutes, or until the fruit is soft and the chutney fairly thick. Stir occasionally during cooking.

4 Stir in the lemon rind and juice, mixed spice, coriander, cayenne pepper and salt. Simmer for a further 15 minutes, stirring frequently towards the end of the cooking, until the chutney is thick and no excess liquid remains.

VARIATIONS

If you prefer, substitute dried sour cherries for the dried cranberries. Apple juice can be used instead of the cranberry juice.

5 Spoon the chutney into warmed sterilized jars, cover and seal. Store in a cool, dark place and allow to mature for at least 1 month before eating. Use within 1 year. Once opened, store in the refrigerator and use within 2 months.

pickled peach and chilli chutney

This is a spicy, rich chutney with a succulent texture. It is great served traditional-style, with cold roast meats such as ham, pork or turkey; it is also good with pan-fried chicken served in warm wraps. Try it with ricotta cheese as a filling for pitta bread.

Makes about 450g/1lb

INGREDIENTS

475ml/16fl oz/2 cups cider vinegar

275g/10oz/1¼ cups light muscovado (brown) sugar

225g/8oz/1⅓ cups dried dates, stoned (pitted) and finely chopped

5ml/1 tsp ground allspice

5ml/1 tsp ground mace

450g/1lb ripe peaches, stoned and cut into small chunks

3 onions, thinly sliced

4 fresh red chillies, seeded and finely chopped

4 garlic cloves, crushed

5cm/2in piece fresh root ginger, peeled and finely grated

5ml/1 tsp salt

1 Place the vinegar, sugar, dates, allspice and mace in a large pan and heat gently, stirring, until the sugar has dissolved. Bring to the boil, stirring occasionally.

2 Add the peaches, sliced onions, chopped chillies, crushed garlic, grated ginger and salt, and bring the mixture back to the boil, stirring occasionally.

3 Reduce the heat and simmer for 40–50 minutes, or until the chutney has thickened. Stir frequently to prevent the mixture sticking to the bottom of the pan.

4 Spoon the hot cooked chutney into warmed sterilized jars and seal immediately. When cold, store the jars in a cool, dark place and leave the chutney to mature for at least 2 weeks before eating. Use within 6 months.

COOK'S TIP

To test the consistency of the chutney before bottling, spoon a little of the mixture on to a plate; the chutney should hold its shape.

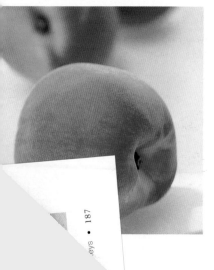

hot yellow plum chutney

It is well worth seeking out yellow plums to make this hot, fragrant chutney. They give it a slightly tart flavour and make it the perfect accompaniment to deep-fried Asian-style snacks such as spring rolls and wontons, or battered vegetables and shellfish.

Makes 1.3kg/3lb

INGREDIENTS

900g/2lb yellow plums, halved and stoned (pitted)

1 onion, finely chopped

7.5cm/3in piece fresh root ginger, peeled and grated

3 whole star anise

350ml/12fl oz/1½ cups white wine vinegar

225g/8oz/1 cup soft light brown sugar

5 celery sticks, thinly sliced

3 green chillies, seeded and finely sliced

2 garlic cloves, crushed

1 Put the halved plums, onion, ginger and star anise in a large pan and pour over half the white wine vinegar. Bring to the boil and simmer gently over a low heat for about 30 minutes, or until the plums have softened.

2 Stir the remaining vinegar, sugar, sliced celery, chillies and crushed garlic into the plum mixture. Cook very gently over a low heat, stirring frequently, until the sugar has completely dissolved.

3 Bring the mixture to the boil, then simmer for 45–50 minutes, or until thick, with no excess liquid. Stir frequently during the final stages of cooking to prevent the chutney sticking to the pan.

4 Spoon the plum chutney into warmed sterilized jars, then cover and seal immediately.

5 Store the chutney in a cool, dark place and allow to mature for at least 1 month before using. Use within 2 years.

COOK'S TIPS

• Once opened, store the chutney in the refrigerator and use within 3 months.

• Be sure to use jars with non-metallic lids to store the chutney.

mango chutney

No Indian meal would be complete without this classic chutney. Its gloriously sweet, tangy flavour complements the warm taste of Indian spices perfectly, but it is equally good scooped up on crispy fried poppadums. Mango chutney is also great served with chargrilled chicken, turkey or duck breasts; with potato wedges and soured cream; or spread on cheese on toast.

Makes about 1kg/2¼lb

INGREDIENTS

900g/2lb mangoes, halved, peeled and stoned

2.5ml/½ tsp salt

225g/8oz cooking apples, peeled

300ml/½ pint/1¼ cups distilled malt vinegar

200g/7oz/scant 1 cup demerara (raw) sugar

1 onion, chopped

1 garlic clove, crushed

10ml/2 tsp ground ginger

COOK'S TIPS

• Once opened, store the chutney in the refrigerator and use within 3 months.

• When serving mango chutney with crispy popadoms, also offer a selection of other condiments such as salty lime pickle, finely chopped fresh onion salad and minty yogurt.

1 Using a sharp knife, slice the mango flesh into chunks and place in a large, non-metallic bowl. Sprinkle with salt and set aside while you prepare the apples.

2 Using a sharp knife, cut the apples into quarters, then remove and discard the cores and peel. Chop the flesh roughly.

3 Put the malt vinegar and sugar in a preserving pan and heat very gently, stirring occasionally, until the sugar has dissolved completely.

4 Add the mangoes, apple, onion, garlic and ginger to the pan and slowly bring the mixture to the boil, stirring occasionally.

5 Reduce the heat and simmer gently for about 1 hour, stirring frequently towards the end of the cooking time, until the chutney is reduced to a thick consistency and no excess liquid remains.

6 Spoon the chutney into warmed sterilized jars, cover and seal. Store in a cool, dark place and allow to mature for at least 2 weeks before eating. Use within 1 year of making.

VARIATION

To make a chutney with a fiery, spicy kick to serve with cheeses and cold meats, seed and finely slice two green chillies and stir into the chutney with the garlic and ginger.

chunky pear and walnut chutney

This chutney recipe is ideal for using up hard windfall pears. Its mellow flavour is excellent with cheese and also good with grains such as in pilaff or with tabbouleh.

Makes about 1.8kg/4lb

INGREDIENTS

1.2kg/2½lb firm pears
225g/8oz tart cooking apples
225g/8oz onions
450ml/¾ pint/scant 2 cups cider vinegar
175g/6oz/generous 1 cup sultanas
  (golden raisins)
finely grated rind and juice
  of 1 orange
400g/14oz/2 cups granulated sugar
115g/4oz/1 cup walnuts,
  roughly chopped
2.5ml/½ tsp ground cinnamon

1 Peel and core the fruit, then chop into 2.5cm/1in chunks. Peel and quarter the onions, then chop into pieces the same size. Place in a preserving pan with the vinegar.

2 Slowly bring to the boil, then reduce the heat and simmer for 40 minutes, until the apples, pears and onions are tender, stirring the mixture occasionally.

3 Meanwhile, put the sultanas in a small bowl, pour over the orange juice and leave to soak.

4 Add the sugar, sultanas, and orange rind and juice to the pan. Gently heat until the sugar has dissolved, then simmer for 30–40 minutes, or until the chutney is thick and no excess liquid remains. Stir frequently towards the end of cooking to prevent the chutney sticking on the bottom of the pan.

5 Gently toast the walnuts in a non-stick pan over a low heat for 5 minutes, stirring frequently, until lightly coloured. Stir the nuts into the chutney with the cinnamon.

6 Spoon the chutney into warmed sterilized jars, cover and seal. Store in a cool, dark place and leave to mature for at least 1 month. Use within 1 year.

green grape chutney

A hint of lime heightens the fragrant grape flavour and complements the sweetness of this chutney. It is delicious warmed with a knob of butter and served with roast pork.

Makes 1.2kg/2½lb

INGREDIENTS

900g/2lb/6 cups seedless green grapes
900g/2lb tart cooking apples
450g/1lb/2¼ cups granulated sugar
450ml/¾ pint/scant 2 cups white wine vinegar
finely grated rind and juice of 1 lime
1.5ml/¼ tsp salt

COOK'S TIP

Once opened, store the chutney in the refrigerator and use within 1 month.

1 Halve the grapes if large, then peel, core and finely chop the apples. Put the fruit in a preserving pan with the sugar and vinegar and slowly bring to the boil.

2 Reduce the heat and simmer the chutney for about 45 minutes, or until the fruit is tender and the chutney fairly thick.

3 Stir the lime rind and juice and salt into the chutney and simmer for 15 minutes until the chutney is thick and no excess liquid remains.

4 Spoon the chutney into warmed sterilized jars, cover and seal. Store in a cool, dark place and leave to mature for at least 1 month before eating. Use within 18 months.

beetroot and orange preserve

With its vibrant red colour and rich earthy flavour, this distinctive chutney is good with salads as well as full-flavoured cheeses such as mature Cheddar, Stilton or Gorgonzola. You might also like to try it with cream cheese in baked potatoes.

Makes about 1.4kg/3lb

INGREDIENTS

350g/12oz raw beetroot (beets)

350g/12oz eating apples

300ml/½ pint/1¼ cups malt vinegar

200g/7oz/1 cup granulated sugar

225g/8oz red onions,
   finely chopped

1 garlic clove, crushed

finely grated rind and juice
   of 2 oranges

5ml/1 tsp ground allspice

5ml/1 tsp salt

1 Scrub or, if necessary, thinly peel the beetroot, then cut into 1cm/½in pieces. Peel, quarter and core the apples and cut into 1cm/½in pieces.

2 Put the vinegar and sugar in a preserving pan and heat gently, stirring occasionally, until the sugar has dissolved.

3 Add the beetroot, apples, onions, garlic, orange rind and juice, ground allspice and salt to the pan. Bring to the boil, reduce the heat, then simmer for 40 minutes.

4 Increase the heat slightly and boil for 10 minutes, or until the chutney is thick and no excess liquid remains. Stir frequently to prevent the chutney catching on the base of the pan.

5 Spoon the chutney into warmed sterilized jars, cover and seal. Store in a cool, dark place and allow to mature for at least 2 weeks before eating. Use within 6 months of making. Refrigerate once opened and use within 1 month.

COOK'S TIP

For speedy preparation and a fine-textured chutney, put the peeled beetroot through the coarse grating blade of a food processor.

rhubarb and tangerine chutney

The rhubarb in this soft-textured chutney is added partway through the cooking, so that it retains its attractive colour and shape. It works especially well when partnered with Chinese-style roast duck, or with cold meats such as ham or gammon.

Makes about 1.3kg/3lb

INGREDIENTS

1 large onion, finely chopped

300ml/½ pint/1¼ cups distilled malt vinegar

4 whole cloves

7.5cm/3in cinnamon stick

1 tangerine

400g/14oz/2 cups granulated sugar

150g/5oz/1 cup sultanas (golden raisins)

1kg/2¼lb rhubarb, cut into 2.5cm/1in lengths

1 Put the onion in a preserving pan with the vinegar, whole cloves and cinnamon stick. Bring to the boil, then reduce the heat and simmer for 10 minutes, or until the onions are just tender.

2 Meanwhile, thinly pare the rind from the tangerine. (It is often easier to peel the fruit first, then slice the white pith from the rind.) Finely shred the rind.

3 Add the tangerine rind, sugar and sultanas to the pan. Stir until all the sugar has dissolved, then simmer for 10 minutes, or until the syrup is thick.

4 Add the rhubarb to the pan. Cook gently for about 15 minutes, stirring carefully from time to time, until the rhubarb is soft but still retains its shape, and just a little spare liquid remains.

5 Remove the pan from the heat and leave to cool for 10 minutes, then stir gently to distribute the fruit. Spoon the chutney into warmed sterilized jars, cover and seal. Store in a cool, dark place and allow to mature for at least 1 month. Use within 1 year. Once opened, store in the refrigerator and use within 2 months.

COOK'S TIP

The finely shredded rind of half an orange may be used in place of the shredded tangerine rind.

relishes

These versatile condiments can be fresh and quick to prepare or rich and slowly simmered. They usually have bold, striking flavours with a piquant, sharp and spicy taste balanced by sweet and tangy tones. They are perfect for serving with cheese, cold or grilled meats or for jazzing up plain sandwich fillings.

tart tomato relish

Adding lime to this relish gives it a wonderfully tart, tangy flavour and a pleasantly sour after-taste. It is particularly good served with grilled or roast meats such as pork or lamb.

Makes about 500g/1¼lb

INGREDIENTS

2 pieces preserved stem ginger

1 lime

450g/1lb cherry tomatoes

115g/4oz/½ cup muscovado (molasses) sugar

120ml/4fl oz/½ cup white wine vinegar

5ml/1 tsp salt

VARIATION

Use chopped tomatoes in place of the cherry tomatoes, if you prefer.

1 Coarsely chop the preserved stem ginger. Slice the lime thinly, including the rind, then chop the slices into small pieces.

2 Place the cherry tomatoes, sugar, vinegar, salt, ginger and lime in a large heavy pan.

3 Bring the mixture to the boil, stirring until the sugar dissolves, then simmer rapidly for about 45 minutes. Stir frequently until the liquid has evaporated and the relish is thick and pulpy.

4 Leave the relish to cool for about 5 minutes, then spoon into sterilized jars. Leave to cool, then cover and store in the refrigerator for up to 1 month.

COOK'S TIP

There is always discussion between preserving enthusiasts as to the best choice of covering for chutneys and pickles. While cellophane covers are vinegarproof, they are difficult to secure for a good airtight seal, and not very good once opened. Screw-top lids with a plastic coating inside are best: put them on as soon as the piping hot preserve is potted and they will provide a hygienic, air-tight seal. New lids can be purchased for standard-size glass jars.

red hot relish

Make this relish during the summer months when tomatoes and peppers are plentiful.
It enhances simple, plain dishes such as a cheese or mushroom omelette.

Makes about 1.3kg/3lb

800g/1¾lb ripe tomatoes, skinned
    and quartered

450g/1lb red onions, chopped

3 red (bell) peppers, seeded
    and chopped

3 fresh red chillies, seeded
    and finely sliced

200g/7oz/1 cup granulated sugar

200ml/7fl oz/scant 1 cup red
    wine vinegar

30ml/2 tbsp mustard seeds

10ml/2 tsp celery seeds

15ml/1 tbsp paprika

5ml/1 tsp salt

1 Put the chopped tomatoes, onions, peppers and chillies in a preserving pan, cover with a lid and cook over a very low heat for about 10 minutes, stirring once or twice, until the tomato juices start to run.

2 Add the sugar and vinegar to the tomato mixture and slowly bring to the boil, stirring occasionally until the sugar has dissolved completely. Add the mustard seeds, celery seeds, paprika and salt and stir well to combine.

3 Increase the heat under the pan slightly and cook the relish, uncovered, for about 30 minutes, or until most of the liquid has evaporated and the mixture has a thick, but moist consistency. Stir frequently towards the end of cooking time to prevent the mixture sticking to the pan.

4 Spoon the relish into warmed sterilized jars, cover and seal. Store in a cool, dark place and leave to mature for at least 2 weeks before eating. Use the relish within 1 year of making.

COOK'S TIP

Once opened, store the relish in the refrigerator and use within 2 months.

bloody mary relish

This fresh-tasting relish with contrasting textures of tomatoes, celery and cucumber is perfect for al fresco *summer eating. For a special occasion, serve it with freshly shucked oysters.*

Makes about 1.3kg/3lb

INGREDIENTS

1.3kg/3lb ripe well-flavoured tomatoes
1 large cucumber
30–45ml/2–3 tbsp salt
2 celery sticks, chopped
2 garlic cloves, peeled and crushed
175ml/6fl oz/¾ cup white wine vinegar
15ml/1 tbsp granulated sugar
60ml/4 tbsp vodka
5ml/1 tsp Tabasco sauce
10ml/2 tsp Worcestershire sauce

COOK'S TIP

To skin the tomatoes, plunge them in a bowl of just-boiled water for 30 seconds. The skins will split and will be easy to peel off.

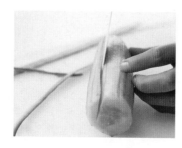

1 Skin and chop the tomatoes. Peel the cucumber and slice the flesh from around the seeds. Discard the seeds and chop the flesh. Layer the vegetables in a colander placed over a bowl, lightly sprinkling each layer with salt. Cover, put in the refrigerator and leave to drain overnight.

2 The next day, rinse the tomatoes and cucumber thoroughly under cold running water to remove as much salt as possible. Drain well, then place in a pan. Discard the salty vegetable juices in the bowl.

3 Add the celery, garlic, vinegar and sugar to the pan and slowly bring to the boil over a low heat.

4 Cook the vegetables, uncovered, for about 30 minutes, stirring occasionally, until the vegetables have softened and most of the liquid has evaporated.

5 Remove the pan from the heat and leave to cool for about 5 minutes. Add the vodka, and Tabasco and Worcestershire sauces and stir well to combine.

6 Spoon the hot relish into warmed sterilized jars, cool, cover and seal. Store in the refrigerator for at least 1 week.

COOK'S TIP

Use the relish within 3 months. Once opened, store it in the refrigerator and use within 1 month.

yellow pepper and coriander relish

Fresh relishes are quick and easy to make although they do not have a long shelf life. Try this relish with mild, creamy cheeses or with grilled tuna or other firm fish, poultry or meat.

Makes 1 small jar

INGREDIENTS

1 large yellow (bell) pepper
45ml/3 tbsp sesame oil
1 large mild fresh red chilli
small handful of fresh coriander (cilantro)
salt

1 Seed and coarsely chop the yellow peppers. Heat the oil in a pan, add the peppers and cook, stirring frequently, for 8–10 minutes, until lightly coloured.

2 Meanwhile, seed the chilli, slice it very thinly and set aside. Transfer the peppers to a food processor and process until chopped, but not puréed. Transfer half the peppers to a bowl, leaving the rest in the food processor.

3 Using a sharp knife, chop the fresh coriander, then add it to the mixture in the food processor and process briefly to combine. Tip the mixture into the bowl with the rest of the peppers, add the sliced chilli and stir well to combine.

4 Season the relish with salt to taste and stir well to combine. Cover the bowl with clear film (plastic wrap) and chill in the refrigerator until ready to serve.

COOK'S TIPS

• Red and orange sweet peppers work just as well as yellow, though green peppers are unsuitable as they are not sweet enough in flavour.
• This relish does not keep well, so use within 3 or 4 days of making.
• If you find the flavour of chilli too hot, use only half a chilli and chop into tiny pieces.

sweet piccalilli

Undoubtedly one of the most popular relishes, piccalilli can be eaten with grilled sausages, ham or chops, cold meats or a strong, well-flavoured cheese such as Cheddar. It should contain a good selection of fresh crunchy vegetables in a smooth, mustard sauce.

Makes about 1.8kg/4lb

INGREDIENTS

1 large cauliflower

450g/1lb pickling (pearl) onions

900g/2lb mixed vegetables, such as marrow (large zucchini), cucumber, French (green) beans

225g/8oz/1 cup salt

2.4 litres/4 pints/10 cups cold water

200g/7oz/1 cup granulated sugar

2 garlic cloves, peeled and crushed

10ml/2 tsp mustard powder

5ml/1 tsp ground ginger

1 litre/1¾ pints/4 cups distilled (white) vinegar

25g/1oz/¼ cup plain (all-purpose) flour

15ml/1 tbsp turmeric

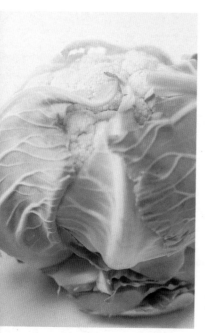

1 Prepare the vegetables. Divide the cauliflower into small florets; peel and quarter the pickling onions; seed and finely dice the marrow and cucumber; top and tail the French beans, then cut them into 2.5cm/1in lengths.

2 Layer the vegetables in a large glass or stainless steel bowl, generously sprinkling each layer with salt. Pour over the water, cover the bowl with clear film (plastic wrap) and leave to soak for about 24 hours.

3 Drain the soaked vegetables, and discard the brine. Rinse well in several changes of cold water to remove as much salt as possible, then drain them thoroughly.

4 Put the sugar, garlic, mustard, ginger and 900ml/1½ pints/3¾ cups of the vinegar in a preserving pan. Heat gently, stirring occasionally, until the sugar has dissolved.

5 Add the vegetables to the pan, bring to the boil, reduce the heat and simmer for 10–15 minutes, or until they are almost tender.

6 Mix the flour and turmeric with the remaining vinegar and stir into the vegetables. Bring to the boil, stirring, and simmer for 5 minutes, until the piccalilli is thick.

7 Spoon the piccalilli into warmed sterilized jars, cover and seal. Store in a cool, dark place for at least 2 weeks. Use within 1 year.

corn relish

When golden sweetcorn cobs are in season, try preserving their kernels in this delicious relish. It has a lovely crunchy texture and a wonderfully bright, appetizing appearance.

Makes about 1kg/2¼lb

INGREDIENTS

6 large fresh corn on the cob

½ small white cabbage, weighing about 275g/10oz, very finely shredded

2 small onions, halved and very finely sliced

475ml/16fl oz/2 cups distilled malt vinegar

200g/7oz/1 cup golden granulated sugar

1 red (bell) pepper, seeded and finely chopped

5ml/1 tsp salt

15ml/1 tbsp plain (all-purpose) flour

5ml/1 tsp mustard powder

2.5ml/½ tsp turmeric

1 Put the corn in a pan of boiling water and cook for 2 minutes. Drain and, when cool enough to handle, use a sharp knife to strip the kernels from the cobs.

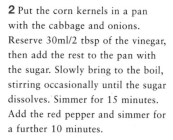

2 Put the corn kernels in a pan with the cabbage and onions. Reserve 30ml/2 tbsp of the vinegar, then add the rest to the pan with the sugar. Slowly bring to the boil, stirring occasionally until the sugar dissolves. Simmer for 15 minutes. Add the red pepper and simmer for a further 10 minutes.

3 Blend the salt, flour, mustard and turmeric with the reserved vinegar to make a smooth paste.

4 Stir the paste into the vegetable mixture and bring back to the boil. Simmer for 5 minutes, until the mixture has thickened.

5 Spoon the relish into warmed sterilized jars, cover and seal. Store in a cool dark place. Use within 6 months of making. Once opened, store in the refrigerator and use within 2 months.

COOK'S TIP

This tangy relish is the perfect barbecue preserve. It is perfect for enlivening barbecued meats such as chicken, sausages and burgers.

cool cucumber and green tomato relish

This is a great way to use up those green tomatoes that seem as though they're never going to ripen. Combined with cucumber, they make a pale green relish that is great for barbecues.

Makes about 1.6kg/3½lb

INGREDIENTS

2 cucumbers

900g/2lb green tomatoes

4 onions

7.5ml/1½ tsp salt

350ml/12fl oz/1½ cups distilled (white) vinegar

150g/5oz/scant ¾ cup demerara (raw) sugar

200g/7oz/1 cup granulated sugar

15ml/1 tbsp plain (all-purpose) flour

2.5ml/½ tsp mustard powder

1 Wash the cucumbers and green tomatoes. Cut into 1cm/½in cubes. Peel and finely chop the onions.

2 Layer the vegetables in a strainer or colander placed over a bowl, lightly sprinkling each layer with salt, then cover and leave to drain for at least 6 hours, or overnight.

3 Discard the salty liquid and tip the salted vegetables into a large heavy pan. Reserve 30ml/2 tbsp of the vinegar and add the rest to the pan with the demerara and granulated sugars.

4 Slowly bring the vegetable mixture to the boil, stirring occasionally until the sugar has dissolved completely. Reduce the heat slightly and cook, uncovered, for about 30 minutes, or until the vegetables are tender.

5 In a small bowl, blend the flour and mustard to a paste with the reserved vinegar. Stir the mixture into the relish and simmer for about 20 minutes, or until the mixture is very thick.

6 Spoon the relish into warmed sterilized jars, cover and seal. Store in a cool, dark place for at least 1 week. Use the relish within 6 months. Once opened, keep in the refrigerator and use within 2 months.

malay mixed vegetable relish

This traditional, full-flavoured relish, with its crunchy texture and spicy kick, is known as acar
kuning *in Malaysia. It is served in very generous portions, almost like a side salad.*

Makes about 900g/2lb

INGREDIENTS

12 small pickling (pearl) onions,
  quartered

225g/8oz French (green) beans, cut into
  2.5cm/1in lengths

225g/8oz carrots, cut into 2.5cm/1in
  long thin sticks

225g/8oz cauliflower, cut into
  small florets

5ml/1 tsp mustard powder

5ml/1 tsp salt

10ml/2 tsp granulated sugar

60ml/4 tbsp sesame seeds

For the spice paste

2 shallots, finely chopped

2 garlic cloves, crushed

2 fresh green chillies, seeded and
  finely chopped

115g/4oz/1 cup dry-roasted peanuts

5ml/1 tsp turmeric

5ml/1 tsp chilli powder

60ml/4 tbsp distilled (white) vinegar

30ml/2 tbsp vegetable oil

175ml/6fl oz/¾ cup boiling water

2 Transfer the mixture to a large
heavy pan and slowly bring to the
boil. Reduce the heat and simmer
gently for 2 minutes, stirring all
the time. Gradually stir in the
water and simmer the mixture for
a further 3 minutes.

5 Meanwhile, toast the sesame
seeds in a non-stick pan over a
medium heat until golden, stirring
frequently. Stir the seeds into the
vegetable mixture.

6 Spoon the relish into warmed
sterilized jars, cover and seal.
Leave until completely cold, then
store in the refrigerator.

COOK'S TIP

The relish can be served immediately
and should be used within 4 weeks.

3 Add the onions to the pan, cover
and simmer for 5 minutes, then
add the beans and carrots. Cover
the pan again and cook for a
further 3 minutes.

4 Finally, add the cauliflower,
mustard, salt and sugar to the pan
and simmer, uncovered, for about
5 minutes, or until the vegetables
are tender and have absorbed most
of the sauce. Remove the pan from
the heat and set aside to cool for
a few minutes.

1 Make the spice paste. Put the
shallots, garlic, chillies, peanuts,
turmeric, chilli powder, vinegar
and oil in a food processor or
blender and process to a fairly
smooth paste.

carrot and almond relish

This is a Middle Eastern classic, usually made with long fine strands of carrot, available from many supermarkets. Alternatively, grate large carrots lengthways on a medium grater.

Makes about 675g/1½lb

INGREDIENTS

15ml/1 tbsp coriander seeds

500g/1¼lb carrots, grated

50g/2oz fresh root ginger,
  finely shredded

200g/7oz/1 cup caster (superfine) sugar

finely grated rind and juice
  of 1 lemon

120ml/4fl oz/½ cup white wine vinegar

75ml/5 tbsp water

30ml/2 tbsp clear honey

7.5ml/1½ tsp salt

50g/2oz/½ cup flaked (sliced) almonds

1 Crush the coriander seeds using a mortar and pestle. Put them in a bowl with the carrots, ginger, sugar and lemon rind and mix together well to combine.

2 Put the lemon juice, vinegar, water, honey and salt in a jug (pitcher) and stir until the salt has dissolved. Pour over the carrot mixture. Mix well, cover and leave in the refrigerator for 4 hours.

3 Transfer the chilled mixture to a preserving pan. Slowly bring to the boil, then reduce the heat and simmer for 15 minutes until the carrots and ginger are tender.

4 Increase the heat and boil for 15 minutes, or until most of the liquid has evaporated and the mixture is thick. Stir frequently towards the end of the cooking time to prevent the mixture from sticking to the pan.

5 Put the almonds in a frying pan and toast over a low heat until just beginning to colour. Gently stir into the relish, taking care not to break the almonds.

6 Spoon the relish into warmed sterilized jars, cover and seal. Leave for at least 1 month and use within 18 months. Once opened, store in the refrigerator.

lemon and garlic relish

This powerful relish is flavoured with North African spices and punchy preserved lemons, which are widely available in Middle Eastern stores. It is great served with Moroccan tagines.

Makes 1 small jar

INGREDIENTS

45ml/3 tbsp olive oil

3 large red onions, sliced

2 heads of garlic, separated into cloves and peeled

10ml/2 tsp coriander seeds, crushed

10ml/2 tsp light muscovado (brown) sugar, plus a little extra

pinch of saffron threads

5cm/2in piece cinnamon stick

2–3 small whole dried red chillies (optional)

2 fresh bay leaves

30–45ml/2–3 tbsp sherry vinegar

juice of ½ small orange

30ml/2 tbsp chopped preserved lemon

salt and ground black pepper

1 Gently heat the oil in a large heavy pan. Add the onions and stir, then cover and cook on the lowest setting for 10–15 minutes, stirring occasionally, until soft.

2 Add the garlic cloves and the coriander seeds. Cover and cook for 5–8 minutes, until soft.

3 Add a pinch of salt, lots of ground black pepper and the sugar to the onions and cook, uncovered, for a further 5 minutes.

4 Soak the saffron threads in about 45ml/3 tbsp warm water for 5 minutes, then add to the onions, with the soaking water. Add the cinnamon stick, dried chillies, if using, and bay leaves. Stir in 30ml/2 tbsp of the sherry vinegar and the orange juice.

5 Cook very gently, uncovered, until the onions are very soft and most of the liquid evaporated. Stir in the preserved lemon and cook gently for 5 minutes.

6 Taste the relish and adjust the seasoning, adding more salt, sugar and/or vinegar to taste.

7 Serve warm or cold (not hot or chilled). The relish tastes best if left to stand for 24 hours.

COOK'S TIP

You can store the relish in a tightly covered bowl or jar for up to a week in the refrigerator. Allow it to stand at room temperature for about an hour before serving.

cranberry and red onion relish

This wine-enriched relish is perfect for serving with hot roast turkey at Christmas or Thanksgiving. It is also good served with cold meats or stirred into a beef or game casserole for a touch of sweetness. It can be made several months in advance of the festive season.

Makes about 900g/2lb

INGREDIENTS

450g/1lb small red onions

30ml/2 tbsp olive oil

225g/8oz/1 cup soft light
   brown sugar

450g/1lb/4 cups fresh or
   frozen cranberries

120ml/4fl oz/½ cup red wine vinegar

120ml/4fl oz/½ cup red wine

15ml/1 tbsp mustard seeds

2.5ml/½ tsp ground ginger

30ml/2 tbsp orange liqueur or port

salt and ground black pepper

VARIATION

Redcurrants make a very good substitute for cranberries in this recipe. They produce a relish with a lovely flavour and pretty colour.

1 Halve the red onions and slice them very thinly. Heat the oil in a large pan, add the onions and cook them over a very low heat for about 15 minutes, stirring occasionally until softened. Add 30ml/2 tbsp of the sugar and cook for a further 5 minutes, or until the onions are caramelized.

4 Increase the heat slightly and cook uncovered for a further 10 minutes, stirring the mixture frequently until it is well reduced and thickened. Remove the pan from the heat, then season with salt and pepper to taste.

2 Meanwhile, put the cranberries in a pan with the remaining sugar, and the vinegar, red wine, mustard seeds and ginger. Heat gently until the sugar has dissolved, then cover and bring to the boil.

3 Simmer the relish mixture for 12–15 minutes, until the berries have burst and are tender, then stir in the caramelized onions.

5 Transfer the relish to warmed sterilized jars. Spoon a little of the orange liqueur or port over the top of each, then cover and seal. Store in a cool place for up to 6 months. Store in the refrigerator once opened and use within 1 month.

COOK'S TIP

It is important to cover the pan when cooking the cranberries because they can sometimes pop out of the pan during cooking and are very hot.

mango and papaya relish

Brightly coloured pieces of dried papaya adds taste and texture to this anise-spiced mango preserve. The fruit is cooked for only a short time to retain its juicy texture and fresh flavour.

Makes about 800g/1¾lb

INGREDIENTS

115g/4oz/½ cup dried papaya

30ml/2 tbsp orange or
 apple juice

2 large slightly underripe mangoes

2 shallots, very finely sliced

4cm/1½in piece fresh root
 ginger, grated

1 garlic clove, crushed

2 whole star anise

150ml/¼ pint/⅔ cup cider vinegar

75g/3oz/scant ½ cup light muscovado
 (brown) sugar

1.5ml/¼ tsp salt

1 Using a sharp knife or scissors, roughly chop the papaya and place in a small bowl. Sprinkle over the orange or apple juice and leave to soak for at least 10 minutes.

2 Meanwhile, peel and slice the mangoes, cutting the flesh away from the stone (pit) in large slices. Cut into 1cm/½in chunks, then set the flesh aside.

3 Put the sliced shallots, ginger, garlic and star anise in a large pan. Pour over the vinegar. Slowly bring to the boil, then reduce the heat, cover and simmer for 5 minutes, or until the shallots are just beginning to soften.

4 Add the sugar and salt to the pan and stir over a low heat until dissolved. When the mixture is simmering, add the papaya and mango and cook for a further 20 minutes, or until the fruit is just tender and the relish mixture has reduced and thickened.

5 Allow the relish to cool for about 5 minutes, then spoon into warmed sterilized jars. Allow to cool completely before covering and sealing. Store in a cool, dark place and use within 3 months of making. Once opened, keep the jars in the refrigerator and use within 1 month.

sweet and sour pineapple relish

This simple preserve is an excellent condiment for perking up grilled chicken or bacon chops. Using canned pineapple means it can be made mainly from store-cupboard ingredients.

Makes about 675g/1½lb

INGREDIENTS

2 x 400g/14oz cans pineapple rings
  or pieces in natural juice

1 lemon

115g/4oz/½ cup granulated sugar

45ml/3 tbsp white wine vinegar

6 spring onions (scallions),
  finely chopped

2 fresh red chillies, seeded and
  finely chopped

salt and ground black pepper

1 Drain the pineapple, reserving 120ml/4fl oz/½ cup of the juice. Pour the juice into a preserving pan. Finely chop the pineapple, if necessary, and place in a sieve (strainer) set over a bowl.

2 Pare a strip of rind from the lemon. Squeeze the lemon juice and add to the pan with the lemon rind, sugar and vinegar.

3 Heat over a low heat, stirring occasionally, until the sugar has dissolved, then bring to the boil. Cook, uncovered, over a medium heat for about 10 minutes, or until the sauce has thickened slightly.

4 Add the chopped onions and chillies to the pan, together with any juice that has been drained from the chopped pineapple.

5 Cook the sauce for 5 minutes, until thick and syrupy, stirring frequently towards the end of the cooking time.

6 Increase the heat slightly, add the pineapple and cook for about 4 minutes, or until most of the liquid has evaporated. Season.

7 Spoon the relish into warmed sterilized jars, cover and seal. Store in the refrigerator and eat within 3 months of making.

plum and cherry relish

This simple sweet and sour fruity relish complements rich poultry, game or meat such as roast duck or grilled duck breasts. Sieve a few spoonfuls into a sauce or gravy to add fruity zest and flavour, as well as additional colour.

Makes about 350g/12oz

INGREDIENTS

350g/12oz dark-skinned red plums

350g/12oz/2 cups cherries

2 shallots, finely chopped

15ml/1 tbsp olive oil

30ml/2 tbsp dry sherry

60ml/4 tbsp red wine vinegar

15ml/1 tbsp balsamic vinegar

1 bay leaf

90g/3½oz/scant ½ cup demerara (raw) sugar

1 Halve and stone (pit) the plums, then roughly chop the flesh. Stone all the cherries.

2 Cook the shallots gently in the oil for 5 minutes, or until soft. Add the fruit, sherry, vinegars, bay leaf and sugar.

3 Slowly bring the mixture to the boil, stirring until the sugar has dissolved completely. Increase the heat and cook briskly for about 15 minutes, or until the relish is very thick and the fruit tender.

4 Remove the bay leaf and spoon the relish into warmed sterilized jars. Cover and seal. Store the relish in the refrigerator and use within 3 months.

nectarine relish

This sweet and tangy fruit relish goes very well with hot roast meats such as pork and game birds such as guinea fowl and pheasant. Make it while nectarines are plentiful and keep tightly covered in the refrigerator to serve for Christmas, or even to give as a seasonal gift.

Makes about 450g/1lb

INGREDIENTS

45ml/3 tbsp olive oil

2 Spanish onions, thinly sliced

1 fresh green chilli, seeded and finely chopped

5ml/1 tsp finely chopped fresh rosemary

2 bay leaves

450g/1lb nectarines, stoned (pitted) and cut into chunks

150g/5oz/1 cup raisins

10ml/2 tsp crushed coriander seeds

350g/12oz/1½ cups demerara (raw) sugar

200ml/7fl oz/scant 1 cup red wine vinegar

1 Heat the oil in a large pan. Add the onions, chilli, rosemary and bay leaves. Cook, stirring frequently, for about 15 minutes, or until the onions are soft.

COOK'S TIP

Pots of this relish make a lovely gift. Store it in pretty jars and add a colourful label identifying the relish, and reminding the recipient that it should be stored in the refrigerator, and when it should be used by.

2 Add the nectarines, raisins, coriander seeds, sugar and vinegar to the pan, then slowly bring to the boil, stirring frequently.

3 Reduce the heat under the pan and simmer gently for 1 hour, or until the relish is thick and sticky. Stir occasionally during cooking, and more frequently towards the end of cooking time to prevent the relish sticking to the pan.

4 Spoon the relish into warmed, sterilized jars and seal. Leave the jars to cool completely, then store in the refrigerator. The relish will keep well in the refrigerator for up to 5 months.

savoury jellies

Although many of the jellies in this chapter contain sugar, they are all prepared as a condiment to serve with savoury foods such as meat, fish or cheese. Soft or firmly set, these interesting jellies are made from fruits and vegetables and usually have a tangy, sweet-and-sour taste. Many are flavoured with zesty citrus fruits and are spiked with herbs and spices to produce wonderful aromatic flavours. They really are a true gourmet treat – enjoy!

lemon grass and ginger jelly

This aromatic jelly is delicious with Asian-style roast meat and poultry such as Chinese crispy duck. It is also the perfect foil for rich fish, especially cold smoked trout or mackerel.

2 Put the chopped lemon grass in a preserving pan and pour over the water. Add the lemons and ginger. Bring to the boil, then reduce the heat, cover and simmer for 1 hour, or until the lemons are pulpy.

3 Pour the fruit and juices into a sterilized jelly bag suspended over a large bowl. Leave to drain for at least 3 hours, or until the juice stops dripping.

4 Measure the juice into the cleaned preserving pan, adding 450g/1lb/2¼ cups sugar for every 600ml/1 pint/2½ cups juice.

5 Heat the mixture gently, stirring occasionally, until the sugar has dissolved completely. Boil rapidly for about 10 minutes until the jelly reaches setting point (105°C/220°F). Remove from the heat.

6 Skim any scum off the surface using a slotted spoon, then pour the jelly into warmed sterilized jars, cover and seal. Store in a cool, dark place and use within 1 year. Once opened, keep in the refrigerator. Eat within 3 months.

Makes about 900g/2lb

INGREDIENTS

2 lemon grass stalks

1.5 litres/2½ pints/6¼ cups water

1.3kg/3lb lemons, washed and cut into small pieces

50g/2oz fresh root ginger, unpeeled, thinly sliced

about 450g/1lb/2¼ cups preserving or granulated sugar

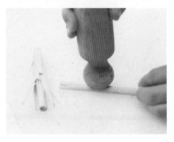

1 Using a rolling pin, bruise the lemon grass, then chop roughly.

roasted red pepper and chilli jelly

The hint of chilli in this glowing red jelly makes it ideal for spicing up hot or cold roast meat, sausages or hamburgers. The jelly is also good stirred into sauces or used as a glaze for poultry.

Makes about 900g/2lb

INGREDIENTS

8 red (bell) peppers, quartered and seeded

4 fresh red chillies, halved and seeded

1 onion, roughly chopped

2 garlic cloves, roughly chopped

250ml/8fl oz/1 cup water

250ml/8fl oz/1 cup white wine vinegar

7.5ml/1½ tsp salt

450g/1lb/2¼ cups preserving or granulated sugar

25ml/1½ tbsp powdered pectin

4 Scrape the purée into a large stainless steel pan, then stir in the white wine vinegar and salt.

5 In a bowl, combine the sugar and pectin, then stir it into the pepper mixture. Heat gently, stirring, until the sugar and pectin have dissolved completely, then bring to a rolling boil. Cook the jelly, stirring frequently, for exactly 4 minutes, then remove the pan from the heat.

6 Pour the jelly into warmed, sterilized jars. Leave to cool and set, then cover, label and store.

1 Arrange the peppers, skin side up, on a rack in a grill (broiling) pan and grill (broil) until the skins blister and blacken.

2 Put the peppers in a polythene bag until they are cool enough to handle, then remove the skins.

3 Put the skinned peppers, chillies, onion, garlic and water in a food processor or blender and process to a purée. Press the purée through a nylon sieve set over a bowl, pressing hard with a wooden spoon, to extract as much juice as possible. There should be about 750ml/1¼ pints/3 cups.

tomato and herb jelly

This dark golden jelly is delicious served with roast and grilled meats, especially lamb. It is also great for enlivening tomato-based pasta sauces: stirring a couple of teaspoons of the jelly into sauces helps to heighten their flavour and counteract acidity.

Makes about 1.3kg/3lb

INGREDIENTS

1.8kg/4lb tomatoes

2 lemons

2 bay leaves

300ml/½ pint/1¼ cups cold water

250ml/8fl oz/1 cup malt vinegar

bunch of fresh herbs such as rosemary, thyme, parsley and mint, plus a few extra sprigs for the jars

about 900g/2lb/4½ cups preserving or granulated sugar

COOK'S TIP

Once you have opened a jar of this jelly, store it in the refrigerator and use within 3 months.

1 Wash the tomatoes and lemons well, then cut the tomatoes into quarters and the lemons into small pieces. Put the chopped tomatoes and lemons in a large heavy pan with the bay leaves and pour over the water and vinegar.

2 Add the herbs, either one herb or a mixture if preferred. (If you are using pungent woody herbs such as rosemary and thyme, use about six sprigs; if you are using milder leafy herbs such as parsley or mint, add about 12 large sprigs.)

3 Bring the mixture to the boil, then reduce the heat. Cover the pan with a lid and simmer for about 40 minutes, or until the tomatoes are very soft.

4 Pour the tomato mixture and all the juices into a sterilized jelly bag suspended over a large bowl. Leave to drain for about 3 hours, or until the juices stop dripping.

5 Measure the juice into the cleaned pan, adding 450g/1lb/2¼ cups sugar for every 600ml/1 pint/2½ cups juice. Heat gently, stirring, until the sugar dissolves. Boil rapidly for 10 minutes, to setting point (105°C/220°F), then remove from the heat. Skim off any scum.

6 Leave the jelly for a few minutes until a skin forms. Place a herb sprig in each warmed sterilized jar, then pour in the jelly. Cover and seal when cold. Store in a cool, dark place and use within 1 year.

citrus thyme jelly

You can vary the sharpness of this jelly by altering the proportions of fruit. Use more oranges and fewer lemons and limes to obtain a milder, sweeter-tasting jelly.

2 Bring the mixture to the boil, then reduce the heat, cover and simmer for 1 hour, or until pulpy. Discard the bay leaves, then pour the fruit and juices into a sterilized jelly bag suspended over a large bowl. Leave to drain for 3 hours, or until the juices stop dripping.

3 Measure the juice into the cleaned pan, adding 450g/1lb/ 2¼ cups sugar for every 600ml/ 1 pint/2½ cups juice. Heat gently until the sugar has dissolved. Bring to the boil, then boil rapidly for about 10 minutes, or until setting point is reached (105°C/220°F). Remove the pan from the heat.

Makes about 1.3kg/3lb

INGREDIENTS

675g/1½lb lemons
675g/1½lb limes
450g/1lb oranges
2 bay leaves
2 litres/3½ pints/8¾ cups water
about 800g/1¾lb/4 cups preserving
  or granulated sugar
60ml/4 tbsp fresh thyme leaves

COOK'S TIP

It is important to stir the jelly before potting to re-distribute the herbs.

1 Wash all the fruit, then cut into small pieces. Place in a large heavy pan with the bay leaves and pour over the water.

4 Skim any scum off the surface, then stir in the thyme leaves. Leave to cool for a few minutes until a thin skin forms, then gently stir again to make sure the thyme is evenly distributed.

5 Pour the jelly into warmed sterilized jars. Cover and seal when cold. Store in a cool, dark place and use within 1 year. Once opened, store in the refrigerator and eat within 3 months.

bitter lime and juniper jelly

In this sharp, aromatic jelly the distinctive taste of zesty lime and the rich, resinous flavour of juniper berries is enhanced with a hint of aniseed from the splash of Pernod.

Makes about 1.6kg/3½lb

INGREDIENTS

6 limes

1.3kg/3lb tart cooking apples

6 juniper berries, crushed

1.75 litres/3 pints/7½ cups water

about 800g/1¾lb/4 cups preserving
  or granulated sugar

45ml/3 tbsp Pernod (optional)

1 Wash the limes and apples, then cut them into small pieces. Put them in a large heavy pan with the juniper berries. Pour over the water, then bring to the boil and simmer for about 1 hour, or until the fruit is very tender and pulpy.

2 Pour the fruit and juices into a sterilized jelly bag suspended over a large bowl. Leave the fruit to drain for at least 3 hours, until the juices stop dripping.

3 Measure the juice into the cleaned pan, adding 450g/1lb/ 2¼ cups sugar for every 600ml/ 1 pint/2½ cups juice. Heat gently, stirring occasionally, until the sugar has dissolved. Boil rapidly for about 10 minutes, to setting point (105°C/220°F), then remove the pan from the heat.

4 Skim any scum off the surface using a slotted spoon, then stir in the Pernod, if using. Pour the jelly into warmed sterilized jars, cover and seal immediately.

5 Store the jelly in a cool, dark place and use within 1 year. Once opened, keep in the refrigerator and eat within 3 months.

COOK'S TIP

When using citrus fruits for preserves, try to use unwaxed ones. If they are unavailable, scrub waxed fruits well.

apple, orange and cider jelly

A spoonful or two of this tangy amber jelly adds a real sparkle to a plate of cold meats, especially ham and pork or rich game pâtés. Tart cooking apples make the best-flavoured jelly, while the addition of cloves gives it a wonderfully warm, spicy taste and aroma.

Makes about 1.8kg/4lb

INGREDIENTS

1.3kg/3lb tart cooking apples

4 oranges

4 whole cloves

1.2 litres/2 pints/5 cups sweet cider

about 600ml/1 pint/2½ cups cold water

about 800g/1¾lb/4 cups preserving
  or granulated sugar

VARIATION

Replace some of the apples with crab apples for a more distinctive taste.

1 Wash and chop the apples and oranges, then put in a preserving pan with the cloves, cider and water to barely cover the fruit.

2 Bring the mixture to the boil, cover and simmer gently for 1 hour, stirring occasionally.

3 Pour the fruit and juices into a sterilized jelly bag suspended over a large bowl. Leave to drain for at least 4 hours, or overnight, until the juices stop dripping.

4 Measure the juice into the cleaned preserving pan, adding 450g/1lb/2¼ cups sugar for every 600ml/1 pint/2½ cups juice.

5 Heat the mixture gently stirring, until the sugar has dissolved. Boil rapidly for about 10 minutes until setting point is reached (105°C/ 220°F). Remove from the heat.

6 Skim any scum off the surface, then pour the jelly into warmed sterilized jars. Cover and seal. Store in a cool, dark place and use within 18 months. Once opened, store in the refrigerator and eat within 3 months.

quince and rosemary jelly

The amount of water needed for this jelly varies according to the ripeness of the fruit. For a good set, hard under-ripe quinces should be used as they contain the most pectin. If the fruit is soft and ripe, add a little lemon juice along with the water.

Makes about 900g/2lb

INGREDIENTS

900g/2lb quinces, cut into small pieces, with bruised parts removed

900ml–1.2 litres/1½–2 pints/ 3¾–5 cups water

lemon juice (optional)

4 large sprigs of fresh rosemary

about 900g/2lb/4½ cups preserving or granulated sugar

1 Put the chopped quinces in a large heavy pan with the water, using the smaller volume if the fruit is ripe and the larger volume plus lemon juice if it is hard.

2 Reserve a few small sprigs of rosemary, then add the rest to the pan. Bring to the boil, reduce the heat, cover with a lid and simmer gently until the fruit becomes pulpy.

3 Remove and discard all the rosemary sprigs. (Don't worry about any tiny leaves that have fallen off during cooking). Pour the fruit and juices into a sterilized jelly bag suspended over a large bowl. Leave for 3 hours, or until the juices stop dripping.

4 Measure the drained juice into the cleaned pan, adding 450g/1lb/ 2¼ cups sugar for every 600ml/ 1 pint/2½ cups juice.

5 Heat the mixture gently over a low heat, stirring occasionally, until the sugar has dissolved completely. Bring to the boil, then boil rapidly for about 10 minutes until the jelly reaches setting point (105°C/220°F). Remove the pan from the heat.

6 Skim any scum from the surface using a slotted spoon, then leave the jelly to cool for a few minutes until a thin skin begins to form on the surface.

7 Place a sprig of rosemary in each warmed sterilized jar, then pour in the jelly. Cover and seal when cold. Store in a cool, dark place and use within 1 year. Once the jelly is opened, keep it in the refrigerator and use within 3 months.

minted gooseberry jelly

This classic, tart jelly is an ideal complement to roast lamb. Rather surprisingly, the gooseberry juice takes on a pinkish tinge during cooking so does not produce a green jelly as one would expect.

Makes about 1.2kg/2½lb

INGREDIENTS

1.3kg/3lb/12 cups gooseberries
1 bunch fresh mint
750ml/1¼ pints/3 cups cold water
400ml/14fl oz/1⅔ cups white wine vinegar
about 900g/2lb/4½ cups preserving or
    granulated sugar
45ml/3 tbsp chopped fresh mint

1 Place the gooseberries, mint and water in a preserving pan. Bring to the boil, reduce the heat, cover and simmer for about 30 minutes, until the gooseberries are soft. Add the vinegar and simmer uncovered for a further 10 minutes.

2 Pour the fruit and juices into a sterilized jelly bag suspended over a large bowl. Leave to drain for at least 3 hours, or until the juices stop dripping, then measure the strained juices back into the cleaned preserving pan.

3 Add 450g/1lb/2½ cups sugar for every 600ml/1 pint/2½ cups juice, then heat gently, stirring, until the sugar has dissolved. Bring to the boil and cook for 15 minutes, or to setting point (105°C/220°F). Remove the pan from the heat.

4 Skim any scum from the surface. Leave to cool until a thin skin forms, then stir in the mint.

5 Pour the jelly into warmed sterilized jars, cover and seal. Store and use within 1 year. Once opened, store in the refrigerator and eat within 3 months.

plum and apple jelly

Use dark red cooking plums, damsons or wild plums such as bullaces to offset the sweetness of this deep-coloured jelly. Its flavour complements rich roast meats such as lamb and pork.

Makes about 1.3kg/3lb

INGREDIENTS

900g/2lb plums
450g/1lb tart cooking apples
150ml/¼ pint/⅔ cup cider vinegar
750ml/1¼ pints/3 cups water
about 675g/1½lb/scant 3½ cups
    preserving or granulated sugar

COOK'S TIP

This jelly can be stored for up to 2 years. However, once opened, it should be stored in the refrigerator and eaten within 3 months.

1 Cut the plums in half along the crease, twist the two halves apart, then remove the stones (pits) and roughly chop the flesh. Chop the apples, including the cores and skins. Put the fruit in a large heavy pan with the vinegar and water.

2 Bring the mixture to the boil, reduce the heat, cover and simmer for 30 minutes or until the fruit is soft and pulpy.

3 Pour the fruit and juices into a sterilized jelly bag suspended over a large bowl. Leave to drain for at least 3 hours, or until the fruit juices stop dripping.

4 Measure the juice into the cleaned pan, adding 450g/1lb/ 2¼ cups sugar for every 600ml/ 1 pint/2½ cups juice.

5 Bring the mixture to the boil, stirring occasionally, until the sugar has dissolved, then boil rapidly for about 10 minutes, or until the jelly reaches setting point (105°C/220°F). Remove the pan from the heat.

6 Skim any scum from the surface, then pour the jelly into warmed sterilized jars. Cover and seal while hot. Store in a cool, dark place and use within 2 years.

blackberry and sloe gin jelly

Although they have a wonderful flavour, blackberries are full of pips, so turning them into a deep-coloured jelly is a good way to make the most of this full-flavoured hedgerow harvest. This preserve is delicious served with richly flavoured roast meats such as lamb.

Makes about 1.3kg/3lb

INGREDIENTS

450g/1lb sloes (black plums)
600ml/1 pint/2½ cups cold water
1.8kg/4lb/16 cups blackberries
juice of 1 lemon
about 900g/2lb/4½ cups preserving
  or granulated sugar
45ml/3 tbsp gin

VARIATION

Sloes are much harder to come by than blackberries and you will usually need to find them growing in the wild. If you can't find sloes, use extra blackberries in their place.

1 Wash the sloes and prick with a fine skewer. Put them in a large heavy pan with the water and bring to the boil. Reduce the heat, cover and simmer for 5 minutes.

2 Briefly rinse the blackberries in cold water and add them to the pan with the lemon juice.

3 Bring the fruit mixture back to a simmer and cook gently for about 20 minutes, or until the sloes are tender and the blackberries very soft, stirring once or twice.

4 Pour the fruit and juices into a sterilized jelly bag suspended over a large bowl. Leave to drain for at least 4 hours or overnight, until the juices have stopped dripping.

5 Measure the fruit juice into the cleaned preserving pan, adding 450g/1lb/2¼ cups sugar for every 600ml/1 pint/2½ cups juice.

6 Heat the mixture gently, stirring occasionally, until the sugar has dissolved completely. Bring to the boil, then boil rapidly for about 10 minutes until the jelly reaches setting point (105°C/220°F). Remove the pan from the heat.

7 Skim off any scum from the surface of the jelly using a slotted spoon, then stir in the gin.

8 Pour the jelly into warmed sterilized jars, cover and seal. Store in a cool, dark place and use within 2 years. Once opened, keep the jelly in the refrigerator and eat within 3 months.

COOK'S TIP

Sloes bring a good level of pectin to the jelly. If all blackberries are used without sloes, select some under-ripe fruit and use preserving sugar with added pectin for a good set.

cranberry and claret jelly

The slight sharpness of cranberries makes this a superb jelly for serving with rich meats such as lamb or game. Together with claret, the cranberries give the jelly a beautiful deep red colour.

Makes about 1.2kg/2½lb

INGREDIENTS

900g/2lb/8 cups fresh or
  frozen cranberries
350ml/12fl oz/1½ cups water
about 900g//2lb/4½ cups preserving
  or granulated sugar
250ml/8fl oz/1 cup claret

COOK'S TIP

When simmering the cranberries,
keep the pan covered until they stop
"popping", as they can occasionally
explode and jump out of the pan.

1 Wash the cranberries, if fresh, and put them in a large heavy pan with the water. Cover the pan and bring to the boil.

2 Reduce the heat under the pan and simmer for about 20 minutes, or until the cranberries are soft.

3 Pour the fruit and juices into a sterilized jelly bag suspended over a large bowl. Leave to drain for at least 3 hours or overnight, until the juices stop dripping.

4 Measure the juice and wine into the cleaned preserving pan, adding 400g/14oz/2 cups preserving or granulated sugar for every 600ml/1 pint/2½ cups liquid.

5 Heat the mixture gently, stirring occasionally, until the sugar has dissolved, then bring to the boil and boil rapidly for 10 minutes until the jelly reaches setting point (105°C/220°F). Remove the pan from the heat.

6 Skim any scum from the surface using a slotted spoon and pour the jelly into warmed sterilized jars. Cover and seal. Store in a cool, dark place and use within 2 years. Once opened, keep the jelly in the refrigerator and eat within 3 months.

red grape, plum and cardamom jelly

Enhance the flavour of roast beef and steaks with a spoonful of deep ruby-coloured jelly. You may need to add a little pectin to the jelly to ensure you achieve a really good set.

Makes about 1.3kg/3lb

INGREDIENTS

1.8kg/4lb plums
450g/1lb/3 cups red grapes
15ml/1 tbsp cardamom pods
600ml/1 pint/2½ cups cold water
350–450ml/12fl oz–¾ pint/1½ cups–
    scant 2 cups pectin stock (optional)
about 1kg/2¼lb/5 cups preserving
    or granulated sugar

1 Cut the plums in half, then twist the two halves apart and remove the stone (pit). Roughly chop the flesh and halve the grapes. Remove the cardamom seeds from the pods and crush them in a mortar.

2 Put the fruit and cardamom seeds in a large heavy pan and pour over the water. Slowly bring to the boil, then simmer for about 30 minutes, or until very tender.

3 Check the pectin content of the fruit (see below); if it is low, stir the pectin stock into the fruit mixture and simmer for 5 minutes.

COOK'S TIP

To check the pectin content of the fruit, spoon 5ml/1 tsp of the juices into a glass. Add 15ml/1 tbsp of methylated spirits (denatured alcohol) and shake gently. After about a minute a clot should form. If the clot is large and jelly-like or if two or three smaller clots form, the pectin content should be sufficient for a set. If there are lots of small clots, or none at all, the pectin content is low and additional pectin will be needed.

4 Pour the fruit into a sterilized jelly bag suspended over a large bowl. Leave to drain for 3 hours, or until the juices stop dripping. Measure the juice into a clean pan, adding 450g/1lb/2¼ cups sugar for every 600ml/1 pint/2½ cups juice.

5 Heat the mixture gently, stirring occasionally, until the sugar has completely dissolved.

6 Bring the mixture to the boil, then boil rapidly for 10 minutes until setting point is reached (105°C/220°F). Remove the pan from the heat.

7 Skim off any scum from the surface, then pour the jelly into warmed sterilized jars, cover and seal. Store in a cool, dark place and use within 2 years. Keep in the refrigerator once opened, and eat within 3 months.

pear and pomegranate jelly

This delicate jelly has a faintly exotic perfume. Pears are not naturally rich in pectin so liquid pectin needs to be added to the jelly during cooking to help it achieve a good set.

Makes about 1.2kg/2½lb

INGREDIENTS

900g/2lb pears
pared rind and juice of 2 lemons
1 cinnamon stick
750ml/1¼ pints/3 cups water
900g/2lb red pomegranates
about 900g/2lb/4½ cups preserving or
  granulated sugar
250ml/8fl oz/1 cup liquid pectin
15ml/1 tbsp rose water (optional)

COOK'S TIP

Once opened, store the jelly in the refrigerator and use within 3 months.

1 Wash and remove the stalks from the pears and chop the fruit roughly. Put the chopped fruit in a large heavy pan with the lemon rind and juice, cinnamon stick and measured water.

2 Bring the mixture to the boil, then reduce the heat to low, cover with a lid and simmer gently for about 15 minutes.

3 Remove the lid from the pan, stir the fruit mixture, then leave to simmer, uncovered, for a further 15 minutes.

4 While the pears are simmering, cut the pomegranates in half horizontally, and use a lemon squeezer to extract all the juice: there should be about 250ml/ 8fl oz/1 cup.

5 Add the pomegranate juice to the pan and bring back to the boil. Reduce the heat and simmer for 2 minutes. Pour the fruit and juices into a sterilized jelly bag suspended over a large bowl. Leave to drip for at least 3 hours.

6 Measure the strained juice into the cleaned pan, adding 450g/1lb/ 2¼ cups sugar for every 600ml/ 1 pint/2½ cups juice.

7 Heat gently, stirring occasionally, until the sugar has dissolved. Bring to the boil, then boil rapidly for 3 minutes. Remove the pan from the heat and stir in the liquid pectin.

8 Skim any scum from the surface, then stir in the rose water, if using. Pour the jelly into warmed sterilized jars. Cover and seal. Store in a cool, dark place and use within 18 months.

guava jelly

Fragrant guava makes an aromatic, pale rust-coloured jelly with a soft set and a slightly sweet-sour flavour that is enhanced by lime juice. Guava jelly goes well with goat's cheese.

Makes about 900g/2lb

INGREDIENTS

900g/2lb guavas
juice of 2–3 limes
about 600ml/1 pint/2½ cups cold water
about 500g/1¼lb/2½ cups preserving
  or granulated sugar

1 Thinly peel and halve the guavas. Using a spoon, scoop out the seeds (pips) from the centre of the fruit and discard them.

2 Place halved guavas in a large heavy pan with 15ml/1 tbsp lime juice and the water – there should be just enough to cover the fruit. Bring the mixture to the boil, then reduce the heat, cover with a lid and simmer for 30 minutes, or until the fruit is tender.

3 Pour the fruit and juices into a sterilized jelly bag suspended over a large bowl. Leave to drain for at least 3 hours.

COOK'S TIP

Do not be tempted to squeeze the jelly bag while the fruit juices are draining from it; this will result in a cloudy jelly.

4 Measure the juice into the cleaned preserving pan, adding 400g/14oz/2 cups sugar and 15ml/1 tbsp lime juice for every 600ml/1 pint/2½ cups guava juice.

5 Heat gently, stirring occasionally, until the sugar has dissolved. Boil rapidly for about 10 minutes. When the jelly reaches setting point, remove the pan from the heat.

6 Skim any scum from the surface of the jelly using a slotted spoon, then pour the jelly into warmed sterilized jars. Cover and seal.

7 Store the jelly in a cool, dark place and use within 1 year. Once opened, keep in the refrigerator and eat within 3 months.

sauces and mustards

No store cupboard is complete without a bottle of tangy sauce and a jar of peppery mustard for serving with hot and cold meats, spreading over cheese on toast, or smearing in a sandwich for an extra spicy bite. Mustard is also indispensable for enlivening mild sauces and dressings – even the smallest spoonful can completely transform a plain cheese sauce or a simple vinaigrette.

sherried plum sauce

Here, plums are cooked with their skins, then strained to make a smooth sauce. Sharp cooking plums, damsons or bullaces give the best flavour and help counteract the sweetness of the sauce, which is wonderful served with roast duck or goose.

2 Roughly chop the flesh and put in a large, heavy pan. If you're using damsons or bullaces, you may find it easier simply to chop them, leaving in the stones. Stir in the sherry and vinegar.

3 Slowly bring the mixture to the boil, then cover and cook over a gentle heat for about 10 minutes, or until the plums are very soft. Push the fruit through a food mill or sieve to remove the skins.

4 Return the plum purée to the pan and add the sugar, garlic, salt and ginger. Stir until the sugar has dissolved, then bring back to the boil and simmer uncovered for about 15 minutes, until thickened.

Makes about 400ml/14fl oz/1⅔ cups

INGREDIENTS

450g/1lb dark plums or damsons
120ml/4fl oz/½ cup dry sherry, plus extra
30ml/2 tbsp sherry vinegar
175g/6oz/scant 1 cup light muscovado (brown) sugar
1 garlic clove, crushed
1.5ml/¼ tsp salt
2.5cm/1in piece fresh root ginger, finely chopped
3–4 drops of Tabasco sauce

1 Cut each plum in half, then twist apart and remove the stone (pit).

5 Remove the pan from the heat and stir in the Tabasco sauce. Ladle the sauce into hot sterilized jars. Add 5–10ml/1–2 tsp sherry to the top of each jar, then cover and seal. The sauce will keep for several weeks in the refrigerator or, if heat treated, for 6 months. Once opened, store in the refrigerator and use within 3 weeks.

cumberland sauce

This sauce is thought to have been named after the Duke of Cumberland who became ruler of Hanover at a time when fruit sauces were served with meat and game in Germany. It goes well with cold cuts, pâtés and terrines, and Christmas or Thanksgiving turkey.

Makes about 750ml/1¼ pints/3 cups

INGREDIENTS

4 oranges
2 lemons
450g/1lb redcurrant or rowan jelly
150ml/¼ pint/⅔ cup port
20ml/4 tsp cornflour (cornstarch)
pinch of ground ginger

1 Scrub the oranges and lemons, then remove the rind thinly, paring away any white pith.

2 Cut the orange and lemon rind into very thin matchstick strips. Put the strips in a heavy pan, cover them with cold water and bring the water to the boil.

3 Simmer the rind for 2 minutes, then drain, cover with cold water, bring to the boil and simmer for about 3 minutes. Drain well and return the rind to the pan.

4 Squeeze the juice from the fruits, then add it to the pan with the redcurrant or rowan jelly. Reserve 30ml/2 tbsp of the port and add the rest to the pan.

5 Slowly bring the mixture to the boil, stirring until the jelly has melted. Simmer for 10 minutes until slightly thickened. Blend the cornflour and ginger with the reserved port and stir into the sauce. Cook over a low heat, stirring until the sauce thickens and boils. Simmer for 2 minutes.

6 Leave the sauce to cool for about 5 minutes, then stir again briefly. Pour into warmed sterilized wide-necked bottles or jars, cover and seal. The sauce will keep for several weeks in the refrigerator or, if heat treated, for 6 months. Once opened, store in the refrigerator and use within 3 weeks.

mint sauce

In England, mint sauce is the traditional and inseparable accompaniment to roast lamb. Its fresh, tart, astringent flavour is the perfect foil to rich, strongly flavoured lamb. It is extremely simple to make and is infinitely preferable to the ready-made varieties.

Makes about 250ml/8fl oz/1cup

INGREDIENTS

1 large bunch mint
105ml/7 tbsp boiling water
150ml/¼ pint/⅔ cup wine vinegar
30ml/2 tbsp granulated sugar

COOK'S TIP

To make a quick and speedy Indian raita for serving with crispy poppadums, simply stir a little mint sauce into a small bowl of natural (US plain) yogurt. Serve the raita alongside a bowl of tangy mango chutney.

1 Using a sharp knife, chop the mint very finely and place it in a 600ml/1 pint/2½ cup jug (pitcher). Pour the boiling water over the mint and leave to infuse for about 10 minutes.

2 When the mint infusion has cooled and is lukewarm, stir in the wine vinegar and sugar. Continue stirring (but do not mash up the mint leaves) until the sugar has dissolved completely.

3 Pour the mint sauce into a sterilized bottle or jar, seal and store in the refrigerator.

COOK'S TIP

This mint sauce can keep for up to 6 months stored in the refrigerator, but is best used within 3 weeks.

traditional horseradish sauce

Fiery, peppery horseradish sauce is without doubt the essential accompaniment to roast beef and is also delicious served with smoked salmon. Horseradish, like chillies, is a powerful ingredient so you should take care when handling it and wash your hands straight afterwards.

Makes about 200ml/7fl oz/scant 1 cup

INGREDIENTS

45ml/3 tbsp freshly grated
  horseradish root
15ml/1 tbsp white wine vinegar
5ml/1 tsp granulated sugar
pinch of salt
150ml/¼ pint/⅔ cup thick double
  (heavy) cream, for serving

COOK'S TIP

To counteract the potent fumes of the horseradish, keep the root submerged in water while you chop and peel it. Use a food processor to do the fine chopping or grating, and avert your head when removing the lid.

1 Place the grated horseradish in a bowl, then add the white wine vinegar, granulated sugar and just a pinch of salt.

2 Stir the ingredients together until thoroughly combined.

3 Pour the mixture into a sterilized jar. It will keep in the refrigerator for up to 6 months.

4 A few hours before you intend to serve the sauce, stir the cream into the horseradish and leave to infuse.

tomato ketchup

Sweet, tangy, spicy tomato ketchup is perfect for serving with barbecued or grilled burgers and sausages. This home-made variety is so much better than store-bought tomato ketchup.

2 Tie the onion with the allspice, peppercorns, rosemary and ginger into a double layer of muslin (cheesecloth) and add to the pan. Chop the celery, plus the leaves, and add to the pan with the sugar, raspberry vinegar, garlic and salt.

3 Bring the mixture to the boil over a fairly high heat, stirring occasionally. Reduce the heat and simmer for 1½–2 hours, stirring regularly, until reduced by half. Purée the mixture in a food processor, then return to the pan, bring to the boil and simmer for 15 minutes. Bottle in clean, sterilized jars and store in the refrigerator. Use within 2 weeks.

Makes about 1.3kg/3lb

INGREDIENTS

2.25kg/5lb very ripe tomatoes
1 onion
6 cloves
4 allspice berries
6 black peppercorns
1 fresh rosemary sprig
25g/1oz fresh root ginger, sliced
1 celery heart
30ml/2 tbsp soft light brown sugar
65ml/4½ tbsp raspberry vinegar
3 garlic cloves, peeled
15ml/1 tbsp salt

1 Carefully peel and seed the ripe tomatoes, then chop and place in a large pan. Peel the onion, leaving the tip and root intact and stud it with the cloves.

barbecue sauce

As well as enlivening burgers and other food cooked on the barbecue, this sauce is also good for all manner of grilled meats and savoury pastries.

Makes about 900ml/1½ pints/3¾ cups

INGREDIENTS

30ml/2 tbsp olive oil

1 large onion, chopped

1 garlic clove, crushed

1 fresh red chilli, seeded and sliced

2 celery sticks, sliced

1 large carrot, sliced

1 medium cooking apple, quartered, cored, peeled and chopped

450g/1lb ripe tomatoes, quartered

2.5ml/½ tsp ground ginger

150ml/¼ pint/⅔ cup malt vinegar

1 bay leaf

4 whole cloves

4 black peppercorns

50g/2oz/¼ cup soft light brown sugar

10ml/2 tsp English mustard

2.5ml/½ tsp salt

1 Heat the oil in a large heavy pan. Add the onion and cook over a low heat for 5 minutes.

2 Stir in the garlic, chilli, celery and carrot into the onions and cook for 5 minutes, stirring frequently, until the onion just begins to colour.

3 Add the apple, tomatoes, ground ginger and malt vinegar to the pan and stir to combine.

4 Put the bay leaf, cloves and peppercorns on a square of muslin (cheesecloth) and tie into a bag with fine string. Add to the pan and bring to the boil. Reduce the heat, cover and simmer for about 45 minutes, stirring occasionally.

5 Add the sugar, mustard and salt to the pan and stir until the sugar dissolves. Simmer for 5 minutes. Leave to cool for 10 minutes, then remove the bag and discard.

6 Press the mixture through a sieve and return to the cleaned pan. Simmer for 10 minutes, or until thickened. Adjust the seasoning.

7 Pour the sauce into hot sterilized bottles or jars, then seal. Heat process, cool and, if using cork-topped bottles, dip the corks in wax. Store in a cool, dark place and use within 1 year. Once opened, store in the refrigerator and use within 2 months.

roasted red pepper and chilli ketchup

Roasting the peppers gives this ketchup a richer, smoky flavour. You can add fewer or more chillies according to taste. Once opened, store in the refrigerator and use within 3 months.

Makes about 600ml/1 pint/2½ cups

INGREDIENTS

900g/2lb red (bell) peppers

225g/8oz shallots

1 tart cooking apple, quartered, cored and roughly chopped

4 fresh red chillies, seeded and chopped

1 large sprig each thyme and parsley

1 bay leaf

5ml/1 tsp coriander seeds

5ml/1 tsp black peppercorns

600ml/1 pint/2½ cups water

350ml/12fl oz/1½ cups red wine vinegar

50g/2oz/scant ¼ cup granulated sugar

5ml/1 tsp salt

7.5ml/1½ tsp arrowroot

1 Preheat the grill (broiler). Place the peppers on a baking sheet and grill for 10–12 minutes, turning regularly, until the skins have blackened. Put the peppers in a plastic bag and leave for 5 minutes.

2 When the peppers are cool enough to handle, peel away the skin, then quarter the peppers and remove the seeds. Roughly chop the flesh and place in a large pan.

3 Put the shallots in a bowl, pour over boiling water and leave to stand for 3 minutes. Drain, then rinse under cold water and peel. Chop the shallots and add to the pan with the apple and chillies.

4 Tie the thyme, parsley, bay leaf, coriander and peppercorns together in a square of muslin (cheesecloth).

5 Add the bag of herbs and the water to the pan and bring to the boil. Reduce the heat, cover and simmer for 30 minutes. Leave to cool for 15 minutes, then remove and discard the muslin bag.

6 Purée the mixture in a food processor, then press through a sieve and return the purée to the cleaned pan. Reserve 15ml/1 tbsp of the vinegar and add the rest to the pan with the sugar and salt.

7 Bring to the boil, stirring until the sugar has dissolved, then simmer for 45 minutes, or until the sauce is well reduced. Blend the arrowroot with the reserved vinegar, stir into the sauce, then simmer for a 2–3 minutes, or until slightly thickened.

8 Pour the sauce into hot sterilized bottles, then seal, heat process and store in a cool, dark place and use within 18 months.

aromatic mustard powder

This pungent condiment has the added flavour of herbs and spices and should be served in small quantities with meats and cheese. To serve, simply mix it with a little water.

Makes about 200g/7oz/1⅔ cups

INGREDIENTS

115g/4oz/1 cup mustard powder

25ml/1½ tbsp ground sea salt

5ml/1 tsp dried thyme

5ml/1 tsp dried tarragon

5ml/1 tsp mixed spice (apple pie spice)

2.5ml/½ tsp ground black pepper

2.5ml/½ tsp garlic powder (optional)

1 Put the mustard powder and salt in a small bowl and stir together until evenly blended.

2 Add the dried thyme and tarragon to the mustard with the mixed spice, ground black pepper and garlic powder, if using. Stir until thoroughly mixed.

3 Spoon the mustard powder into small clean, dry jars, then seal tightly. Store it in a cool, dark place and use within 6 months. (Although the mustard powder won't go off, the potency of the herbs and spices will fade with age and the final mustard will not have the same lovely, strong flavour.)

4 To serve, combine the mustard powder with an equal amount of cold water 10 minutes before needed. Mix well until smooth.

COOK'S TIPS

• The mustard is best when freshly made, so mix up small quantities as and when you need it.

• To sharpen the flavour when serving the mustard with rich meats, use about a third cider or tarragon vinegar and two-thirds water. It can also be blended with sherry, white or red wine or port; the latter two will give the mustard a darker colour.

• The mustard powder is also great added to sauces and salad dressings to give extra flavour.

moutarde aux fines herbes

This classic, fragrant mustard may be used either as a delicious condiment or for coating meats such as chicken and pork, or oily fish such as mackerel, before cooking. It is also fabulous smeared thinly on cheese on toast for an added bite.

Makes about 300ml/½ pint/1¼ cups

INGREDIENTS

75g/3oz/scant ½ cup white mustard seeds

50g/2oz/¼ cup soft light brown sugar

5ml/1 tsp salt

5ml/1 tsp whole peppercorns

2.5ml/½ tsp ground turmeric

200ml/7fl oz/scant 1 cup distilled malt vinegar

60ml/4 tbsp chopped fresh mixed herbs, such as parsley, sage, thyme and rosemary

COOK'S TIP

Stir a spoonful of this fragrant mustard into creamy savoury sauces and salad dressings to enhance their flavour.

1 Put the mustard seeds, sugar, salt, whole peppercorns and ground turmeric into a food processor or blender and process for about 1 minute, or until the peppercorns are coarsely chopped.

2 Gradually add the vinegar to the mustard mixture, 15ml/1 tbsp at a time, processing well between each addition, then continue processing until a coarse paste forms.

3 Add the chopped fresh herbs to the mustard and mix well, then leave to stand for 10–15 minutes until the mustard thickens slightly.

4 Spoon the mustard into a 300ml/ ½ pint/1¼ cup sterilized jar. Cover the surface of the mustard with a greaseproof (waxed) paper disc, then seal with a screw-top lid or a cork, and label. Store in a cool, dark place.

honey mustard

Delicious home-made mustards mature to make the most aromatic of condiments. This honey mustard is richly flavoured and is wonderful served with meats and cheeses or stirred into sauces and salad dressings to give an extra, peppery bite. The addition of honey gives the mustard a deliciously rounded, full, slightly sweet flavour.

Makes about 500g/1¼lb

INGREDIENTS

225g/8oz/1 cup mustard seeds

15ml/1 tbsp ground cinnamon

2.5ml/½ tsp ground ginger

300ml/½ pint/1¼ cups white wine vinegar

90ml/6 tbsp dark clear honey

COOK'S TIP

Make sure you use well-flavoured clear, runny honey for this recipe. Set (crystallized) honey does not have the right consistency and will not work well.

1 Put the mustard seeds in a bowl with the spices and pour over the vinegar. Stir well to mix, then leave to soak overnight.

2 The next day, put the mustard mixture in a mortar and pound with a pestle, adding the honey very gradually.

3 Continue pounding and mixing until the mustard resembles a stiff paste. If the mixture is too stiff, add a little extra vinegar to achieve the desired consistency.

4 Spoon the mustard into four sterilized jars, seal and label, then store in the refrigerator and use within 4 weeks.

COOK'S TIP

This sweet, spicy mustard is perfect for adding extra flavour to cheese tarts or quiches. Spread a very thin layer of mustard across the base of the pastry case before adding the filling, then bake according to the recipe. The mustard will really complement the cheese, giving a mouth-watering result.

tarragon and champagne mustard

This delicately flavoured mustard is well worth making and goes particularly well with cold chicken, fish and shellfish. Its mild taste enhances these foods perfectly.

Makes about 250g/9oz

INGREDIENTS

30ml/2 tbsp mustard seeds
75ml/5 tbsp champagne vinegar
115g/4oz/1 cup mustard powder
115g/4oz/½ cup soft light brown sugar
2.5ml/½ tsp salt
50ml/3½ tbsp virgin olive oil
60ml/4 tbsp chopped fresh tarragon

COOK'S TIP

Champagne vinegar has a lovely flavour but can sometimes be hard to find. Look in specialist delicatessens and food stores, or large supermarkets that stock a good range of gourmet foods.

1 Put the mustard seeds and vinegar in a bowl and leave to soak overnight.

2 The next day, tip the mustard seeds and vinegar into a food processor and add the mustard powder, sugar and salt.

3 Blend the mustard mixture until smooth, then slowly add the oil while continuing to blend.

4 Tip the mustard into a bowl, stir in the tarragon, then spoon into sterilized jars, seal and store in a cool, dark place.

horseradish mustard

This tangy mustard has a wonderfully creamy, peppery taste and is an excellent accompaniment to cold meats, smoked fish or cheese. It is also effective spread thinly inside cold roast beef sandwiches – a great alternative to the traditional horseradish sauce.

Makes about 400g/14oz

INGREDIENTS

25ml/1½ tbsp mustard seeds
250ml/8fl oz/1 cup boiling water
115g/4oz/1 cup mustard powder
115g/4oz/scant ½ cup granulated sugar
120ml/4fl oz/½ cup white wine
  or cider vinegar
50ml/2fl oz/¼ cup olive oil
5ml/1 tsp lemon juice
30ml/2 tbsp horseradish sauce

COOK'S TIP

For the best results, use home-made horseradish sauce.

1 Put the mustard seeds in a bowl and pour over the boiling water. Set aside and leave to soak for at least 1 hour.

2 Drain the mustard seeds and discard the soaking liquid, then tip the seeds into a food processor or blender.

3 Add the mustard powder, sugar, white wine or cider vinegar, olive oil, lemon juice and horseradish sauce to the mustard seeds in the food processor or blender.

4 Process the ingredients into a smooth paste, then spoon the mustard into sterilized jars. Store the mustard in the refrigerator and use within 3 months.

spiced tamarind mustard

Tamarind has a distinctive sweet and sour flavour, a dark brown colour and sticky texture. Combined with spices and ground mustard seeds, it makes a wonderful condiment.

Makes about 200g/7oz

INGREDIENTS

115g/4oz tamarind block
150ml/¼ pint/⅔ cup warm water
50g/2oz/¼ cup yellow mustard seeds
25ml/1½ tbsp black or brown
  mustard seeds
10ml/2 tsp clear honey
pinch of ground cardamom
pinch of salt

COOK'S TIP

The mustard will be ready to eat in 3–4 days. It should be stored in a cool, dark place and used within 4 months.

1 Put the tamarind in a small bowl and pour over the water. Leave to soak for 30 minutes. Mash to a pulp with a fork, then strain through a fine sieve into a bowl.

2 Grind the mustard seeds in a spice mill or coffee grinder and add to the tamarind with the remaining ingredients. Spoon into sterilized jars, cover and seal.

clove-spiced mustard

This spicy mustard is the perfect accompaniment to robust red meats such as sausages and steaks, particularly when they are cooked on the barbecue.

Makes about 300ml/½ pint/1¼ cups

INGREDIENTS

75g/3oz/scant ½ cup white
    mustard seeds
50g/2oz/¼ cup soft light brown sugar
5ml/1 tsp salt
5ml/1 tsp black peppercorns
5ml/1 tsp cloves
5ml/1 tsp turmeric
200ml/7fl oz/scant 1 cup distilled
    malt vinegar

COOK'S TIP

Cloves add a lovely, warming taste to this mustard. Make sure you use whole cloves in this mustard – ground cloves tend to have less flavour.

1 Put all the ingredients except the malt vinegar into a food processor or blender and process. Gradually add the vinegar, 15ml/1 tbsp at a time, processing well between each addition. Continue processing the mustard until it forms a fairly thick, coarse paste.

2 Leave the mustard to stand for 10–15 minutes to thicken slightly. Spoon into a 300ml/½ pint/1¼ cup sterilized jar or several smaller jars, using a funnel. Cover the surface with a greaseproof (waxed) paper disc, then seal with a screw-top lid or a cork, and label.

SHOPPING AND FURTHER INFORMATION

AUSTRALIA

Accoutrement Cook Shops
Good selection of general kitchen
equipment.
118 Queen Corner
Woollahra NSW
Tel: (02) 9362 0151
also at:
611 Military Rd
Mosman NSW
Tel: (02) 9969 1031
and:
808 Pacific Highway
Gordon NSW
Tel: (02) 9418 2992

Bop Discount Kitchenware
Good selection of general kitchen
equipment for delivery anywhere
in Australia.
196 Harris Street
Pyrmont NSW
Tel: (02) 9571 4988
Fax: (02) 9571 5688
Email: sucram@ihug.com.au

Kitchen Centre
Online service offering range of
preserving equipment.
Website: kitchen.centre.net.au

CANADA

Farmer's Market Directory
Comprehensive website offering
a state-by-state directory of
farmer's markets.
Website: chef2chef.net/farmer-
markets/canada

Homecanning.com
Online service offering good range
of preserving equipment.
Bernardin Ltd
120 The East Mall
Toronto ON M8Z 5V5
Fax: (416) 239 4424
Website: www.homecanning.com

NEW ZEALAND

Arthur Holmes Limited
Good selection of glass storage jars
and bottles.
10–30 Horner Street
Newtown
Wellington
Tel: (04) 389 4103
Email: email@arthurholmes.co.nz
Website: www.arthurholmes.co.nz

Crofter Supplies
Mail-order and online ordering
service offering range of preserving
jars and bottles, and other equipment.
PO Box 80 212
Green Bay
Auckland
Tel: (09) 817 2216
Website: www.crofter.co.nz

The Scullery
Mail-order service offering good
range of general kitchen equipment.
391 Victoria Street
Hamilton
Tel: (07) 839 9001
Website: www.shop@thescullery.co.nz

Total Food Equipment Limited
Good range of preserve-making
equipment and accessories.
29 Bower Street
Napier
Tel: (06) 834 4004
Fax: (06) 834 2925
Email: totalfood@xtra.co.nz
Website: www.tfe.co.nz

SOUTH AFRICA

Durbanville Market
Good range of fresh fruits, vegetables
and local produce.
Frederick Street
Durbanville
Cape Town
Tel: (021) 976 9250
Fax: (021) 976 544

Hillcrest Berry Orchards
Good range of fresh berries and fruit;
quick-frozen produce also available.
Banhoek Valley
R310
Stellenbosch
Cape Town
Tel: (021) 885 1629
Fax: (021) 885 1624
Website: www.hillcrestberries.co.za

UNITED KINGDOM

Cucina Direct
Mail-order catalogue service offering good range of preserve-making equipment and accessories. Online ordering available.
PO Box 6611
London SW15 2WG
Tel: 0870 420 4300
Fax: 0870 420 4330
Website: www.cucinadirect.com

Divertimenti
Good range of preserve-making equipment and accessories. Home delivery and online ordering available.
139–141 Fulham Road
London SW3 6SD
Tel: 020 7581 8065
Web site: www.divertimenti.co.uk
and also at:
33–34 Marylebone High Street
London W1U 4PT
Tel: 020 7935 0689

Farmer's Market Directory
Comprehensive website offering a directory of farmers markets.
Website: www.farmersmarket.co.uk

Harrison Smith French Flint Limited
Excellent range of plain and fancy-shaped glass jars.
Rich House
40 Crimscott Street
London SE1 5TE
Tel: 020 7231 6777

John Lewis
Good range of preserve-making equipment and accessories. Stores throughout the United Kingom and online ordering available.
Oxford Street
London W1A 1EX
Tel: 020 7629 7711
General enquiries: 08456 049049
Website: www.johnlewis.com

Lakeland Limited
Good range of preserve-making equipment and accessories. Comprehensive mail-order catalogue, over 20 stores in the United Kingdom and telephone/online ordering system.
Alexandra Buildings
Windermere, Cumbria LA23 1BQ
Tel: 01539 488 100
www.lakelandlimited.com

Wares of Knutsford
Good range of traditional preserving equipment. Online ordering available.
36a Princess Street
Knutsford
Cheshire WA16 6BN
Tel: 01565 751 477
Fax: 01565 754 718
Email: sales@waresofknutsford.co.uk
Website: www.waresofknutsford.co.uk

UNITED STATES

Cash-us.com
Online ordering service offering good range of preserving equipment.
Website: www.cash-us.com/products/cookware/Cooks_tools/canning_tools

Chefs Store
Online service offering range of preserving and general kitchen equipment.
Website: www/chefs-store.com

Farmer's Market Directory
Comprehensive website offering a state-by-state directory of farmer's markets.
Website: chef2chef.net/farmer-markets

Kitchen Krafts
Online service offering good supply of specialty kitchen tools including preserving equipment and glass bottles and jars.
PO Box 442-ORD
Waukon
Iowa 52172
Tel: 1 800 776 0575
Fax: 1 800 850 3093
Email: Info@kitchenkrafts.com
Website: www.kitchenkrafts.com

Village Kitchen
Online service offering good range of glass preserving jars and bottles, and other equipment.
2774 Tarmac Rd
Suite 1
Redding CA 96003
Website: www.villagekitchen.com

INDEX

NOTES

NOTES

Notes

NOTES

NOTES

Notes

Notes

NOTES